Management Accounting

Second Edition

PEARSON CUSTOM PUBLISHING

Management Accounting

Compiled by:

Atish Soonucksing
University of Surrey

Selected chapters from:

Managerial Accounting: Decision Making and Performance Improvement
Fourth Edition
by Ray Proctor

Harlow, England • London • New York • Boston • San Francisco • Toronto • Sydney • Auckland • Singapore • Hong Kong
Tokyo • Seoul • Taipei • New Delhi • Cape Town • Sao Paulo • Mexico City • Madrid • Amsterdam • Munich • Paris • Milan

Pearson Education Limited
Edinburgh Gate
Harlow
Essex CM20 2JE

And associated companies throughout the world

Visit us on the World Wide Web at:
www.pearsoned.co.uk

This Custom Book Edition © Pearson Education Limited 2012

Compiled from:
Managerial Accounting: Decision Making and Performance Management
Fourth Edition
by Ray Proctor
ISBN 978 0 27376 448 9
Copyright © Pearson Education Limited 2002, 2006, 2009, 2012.

ISBN 978 1 78273 448 2

ARP impression 98.

Printed and bound by Ashford Colour Press Ltd.

Contents

This following chapters are from:

Managerial Accounting: Decision Making and Performance Improvement

Fourth Edition
by Ray Proctor

CHAPTER 1

Cost behaviour

Chapter contents

Introduction

As a manager, you might find yourself asking your accountant for the cost of one of your products. The answer you expect to be given is probably a specific amount of money, e.g. £49.55. If your accountant replies 'Why do you want to know?' you may think he (or she) is being unnecessarily awkward and assume that he is in a bad mood for some reason or other. However, the accountant's reply is actually very sensible, even though it would have been better for him to reply 'The answer depends on why you want to know.' At first, this may seem very strange to you but a product has several different costs, each of which serves a different purpose. As you will see in the next few chapters of this book, there are several different costing systems in existence, each giving a different answer to your original question.

The absorption costing system gives the absorption cost; the variable costing system gives the variable cost; and the activity-based costing system gives the activity-based cost. They all give the correct cost in the context of their own system. Each system is a financial model based on its own rules and assumptions. Different rules and assumptions result in different numerical answers. For example, the product in question may have an absorption cost of £49.55, a variable cost of £20.95 and an activity-based cost of £142.00. **Each of these three answers is correct.**

The word 'cost' is a general word and is often used in a general sense. However, when a manager asks an accountant for the cost of a product, the manager usually has a specific purpose in mind. The reason why the accountant replied 'Why do you want to know?' is that he wanted to determine the manager's specific purpose so that he could give the right answer. He was actually trying to be helpful rather than awkward! In this chapter, we will look at the different ways in which costs can behave and see how some of these form the bases of the different costing systems.

Learning objectives	**Having worked through this chapter you should be able to:**

- explain the difference between manufacturing, trading and providing services;
- explain the difference between product and period costs;
- explain the difference between variable and fixed costs;
- explain what semi-variable costs and stepped fixed costs are;
- find fixed and variable elements of semi-variable costs using the high–low method;
- draw a scattergraph based on periodic cost and output data and interpret it;
- explain **in outline** what regression analysis is;
- explain the difference between direct and indirect costs;
- compare variable cost analysis with absorption cost analysis;
- explain the basis for analysing activity-based costs;
- say what relevant costs are used for.

Types of business

There are three main categories of businesses: manufacturers, traders and service businesses. Manufacturers make the goods they sell by converting raw materials into finished products. Traders buy in goods and sell them without altering them in any significant way (they may be repackaged and re-presented). Service businesses create intangible products – for example, banks, accountants, lawyers, financial advisers, freight companies, railways, theatrical agents, education and training institutions. So costs can be described as manufacturing costs, trading costs or service costs.

It is worth noting that the type of organization affects the format of the financial accounts. Gross profit is meaningful for a manufacturer or trader but much less so for a

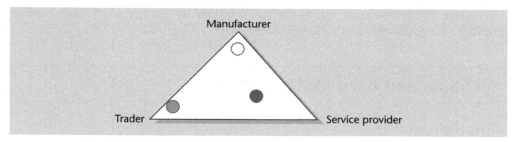

Figure 1.1 Business orientations

service business. Production accounts (to calculate the cost of production) are essential for manufacturers but not applicable to traders or service businesses. However, it is wise not to be too pedantic about this as services tend to be mainly intangible but often include minor tangible items such as chequebooks, sets of accounts, property deeds, share certificates, bills of lading, rail tickets, contracts of employment and degree certificates. In these cases you would probably agree that gross profit is inappropriate.

On the other hand, manufacturers often include a small service element in their products. When you buy a new car, the first two services may be free of charge and there may be a three-year warranty. The price of a new computer usually includes the right to use a selection of software applications for word processing, spreadsheets, databases, etc.

But what about pubs, restaurants and clubs? Are they manufacturers, traders or service providers? The answer is, of course, that they can be all three. The meals are created on the premises, the drinks are bought in and waiting at table, pouring drinks, etc., are pure services. The same applies to residential health clubs and activity holidays where you learn to produce something tangible such as a painting or a piece of pottery.

Figure 1.1 illustrates the relationship between these different types of organization. The darker-coloured circle shows the approximate position of a restaurant. The empty circle represents firms such as furniture makers, and the lighter-coloured circle could represent a national chain of off-licences.

Product and period costs

There are two ways of including costs in the profit and loss account. First, they can be included as part of the production cost of the products made. The production cost of all goods sold in the period gives the total *cost of sales* figure, which is deducted from *sales revenue* to give *gross profit*. Closing stock of finished goods is also valued at production cost. This is how production costs of goods unsold at the year-end are carried forward to the year in which they are sold. (This complies with the accounting rule/concept of realization.) These costs are known as *product costs*.

Second, the full amount of non-production overheads for marketing, administration, etc., appears directly in the profit and loss account of the period in which they were incurred. No attempt is made to apportion them to different financial years. These costs are known as *period costs*.

Product and period costs will be discussed further in Chapter 11, 'Comparison of profits under absorption and variable costing'.

Variable and fixed costs

Variable costs

These are costs which vary **in total** with a measure of activity – for example, the total cost of raw materials increases as output increases (see Figure 1.2b). Take the example of a business making furniture – if the number of chairs produced doubles then the cost of raw materials also doubles.

Note that direct labour is always a variable cost when calculating product costs. However, when looking at the overall total costs of a business, it is often thought of as a fixed cost (provided operatives are employed on a 'permanent' basis, e.g. paid monthly).

Fixed costs

These are costs incurred for a period of time, which, within a given range of production and/or sales activity, do not change (see Figure 1.2c). Continuing the furniture-making example above, if the number of chairs produced doubles, the business rates on the premises do **not** change.

Note that variable costs can be calculated per unit of output but that fixed costs refer to the business as a whole. Variable costing assumes that the variable cost **per unit** stays the same over a range of activity (see Figure 1.2a). This means that **total** variable costs increase linearly with activity (see Figure 1.2b).

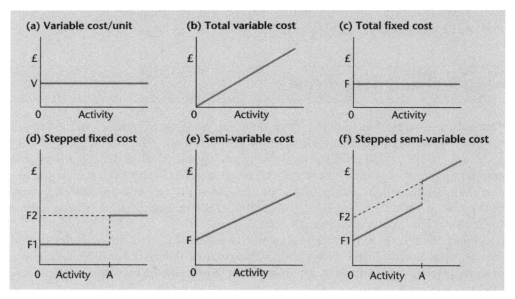

Figure 1.2 **Patterns of variable and fixed cost behaviour**

Great care must be taken if *fixed cost per unit* is used in calculations. This measure will change every time the number of units changes, i.e. fixed cost per unit is **not** fixed!

Stepped fixed costs

When a certain level of production and/or sales activity is reached, there is a sudden increase in fixed costs from F1 to F2 (see Figure 1.2d). For example, when output increases significantly, it may be necessary to put on an extra work shift. This occurs at activity level A and entails extra costs for items such as supervision, security, heating and lighting, etc.

Semi-variable costs

Although there are several costs which are either purely variable or purely fixed, many costs are semi-variable. The utilities, such as telephone and electricity, often have a fixed cost element such as line rental or a standing charge which has to be paid irrespective of usage. In addition, there is also a cost per unit used. The graph of the semi-variable cost (see Figure 1.2e) combines the features of graphs (b) and (c).

If the semi-variable cost covers a range of activity including a stepped fixed cost, it would behave as shown in graph (f). This graph is obtained by combining graphs (b) and (d).

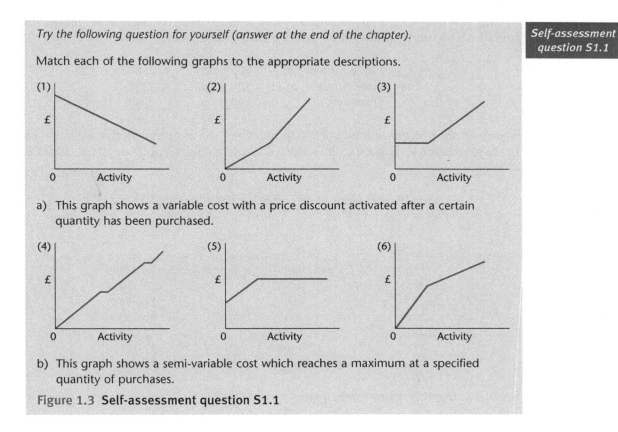

Try the following question for yourself (answer at the end of the chapter).

Self-assessment question S1.1

Match each of the following graphs to the appropriate descriptions.

(1) £ Activity 0   (2) £ Activity 0   (3) £ Activity 0

a) This graph shows a variable cost with a price discount activated after a certain quantity has been purchased.

(4) £ Activity 0   (5) £ Activity 0   (6) £ Activity 0

b) This graph shows a semi-variable cost which reaches a maximum at a specified quantity of purchases.

Figure 1.3 **Self-assessment question S1.1**

c) This graph shows a variable cost with 10 free units for every 100 bought.
d) This graph shows the fixed cost per unit.
e) This graph shows a variable cost which has a minimum charge.
f) This graph shows the variable cost of a scarce item. When local supplies have been exhausted, it has to be purchased abroad, entailing extra transport costs.

Analysis of semi-variable costs into their fixed and variable elements

It is not just the utilities that have semi-variable costs. Many other costs, such as security and maintenance, also follow this pattern. Often, only the **total** amounts of these semi-variable costs are known and the fixed and variable elements have to be worked out mathematically. Three alternative ways of doing this are shown below.

The high–low method

Figure 1.4 shows the machine maintenance costs and the output level of products for the first six monthly periods of the year.

Only two sets of monthly information are used, one from the highest-output month (month 3 = 600 units) and the other from the lowest-output month (month 6 = 500 units).

	Highest (month 3)	600 units	£12,400
Less:	Lowest (month 6)	500 units	£12,000
	Difference	100 units	£400

Since both the £12,400 and the £12,000 include the fixed cost element, this is eliminated by the subtraction and the £400 difference is due solely to the variable cost of the 100 units difference.

Variable cost per unit produced = £400/100 units = £4/unit

Month	Output (units)	Maintenance cost (£)
1	586	12,340
2	503	11,949
3	600	12,400
4	579	12,298
5	550	12,075
6	500	12,000

Figure 1.4 **Monthly maintenance costs**

Using this in month 6,

$$\begin{aligned}
\text{Variable cost of 500 units} = 500 \times \text{£4} = \quad &\text{£2,000} \\
\text{Total cost of 500 units} \qquad\qquad\quad &= \underline{\text{£12,000}} \\
\text{Therefore, fixed cost of 500 units} \qquad &= \underline{\text{£10,000}}
\end{aligned}$$

These cost elements can be checked by applying them to the other month used, month 3:

$$\begin{aligned}
\text{Variable cost of 600 units} = 600 \times \text{£4} = \quad &\text{£2,400} \\
\text{Fixed cost of 600 units} \qquad\qquad\quad &= \underline{\text{£10,000}} \\
\text{Therefore, total cost of 600 units} \qquad &= \underline{\text{£12,400}}
\end{aligned}$$

This shows the calculations to be correct. However, if any of the other months **not** used in the calculation is chosen to test the results, it will probably not work! This is because the high–low method uses the information from only two months. It ignores all the other information. It assumes that the relationship between the cost and production output is a linear one, i.e. if all the monthly points were plotted on a graph, they would all be points on the same straight line. In fact, this is not so, as you can probably see from Figure 1.4. For instance, month 2 has a higher output (503 units) than month 6 (500 units) but a lower maintenance cost.

It can be seen that the high–low method is a fairly crude way of estimating the fixed and variable cost elements of a semi-variable cost. However, its advantage is that it is easy to understand and easy to calculate.

Scattergraphs

If the monthly information shown above (in the high–low method) was plotted on a graph it would look like Figure 1.5.

The line of best fit is drawn on the graph by eye. The intersection of this line and the vertical cost axis gives the fixed cost element. This is **read** from the graph and should be close to £10,000.

The slope of the line

$$\frac{\text{Change in cost}}{\text{Change in output}} = 2{,}384/600 = \text{£3.97}$$

gives the variable cost per unit. You may remember that the equation for a straight line is

$$y = a + bx$$

where a is the intersection with the vertical axis and b is the slope of the line. In this context, the fixed cost is a and the variable cost per unit is b.

The disadvantage of this method is that drawing the line of best fit by eye is subjective and different individuals will produce slightly different lines. However, it does have the advantage of using all the available information and, like the high–low method, a scattergraph will give a workable estimate and is easy to understand.

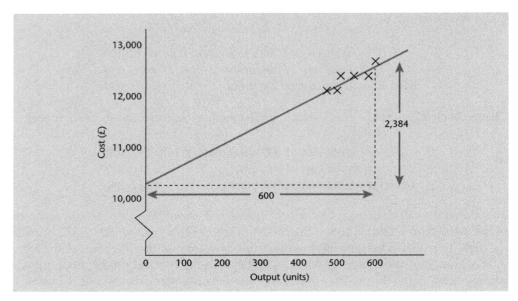

Figure 1.5 **A scattergraph**

Regression analysis

This method is similar to the scattergraph but the line of best fit is not drawn by eye. The equation for the line is calculated by a statistical technique called *regression analysis*. It is sometimes known as *least squares regression*. It is more precise than the other two methods but it is much more complex mathematically. The technique of regression analysis is not covered by this book. It is sufficient for you to know of its existence and availability if needed.

The most important thing to remember is that, although it is more precise than the high–low and scattergraph methods, it still only gives an estimate of the fixed and variable cost elements. The extra complexity involved may not be worth the improvement in accuracy gained.

Self-assessment question S1.2

Try the following question for yourself (answer at the end of the chapter).

As the manager of an Indian restaurant with a take-away service, you have been asked to prepare a detailed budget for next year. To help you with this, you need to know the fixed and variable cost elements of your delivery cost to customers' homes.

The following information is available from the monthly accounts. Calculate the fixed and variable cost elements using the *high–low* method.

Month	No. of deliveries	Total delivery cost (£)
July	403	662.70
August	291	561.90
September	348	613.20
October	364	627.60
November	521	768.90
December	387	648.30

Absorption costs: direct and indirect

Direct cost

This is expenditure which can be economically identified with, and specifically **measured** in, a product.

Consider an advertising agency specializing in the production of television adverts. The cost of hiring a celebrity to appear in one such advert is a measurable direct cost of that advert. Similarly, if the company is a furniture manufacturer, the cost of materials used to make a chair and the pay of the operative assembling it are measurable direct costs of that chair.

Indirect cost (or overhead)

This is expenditure which **cannot** be economically identified with, and specifically **measured** in, a product.

There are many, many different overheads including expenses such as the supervisor's pay, depreciation of fixed assets, business rates and insurance. Somehow, a proportion of these non-measurable expenses has to be included in the total product cost. Absorption costing is one way of doing this. It is based on the assumption that costs can be analysed into their 'direct' and 'indirect' components. For each product, the direct cost is measured but the indirect cost is estimated.

$$\text{Absorption cost} = \text{direct cost} + \text{indirect cost}$$

The estimates of indirect costs are usually based on some connection or correlation between the cost and a measure such as machine hours used, direct labour hours used or total cost of direct materials used. Absorption costing is the subject of Chapter 9.

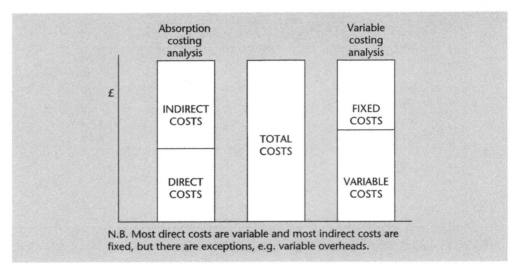

Figure 1.6 **Alternative cost analysis**

Comparison of alternative cost analyses

Variable costing analyses total costs into fixed and variable components. Absorption costing analyses total costs into direct and indirect components. In itself, this is not problematical as these two systems of costing, variable and absorption, are independent financial models. However, it is not unusual to be confused by these terms and how they interrelate. The aim of Figure 1.6 is to clarify these relationships.

Cost analysis by activity

This analysis is based on the principle that costs are **caused** by activities and that activities are caused by products or services. The activity-based cost of a product is a result of determining the costs of all the activities caused by that product. This principle is fundamentally different from the correlation principle used in absorption costing.

Activities are identified and their costs calculated before being attached to products via a measure of the activity called a *cost driver*. Activity-based costing gives significantly more accurate product costs than absorption costing but it has difficulties of its own and does not give 100% accurate costs. This subject is discussed at length in Chapter 10.

Relevant and irrelevant costs

This analysis of costs is very useful in decision making. In brief, it differentiates between those costs which affect a decision (i.e. relevant costs) and those that do not (irrelevant costs). This approach to decision making is discussed further in Chapter 7.

Summary

- Each product can have several different costs.
- The cost of a product depends on the purpose for which this information is required.
- Business types can be divided into three categories: manufacturing, trading and providing services.
- Period costs are written off to the profit and loss account of the period for which they were incurred.
- Product costs are built into the production cost of manufactured items and are either accounted for by the cost of sales figure for the year in which they were incurred or carried forward to the next period in the closing stock valuation figure.
- Total cost can be analysed into variable and fixed cost elements.
- Semi-variable costs have both variable and fixed cost elements.
- Fixed costs are stable only up to a certain level of activity; above this, they step up to a higher level.
- There are three ways of analysing semi-variable costs into their fixed and variable components: the high–low method, scattergraphs and regression analysis.
- Total cost can be analysed into direct and indirect cost elements.
- Costs can be analysed causally according to production activities and activities can be analysed causally by products.
- As an aid to decision making, costs can be analysed into relevant and irrelevant types.
- Direct and indirect costs are similar to, but different from, variable and fixed costs.

Further reading

Anderson, M. C., Banker, R. D. and Janakiraman, S. N. (2003) 'Are selling, general, and administrative costs "sticky"?', *Journal of Accounting Research*, Vol. 41, Issue 1, March.

Drury, C. (2004) *Management and Cost Accounting*, 6th edition, Thomson Learning, London. See chapter 'An introduction to cost terms and concepts'.

Horngren, C., Bhimani, A., Datar, S. and Foster, G. (2002) *Management and Cost Accounting*, Prentice Hall Europe, Harlow. See chapter 'Determining how costs behave'.

Liu, L. and Robinson, J. (2002) 'Double measure', *Financial Management (CIMA)*, October.

Upchurch, A. (2003) *Management Accounting, Principles and Practice*, 2nd edition, Financial Times/Prentice Hall, Harlow. See chapter 'Cost estimation'.

Weetman, P. (2002) *Management Accounting, an Introduction*, 3rd edition, Financial Times/ Prentice Hall, Harlow. See chapter 'Classification of costs'.

Answers to self-assessment questions

S1.1 Cost behaviour graphs

a) Graph 6
b) Graph 5
c) Graph 4
d) Graph 1
e) Graph 3
f) Graph 2

S1.2 Indian take-away delivery costs

Only two sets of monthly information are used, one from the highest-activity month (November = 521 deliveries) and the other from the lowest-activity month (August = 291 deliveries):

	Highest (November)	521 deliveries	£768.90
Less:	Lowest (August)	291 deliveries	£561.90
	Difference	230 deliveries	£207.00

Variable cost per delivery = £207.00/230 = £0.90/delivery

Using this in November,

Variable cost of deliveries = 521 × £0.90 = £468.90
Total cost of 521 deliveries   = £768.90
Therefore, Fixed cost of 521 deliveries   = £300.00

These cost elements can be checked by applying them to the other month used, August:

Variable cost of 291 deliveries = 291 × £0.90 = £261.90
Fixed cost of 291 deliveries   = £300.00
Therefore, Total cost of 291 deliveries   = £561.90

Review questions

1 Explain the difference between manufacturing, trading and providing services.
2 Explain the difference between product costs and period costs.
3 Explain the difference between variable and fixed costs.
4 Explain what semi-variable costs and stepped fixed costs are.
5 Describe the advantages and disadvantages of finding the fixed and variable elements of semi-variable costs using the high–low method.
6 Describe the advantages and disadvantages of finding the fixed and variable elements of semi-variable costs using a scattergraph.
7 Explain **in outline** what regression analysis is.
8 Explain the difference between direct and indirect costs.
9 Compare variable cost analysis with absorption cost analysis.
10 Explain the underlying theory of activity-based costing.
11 Explain the difference between relevant and irrelevant costs.

The answers to all these questions can be found in the text of this chapter.

CHAPTER 2

The difference between profit and cash

Introduction

There are many people, including some business people, who think that profit is the same thing as cash. They use the two words interchangeably, believing there to be no difference in their meaning. They are mistaken.

Profit is **not** the same as cash.

As a manager, it is vital that you understand this. If you do not, studying the many other useful topics in this book may prove to be a waste of time!

Cash is the money that individuals and organizations use to exchange things of value. It consists of bank notes, coins and bank account balances.

Profit is the excess of income over expenditure (incurred to produce that income) in a specified period of time. There are many accounting rules, principles and concepts governing the way profit is calculated. They can be very complex (because business is very complex) and are sometimes controversial.

MG Rover, which collapsed in April 2005, is a good example of a complex organization. The holding company, Phoenix Venture Holdings (PVH), was at the top of a web of 15 or so other companies which were connected to each other in complicated ways. Some of these immediately went into administration when the Shanghai Automotive Industry Corporation (SAIC) of China pulled out of talks to buy a significant part of the UK operation, but others remained trading as solvent entities. In the emotional aftermath of the collapse which resulted in many thousands of people losing their jobs, it was reported in the press that there was a possible 'black hole' in PVH's accounts into which £452 million of cash had disappeared. This figure was the difference between the £1,563 million paid into the company since it started in 2000 and the £1,111 million of capital expenditure and losses during most of that period. This so-called black hole is pure speculation as its calculation mixes together cash flows and profit/losses; these are fundamentally different concepts and cannot be combined in this way. Its creators either do not understand this difference or are mischievously ignoring it.

You may have heard of 'creative accounting' where profits shown by audited company accounts have been manipulated (usually increased) by the dubious, but legal, application of accounting rules. Every few years there is a major court case to test whether a company has gone too far and broken the rules rather than just bent them. This situation is partly due to the way in which the world of business is constantly changing, while the rules lag behind until suitably amended.

One result of creative accounting over the years is that many people do not now trust reported profit figures as much as they used to. They are aware that there are many ways in which profit figures can be manipulated. Also, they acknowledge that to understand published accounts fully, a high degree of accounting knowledge is needed.

Take the example of a new road haulage firm that has bought a small fleet of lorries for £500,000. Reducing balance depreciation at 40% a year will give a depreciation charge of £200,000 (£500,000 × 40%). This gives a net profit of £50,000 (see Figure 2.1a). However, if the owner had told his bank that first-year profits would be in the region of £100,000, he might decide to change the depreciation method to straight line over five years. This would give a depreciation charge of £100,000 (£500,000/5) and a profit of £150,000 (see Figure 2.1b). Note that for exactly the same set of business transactions in the year, two different **legitimate** profits have been produced without breaking any accounting rules! This example of creative accounting (which can be extremely complex) has been kept very simple in order to illustrate the point.

a) Reducing balance depreciation at 40% p.a.

	£
Sales revenue	640,000
Depreciation (500,000 × 40%)	200,000
All other expenses	390,000
Total expenses	590,000
Net profit	50,000

b) Straight-line depreciation over five years

	£
Sales revenue	640,000
Depreciation (500,000/5)	100,000
All other expenses	390,000
Total expenses	490,000
Net profit	**150,000**

Note: No physical change but profits tripled!

Figure 2.1 **Creative accounting in a road haulage firm**

The published accounts contain three major statements: the balance sheet, the profit and loss account and the cash flow statement. Many professional people who use accounts in their work now believe that the cash flow statement is just as important as the profit and loss account, if not more so. They know that, although profits can be manipulated, cash cannot.

Every figure making up the balance sheet totals is subject, to some extent, to subjective opinion, **except cash**. Cash can be, and is, counted and verified for audit purposes. 'The Pizza Wagon' example below illustrates the difference between profit and cash and shows just how critical this difference can be. It can be literally a matter of life or death for a business.

Learning objectives

Having worked through this chapter you should be able to:

- define what is meant by 'cash';
- define what is meant by 'profit';
- explain the importance of cash flow statements;
- convert profits into cash flows (and vice versa);
- reconcile total profit to total cash flow over the lifetime of a business;
- explain the importance of understanding the difference between profit and cash.

Example 2.1

The Pizza Wagon

Olive Napoloni has recently lost her job as a result of her employer going into liquidation and ceasing to trade. She is approaching her 57th birthday but will not be able to access her private pension until she is 60 in three years' time. Because Olive is an active woman with a positive attitude to life, she wants to work for the next three years but in a different way from her last 30 years of office work.

Over the years she has helped a friend run a local business providing the catering for one-off events such as weddings and anniversary parties. She enjoys the catering business but would like to work outdoors and to have the opportunity of meeting new people as well. After much careful thought, she decides to start a business of her own offering a mobile catering facility at outdoor events such as pop festivals, fairs and sporting events. She has always been able to make good pizzas and decides to capitalize on this strength. Her business will be called 'The Pizza Wagon' and will be run from a specially converted parcel van.

The final cost of this van, including all alterations, has been quoted at £19,500. However, after three years' heavy use she believes it will not be worth very much and, to be on the safe side, decides to assume it will be worth nothing at all. Her preliminary costings show that the ingredients for one good-sized pizza will be £1.00 and she decides to sell them for £4.00 each. Her budgeted accounts for the three financial years and for the three-year period as a whole are as follows.

	Year 1	Year 2	Year 3	Three-year period
No. of pizzas sold	15,000	20,000	25,000	60,000
	£	£	£	£
Sales revenue	60,000	80,000	100,000	240,000
Cost of ingredients	15,000	20,000	25,000	60,000
Gross profit	45,000	60,000	75,000	180,000
Van depreciation	6,500	6,500	6,500	19,500
Van running costs	9,000	9,000	9,000	27,000
Site fees	11,000	14,000	19,000	44,000
Advertising	5,000	4,000	4,000	13,000
Administration	3,500	3,500	3,500	10,500
Total overheads	35,000	37,000	42,000	114,000
Net profit	10,000	23,000	33,000	66,000

Olive is very pleased with these projections, especially as she will avoid making a loss in her first year and need not bother asking her bank for a loan to pay herself a salary. Although the £10,000 in year 1 is only about two-thirds of what she is earning now, she believes she will be able to manage on that for one year if she is very careful with her personal expenditure.

However, because she has no track record in business, she is unable to buy her van on credit terms and has to pay the full £19,500 at the start of her first year of trading. Fortunately, she has been able to arrange an overdraft facility to cover this and other business costs by pledging her home as security. She knows it will be a hard three years but is pleased to be in a position to give this new venture a try.

Unfortunately there is a major flaw in Olive's logic. Can you see what it is?

She is assuming that the profit and the net cash inflow for The Pizza Wagon are the same thing. But there is one legitimate item on the budgeted accounts which does not translate into an equivalent cash movement. The sales revenue figures result in cash inflows of those amounts. The cost of ingredients and the overhead expenses translate into cash outflows with the exception of one item, **depreciation**.

Depreciation is a non-cash expense. In Olive's case, the accounts show straight-line depreciation over three years with a zero residual value for the van. Because she has to pay for it in full at the beginning, the cash outflow for the van in year 1 is £19,500 not £6,500. The cash outflow is £13,000 more than the depreciation for year 1, so the profit of £10,000 translates into a net cash **outflow** of £3,000 (see below).

Olive will not receive £10,000 in cash in year 1. In fact, during that year she will have to put **an extra £3,000** into her business. And what is she going to live on? How is she going to pay for her food, electricity, clothes, etc.? She may or may not be able to arrange a loan from some source to cover the £13,000 difference and provide her with adequate living expenses. But unless she understands the difference between profit and cash, her business and personal life will turn into a financial disaster!

Having looked carefully at year 1, let us consider what happens in years 2 and 3. The depreciation in these years (correctly shown in the accounts) does not translate into any cash flows at all. The financial effect of this is shown below.

	Year 1 £	Year 2 £	Year 3 £	Three-year period £
Net profit	10,000	23,000	33,000	66,000
Adjustment	−13,000	+6,500	+6,500	–
Net cash flow	−3,000	+29,500	+39,500	+66,000

So it is not all bad news for Olive. Although her cash flow is negative in year 1, in years 2 and 3 it is not only positive but greater than she expected. The figures show a timing difference between profit and cash. Timing differences are what the accruals accounting concept is all about. Accruals and prepayments are part of this jigsaw and so are provisions such as depreciation and doubtful debts. The above example has been kept very simple in order to illustrate the principle involved. However, in practice detailed cash budgets must be prepared and monitored for the business to survive. Many, many, many **profitable** businesses have had to cease trading due to insufficient cash resources. Lack of cash is one – if not the major – reason for business insolvency.

The lifetime view

Remember that business is about money, i.e. cash. Profit, on the other hand, is the result of an arbitrary set of rules set by people in government, accountancy associations and committees. It is an intangible concept. The financial year is, to some extent, an irrelevant time period imposed upon businesses. Companies are not created specifically to trade for exactly one year. The vast majority of them wish to trade continuously into the future and would be very happy to prepare published audited accounts only every few years instead of every year. Some businesses, like The Pizza Wagon above, are created for a specific purpose and have a set life span. These organizations tend to view financial years as artificial divisions of their existence. They are much more interested in the outcome of the project over its whole life than its annual profits.

Looking at The Pizza Wagon figures above, you can see that, **over the whole lifetime of a business, the total of profit exactly equals the total of cash** (£66,000 in this case). This principle is just as true for the many continuing businesses all around us even though it is far from obvious.

*Self-assessment
question S2.1*

Try the question for yourself (answer at the end of the chapter).

The Bourton Trading Company existed for four years only before being wound up. Its financial record is shown below in the form of summary annual profit and loss accounts.

	Year 1 £000	Year 2 £000	Year 3 £000	Year 4 £000
Sales revenue	400	375	440	380
Cost of sales	225	200	250	220
Gross profit	175	175	190	160
Increase/(decrease) in doubtful debt provision	20	(5)	(5)	(10)
Training expenses	–	3	4	13
Inf'n system depreciation	10	10	10	10
Other admin expenses	45	40	45	50
Co. vehicle depreciation	40	32	26	22
Marketing expenses	25	30	40	35
Bank interest	35	25	30	20
Total overheads	175	135	150	140
Net profit	0	40	40	20

Notes:

1 £10,000 of the £40,000 marketing expenses in year 3 were actually paid in year 2 in order to secure advertising space for a campaign run early in year 3.
2 In order to help the business establish itself, the bank allowed it to defer the payment of 40% of the interest charges it incurred in year 1 until year 2. The profit and loss accounts show the full amounts of interest incurred in each year.
3 In order to get the best discounts, the company always bought its fixed assets for cash with a lump-sum payment.
4 The information system cost £40,000 and was obsolete and worthless when the company closed.
5 The company vehicles cost £140,000 in total. At the end of year 4 they were sold for £20,000 cash.

Tasks:

a) Calculate the net cash flow for each of the four years.
b) Compare the total of profit to the net cash flow for the four-year period as a whole.

The manager's point of view (written by Nigel Burton)

It is an enduring fact of life that you never have enough money to do everything you want. This is as true of companies as it is of individuals. Cash is a company's most precious resource and its stewardship in the best interests of the business is central to the art of management.

Every company has to re-invest in order to survive. If a company were to pay out 100% of its profits in dividends, it would run out of cash in short order. Even a static business will need to spend on renovating or renewing old plant, training replacement staff, and seeking out new customers to replace those that inevitably get lost. Standing still is never an option. And if your company has to change, it may as well become bigger and stronger.

All companies therefore pursue the holy grail of growth. Even Olive in the above example is expecting her little business to show some impressive expansion. Growth demands injections of cash in many different areas: new product developments, new plant on which to manufacture them, new markets into which to sell them, broader infrastructure to support the growing business, and increased working capital to allow the company to operate on a day-to-day basis. It may be several years before even profitable ventures reach the stage of cash-generation rather than cash-consumption.

In the 1980s, our company was one of a number developing components for use in airbag safety systems for motor cars. Here was a product, which, if successful, would quickly become a standard part in every new car. Even with strong competition, the opportunities were clearly enormous. Within just a few years, sales went from zero to multiples of millions. The real challenge to management was to ensure that the plant capacity and administrative infrastructure were continuously upgraded in advance of the ever-growing demand. This meant that every penny generated, together with a good deal of additional outside financing, was ploughed back into the business, and the shareholders, sitting on a hugely profitable venture, saw plenty of capital growth, but precious little cash return in their dividends.

This was, of course, an exceptional circumstance, yet I doubt if there are many companies whose profit projections do not anticipate continuous future growth. How often do we see the 'hockey-stick' graph of a company's projected performance, where actual profits in recent years have remained flat, but future projections show a sharply upward trend? Managers would be accused of, at best, lack of ambition, and, at worst, lack of competence, if their input was not expected to bring improved company results. But how many companies actually achieve these forecasts? If a business fails to make its expected profits, the first casualty may well be cash flow. Budgets are often set as targets, designed to stretch sales efforts and encourage cost savings. Truly realistic estimates might indicate a need for rather higher cash requirements.

So it is easy to overestimate the amount of cash which will become available. Take capital projects for example. In a large, diverse organization, there is always competition between the various businesses for the available capital funds. Senior management will support those projects which give both the greatest rate of return and the quickest payback on their investment. There is pressure on those preparing the supporting documentation to ensure that their project looks attractive, so optimistic salesmen are likely to over-pitch the sales forecasts, while over-confident engineers underestimate the total costs of construction. The result is that the project is far less profitable than forecast, takes much longer to pay back the investment, and in the worst circumstances could pull the entire company down. A business obtaining capital funds on such an unsound basis will almost certainly come unstuck. Every capital investment is, to some degree, a gamble, but the risks can be minimized if a realistic approach to the cash flow requirements is taken.

Perhaps the most common source of liquidity problems today is the failure of management to control working capital, i.e. stocks and debtors, less creditors. This represents the amount of cash needed to oil the wheels of the business, as opposed to investment in capital projects, and is an area which can swallow up large chunks of cash, if it is not properly managed. In fact, it is so frequently neglected, particularly by smaller companies, that the topic warrants a chapter of its own in this book (see Chapter 4).

Sometimes there are external factors which can have a dramatic impact on cash flow. In the early 1970s, a huge increase in the price of oil led to unprecedented levels of inflation, which drove many companies towards insolvency. With inflation in excess of 20% a year, much of the cash generated was needed simply to keep the company standing still. It required 20% more cash than in the previous year to purchase replacement stock, pay the employees wages, or repair a piece of plant. These increases could, of course, be recovered in selling prices, but this was usually too late, as many of the higher costs would be incurred well before the customer had paid up. Any company which was unable to keep pace with the ever increasing cash requirement had to make up the difference through borrowings, which, in turn, hurt profits with continually rising interest costs. During this period, cash generation, rather than profit, became the critical factor to the survival of many companies.

Accounts based on historical costs ceased to give a sufficiently accurate picture of a company's health, so the concept of 'Current Cost Accounting' was introduced. This required balance sheet items to be revalued at their replacement cost, in order to give a better view of the company's solvency and its ability to continue trading on a going-concern basis. This is why the cash flow statement is of such importance. The company may be full of clever people, all pursuing excellent projects which push the overall profits higher and higher, but the sum of their efforts might be bankruptcy. Therefore, a wise manager will always keep an eye on the cash implication of everything he (or she) does.

Finally, a comment on creative accountancy: it is certainly true that there are many different ways of accounting for business activities. Over the years I have had many discussions with the auditors over depreciation rates, accruals, levels of bad debt and obsolete stock reserves, and provisions for other identifiable expenses. There are many areas in a set of accounts where judgement must be applied. But I have never argued for an **increase** in profit unless the underlying circumstances clearly supported it. The prudence concept should be the guiding star for accountants. To anticipate profits, i.e. to take in sales too early, or to underprovide for expenses, is dangerous, irresponsible, unprofessional, does no service to the business, and will get you fired! To be conservative, however, would be regarded as prudent, pragmatic and farsighted. All businesses have to cope with unexpected items of expenditure, such as a bad debt, major repair, exchange loss, etc., and in my experience, managing directors expect their accountants to hold a few 'pots of money', i.e. conservative provisions, which can be released to offset unexpected hits to profit.

The rule is therefore: Keep some provisions up your sleeve for a rainy day, but never, ever, conceal your losses.

Summary

- Cash consists of notes, coins and bank balances.
- Profit is an intangible concept measured by the application of accounting rules.
- Cash is not the same as profit.
- Annual accounts contain many timing differences.
- Timing differences include non-cash expenses, provisions, accruals, prepayments.
- Profits can be manipulated, cash cannot.
- The cash flow figures are at least as important as the profit and loss figures.
- Understanding the difference between profit and cash is vital.
- Many profitable businesses have ceased trading due to lack of cash.
- Over the complete lifetime of a business, total profits equal total net cash flow.

Further reading

Arnold, J. and Turley, S. (1996) *Accounting for Management Decisions*, 3rd edition, Financial Times/Prentice Hall, London. See Chapter 2, 'Accounting and decision making', *section 2.5*: 'The issue of measurement'.

Harrison, W. and Horngren, C. (2001) *Financial Accounting*, 4th edition, Prentice Hall, Englewood Cliffs, NJ. See Chapter 3, 'Accrual accounting and the financial statements', *section*: 'Accrual-basis accounting versus cash-basis accounting'.

Weetman, P. (2002) *Financial Accounting, an Introduction*, 3rd edition, Financial Times/Prentice Hall, Harlow. See chapter 'Who needs accounting', *supplement*: 'Introduction to the terminology of business transactions'.

Answer to self-assessment question

S2.1 The Bourton Trading company

a) Calculate the net cash flow for each of the four years.

	Year 1 £000	Year 2 £000	Year 3 £000	Year 4 £000
Net profit	0	40	40	20
Increase/(decrease) adjustments:				
1 Doubtful debt provision	20	(5)	(5)	(10)
2 Prepaid advertising	–	(10)	10	–
3 Deferred bank interest	14	(14)	–	–
4 Inf'n system depreciation	(30)	10	10	10
5 Co. vehicle depreciation	(100)	32	26	42
Cash in/(out)flow	(96)	53	81	62

Note: The £42,000 vehicle depreciation adjustment in year 4 consists of the £22,000 depreciation charge plus the £20,000 cash received for the sale of the vehicles.

b) Compare the total of profit to the net cash flow for the four-year period as a whole.

Year	Profit	Cash flow
1	0	(96)
2	40	53
3	40	81
4	20	62
Total	100	100

Review questions

1 Define what is meant by 'cash'.
2 Define what is meant by 'profit'.
3 Explain the importance of cash flow statements.
4 Convert profits into cash flows (and vice versa).
5 Reconcile total profit to total cash flow over the lifetime of a business.
6 Explain the importance of understanding the difference between profit and cash.

The answers to all these questions can be found in the text of this chapter.

CHAPTER 5

Variable costing and breakeven analysis

Introduction

Sometimes there are ways of doing things which are so simple they seem almost too easy, too good to be true. Variable costing is one of these. But do not be fooled by its simplicity – it is a very powerful technique. It is used mainly for short-term decision making and calculating the effect of production and sales levels on profitability. Short-term decision making is the subject of the next chapter. This chapter concentrates on the relationship between profit and activity (i.e. production and sales), commonly known as breakeven analysis.

At some point in your life you will probably think seriously about starting your own business. If the type of business you have in mind involves providing the same item for many different customers, breakeven analysis will be very useful to you. Suppose you decide to open a driving school, offering lessons to learner drivers. After much careful thought you will be able to estimate your total annual cost. Dividing this amount by the number of lessons (**estimated conservatively**) will give you the cost per lesson. But what are you going to charge your customers for each lesson? How do you know if you will make a profit or a loss? And how much is it likely to be? These are very important questions for anyone going into business on their own. Breakeven analysis is the financial model designed to answer these questions.

Note that variable costing is also known as *marginal costing and cost–volume–profit (CVP) analysis.*

Learning objectives	Having worked through this chapter you should be able to:

Having worked through this chapter you should be able to:
- differentiate between variable and fixed costs;
- define contribution;
- explain the relationship between contribution, fixed costs and net profit;
- calculate contribution;
- calculate breakeven point;
- draw traditional and contribution breakeven charts;
- define and calculate the margin of safety;
- evaluate different cost structures in terms of their operational gearing;
- calculate the activity level to produce a target profit;
- draw and use a profit–volume chart;
- discuss the assumptions and limitations of breakeven analysis.

Cost behaviour

This section is a brief revision of Chapter 2. Variable costing is based on the difference between fixed and variable costs, which are defined as follows and illustrated in Figure 5.1.

Variable costs – Costs which vary with output (e.g. raw materials)
Fixed costs – Costs which do not change when output changes (e.g. business rates)
Semi-variable costs – Costs which are partly fixed and partly variable (e.g. telephone)

Although there are several costs which are either purely variable or purely fixed, many costs are semi-variable. The utilities, such as telephone and electricity, often have a fixed

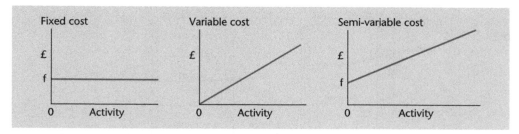

Figure 5.1 **Patterns of cost behaviour**

cost element, such as line rental or a standing charge, which has to be paid irrespective of usage. In addition, there is also a cost per unit used. The graph of the semi-variable cost combines the features of the other two graphs. Sometimes, only the total amounts of semi-variable costs are known for successive periods and the fixed and variable elements have to be worked out. (One way of doing this is the 'high–low method' as detailed in Chapter 1, on cost behaviour.)

Contribution

In the introduction to this chapter, it was pointed out that ignoring fixed costs is sometimes the correct thing to do. As fixed costs cannot be changed **in the short term**, there is no point considering them for short-term decision making. This approach results in something that is like 'profit' but is not 'profit'. To avoid confusion, this new entity is called 'contribution'.

Contribution is defined as the excess of sales revenue over the variable costs.

It can be thought of as the contribution towards paying for the fixed costs. Once all fixed costs have been covered, any further contribution is all net profit, as shown in Figure 5.2.

Contribution calculations

The Grubsteaks restaurant sells 18,000 meals a year at a standard selling price of £5. If each meal has a variable cost of £2, what annual contribution is earned? If the fixed costs are £30,000 in total, what is the net profit?

$$
\begin{array}{rl}
& \text{£} \\
\text{Sales revenue} = & 90,000 \quad (18,000 \times £5) \\
\text{Variable costs} = & \underline{36,000} \quad (18,000 \times £2) \\
\text{Contribution} = & 54,000 \\
\text{Fixed costs} = & \underline{30,000} \\
\text{Net profit} = & \underline{24,000}
\end{array}
$$

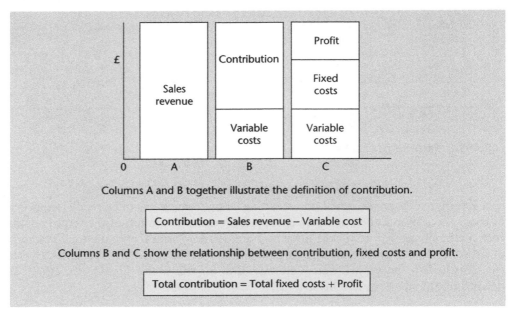

Figure 5.2 **Contribution relationships**

Alternatively, the contribution per unit could have been calculated first to give £3 (= £5 − £2). Multiplying this by 18,000 meals gives the total contribution of £54,000.

Self-assessment question S5.1

Try the following question for yourself (answer at the end of the chapter).

The Good Health drinks tent at a local horse-race meeting sells all its drinks at £2.50 each. The variable cost of each drink is £1.00 and the fixed cost for the one-day event is £2,700. If 4,000 drinks are sold in the day, what is (a) the total contribution, and (b) the net profit?

Breakeven point

Definition and calculation

The total contribution increases as more units are sold. A point will come when the total contribution is just enough to cover the fixed costs. At this precise level of sales, all the costs have been covered and the next unit sold will produce the first profits for the business. This critical point, where the business makes neither a profit nor a loss, is known as the *breakeven point* (BEP). This is a useful concept for planning and control purposes.

At BEP, **Total contribution = total fixed costs**

Continuing with the example used above, the Grubsteaks restaurant sells 18,000 meals a year at a standard selling price of £5 and a variable cost of £2 with fixed costs of £30,000; how many meals will it need to sell to break even?

Let breakeven occur when N meals have been sold – in other words, when N lots of unit contributions have been received.

$$\text{Total contribution} = \text{total fixed costs}$$
$$N \times \text{unit contribution} = \text{total fixed costs}$$
$$N \times (5 - 2) = 30,000$$
$$N = 30,000/3$$
$$N = 10,000 \text{ meals}$$

The relationship between costs and revenues can be illustrated graphically by *breakeven charts*. Figure 5.3 gives the basic structure; this is then added to in two alternative ways in Figures 5.4 and 5.5. It is these two alternatives that are normally seen and used in practice.

Figure 5.4 shows the total cost broken down into its fixed and variable elements.

Figure 5.5 also shows the fixed and variable elements, but with their positions reversed. This enables the contribution to be clearly illustrated by the shaded area. (This is not possible on the traditional breakeven chart.)

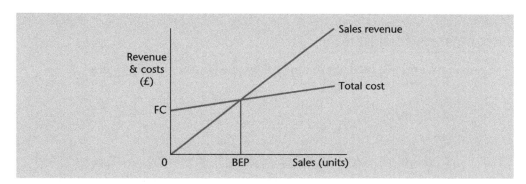

Figure 5.3 **Fundamental structure**

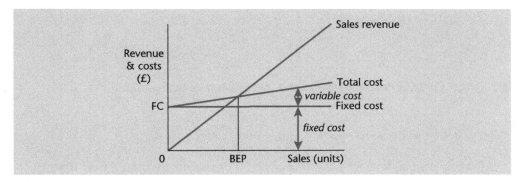

Figure 5.4 **Traditional breakeven chart**

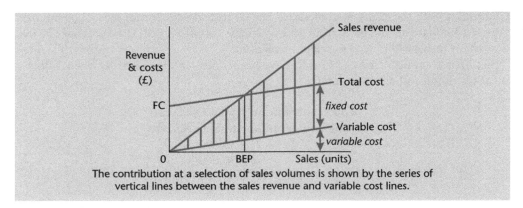

Figure 5.5 **Contribution breakeven chart**

Try the following question for yourself (answer at the end of the chapter).

Continuing with S5.1 above, the Good Health drinks tent at a local horse-race meeting sells all its drinks at £2.50 each. The variable cost of each drink is £1.00 and the fixed cost for the one-day event is £2,700. How many drinks does it need to sell to break even?

Graphical representation

The restaurant example used above can be illustrated by the chart in Figure 5.6.

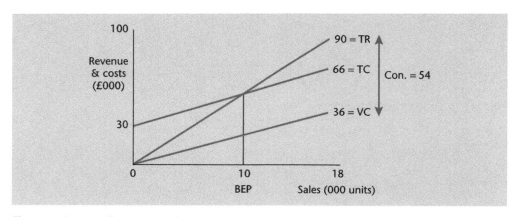

Figure 5.6 **Contribution breakeven chart for the Grubsteaks restaurant**

Try the following question for yourself (answer at the end of the chapter).

Using your answers from S5.1 and S5.2 above, draw a contribution breakeven chart (to scale) for the Good Health drinks tent.

Margin of safety

This is a measure of the amount by which sales can fall before profit turns to loss, i.e. the excess of actual sales over breakeven sales. This can be expressed as a number of units or as a percentage of sales and is illustrated by Figure 5.7.

For the Grubsteaks restaurant example:

$$\begin{aligned} \text{Actual number of meals sold} &= 18{,}000 \\ \text{Breakeven level of sales} &= \underline{10{,}000} \\ \text{Margin of safety} &= \underline{\ \ 8{,}000}\ \text{meals} \end{aligned}$$

or

$$\frac{\text{Margin of safety in units}}{\text{Actual sales in units}} \times 100 = \frac{8{,}000}{18{,}000} \times 100 = 44\% \text{ of sales}$$

So sales could fall by 44% before losses occurred.

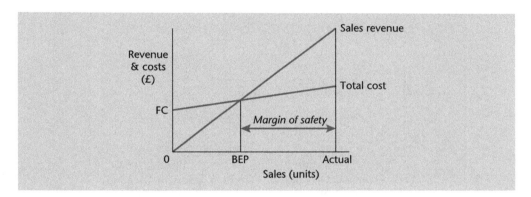

Figure 5.7 **Margin of safety**

Try the following question for yourself (answer at the end of the chapter).

Calculate the margin of safety for the Good Health drinks tent example in S5.3, (a) in units, and (b) as a percentage of sales.

Self-assessment question S5.4

Operational gearing

Operational gearing describes the relationship between fixed costs and total costs. The greater the amount of fixed costs, expressed as a percentage of total costs, the greater the operational gearing. The greater the operational gearing, the greater the effect of changes in sales volume on contribution and profit. The following formula expresses this numerically:

$$\text{Operational gearing} = \frac{\text{change in contribution or profit}}{\text{change in output}}$$

Consider the following situation where two separate businesses make and sell the same item at the same price. They both make cardboard 'outer' boxes to contain, for example, 48 packets of cereal. These large outers are used to transport large volumes of goods around the country.

Business A keeps fixed costs to a minimum but has a high proportion of variable costs. It uses simple bending and gluing devices operated by 12 employees and buys in large sheets of ready-made cardboard as its raw material. On the other hand, business B has invested heavily in automated machinery whose first process is to make its own cardboard sheet. This needs only two people to operate but causes a much larger amount of depreciation (i.e. fixed cost) than in business A. Its raw material is shredded recycled paper and other fibres which are much cheaper to buy than ready-made cardboard. Consequently, business B has a much higher proportion of fixed costs than variable costs compared with A. (See Figure 5.8 and notice the change in slope of the total cost line.)

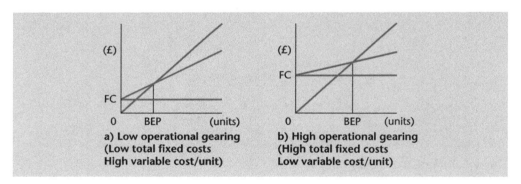

Figure 5.8 **Operational gearing**

As an example, for one outer:

	A	B
	£	£
Selling price	5	5
Variable cost	3	1
Contribution	2	4
Annual fixed cost	£100,000	£300,000

If there is a new order for 3,000 outers the profit will increase by £6,000 (3,000 × £2) for business A but by £12,000 (3,000 × £4) for business B. B will do better than A.

However, if a customer decides to purchase its outers elsewhere and cancels an order for 3,000 outers, the profit will decrease by £6,000 (3,000 × £2) for business A but by £12,000 (3,000 × £4) for business B. This time, A will do better than B.

The greater the operational gearing, the greater the effect of changes in sales volume on profit. In other words, the greater the operational gearing, the greater the risk.

When starting a new business, and sales are not very predictable, low operational gearing is preferable to high operational gearing. Low gearing means that there are fewer fixed costs to be covered before reaching profitability. This strategy helps to minimize risk.

On the other hand, as shown in the above example, provided the business is making profits, high gearing gives a greater increase in profit for each extra item sold.

Activity levels for target profits

Another useful calculation is to determine the number of items that has to be sold to achieve a given net profit. Figure 5.2 at the start of this chapter illustrates the following relationship:

$$\text{Total contribution} = \text{total fixed costs} + \text{profit}$$

If the unit contribution, the total fixed cost and the target profit are known, the activity level can be calculated. Suppose you were given the following information:

	£/unit
Direct materials	4
Direct labour	7
Variable overhead	3
Selling price	24
Total fixed cost	£5,000

How many items need to be sold for the business to make a profit of £10,000?

$$\text{Unit contribution} = \text{sales revenue} - \text{variable costs}$$
$$= 24 - (4 + 7 + 3) = 10$$

Let the number of items needed $= N$. Then

$$\text{Total contribution} = \text{total fixed costs} + \text{profit}$$
$$N \times 10 = 5,000 + 10,000$$
$$10N = 15,000$$
$$N = 1,500$$

Therefore

1,500 items need to be sold to achieve a profit of £10,000

Self-assessment question S5.5

Try the following question for yourself (answer at the end of the chapter).

A new style of electric bass guitar is about to be launched by a well-known instrument company. The materials for each guitar total £25 and 2.5 hours of labour (paid at £12/hour) are needed to assemble one. Variable overheads are charged at £2/labour hour and the associated fixed costs are £600 per month. If the selling price is set at £160, how many guitars need to be sold to achieve an annual profit of £20,000?

Profit–volume relationships

Sometimes it is preferable to bypass the details of sales and costs and compare profit directly with the volume of activity. The profit–volume chart shown in Figure 5.9 has the same horizontal axis as the breakeven chart but the vertical axis is for profit only. The breakeven point is where the profit line crosses the horizontal axis.

In order to draw a profit–volume graph, two points are needed to determine the position of the profit line. One of these points is easy to find. When activity is zero, the loss being made is exactly equal to the total of fixed costs. For the other point, a calculation is needed. The following relationship is used (see Figure 5.2):

Total contribution = total fixed costs + profit

Assuming the total of fixed costs is given, the amount of profit can be calculated for a chosen activity level if the total contribution at that level can be found.

The Grubsteaks restaurant example earlier in this chapter showed the application of this formula. At the activity level of 18,000 meals a year the profit was calculated to be £24,000 (see Figure 5.10).

The advantage of the profit–volume chart over the breakeven chart is that the profit can be determined for any level of activity within the range of the graph. This is done simply by reading the graph.

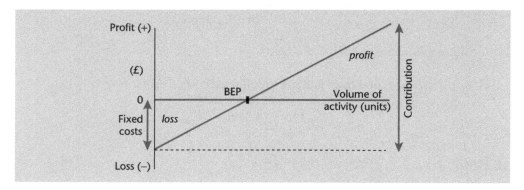

Figure 5.9 **Profit–volume chart**

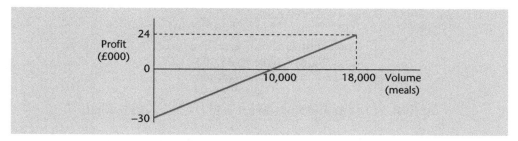

Figure 5.10 Profit–volume chart for the Grubsteaks restaurant

Try the following question for yourself (answer at the end of the chapter).

Using the answer to S5.1, draw a profit–volume graph for the Good Health drinks tent. From this graph, **read** the profit for sales of (a) 1,200 drinks and (b) 2,500 drinks.

Self-assessment question S5.6

Effect of alternative sales mixes

The vast majority of businesses sell more than one product and many of these sell lots of different products. As different products tend to have different unit contributions and no one knows for sure the sales mix that will occur in the next period, it is impossible to determine the breakeven level of output for the whole business. Different sales mixes will have different breakeven points. However, if the sales mix tends not to change much, it is possible to make an estimate with some degree of reliability.

Consider a business with just two products, As and Bs. Product B has a higher price and unit contribution, but a lower volume, than product A. The current sales mix is three As are sold for every B (A:B = 3:1).

Product	A	B	Total
Sales price	10	18	
Variable cost	4	9	
Unit contribution	6	9	
Quantities	30,000	10,000	40,000
Total contribution	180,000	90,000	270,000
Total fixed costs			148,500
Profit			121,500

To calculate the breakeven point, let N = number of Bs sold at BEP:

$$\text{Total contribution} = \text{total fixed cost}$$
$$3N(6) + N(9) = 148,500$$
$$27N = 148,500$$
$$N = 5,500$$
At BEP, 16,500 As and 5,500 Bs are sold (22,000 units in total)

But if the sales mix is changed to 2:1 (= A:B),

$$\text{Total contribution} = \text{total fixed cost}$$
$$2N(6) + N(9) = 148,500$$
$$21N = 148,500$$
$$N = 7,071$$

At BEP, 14,142 As and 7,071 Bs are sold (21,243 units in total)

Note that this is 757 items less in total than the previous sales mix.
What if the original volume was sold in total (40,000 units) but in the new sales mix of 2:1?

Product	A	B	Total
Sales price	10	18	
Variable cost	4	9	
Unit contribution	6	9	
Quantities	26,667	13,333	40,000
Total contribution	160,002	119,998	280,000
Total fixed costs			148,500
Profit			131,500

Note that this is £10,000 greater than with the original sales mix.

Try the following question for yourself (answer at the end of the chapter).

Hoffman Limited makes and sells only two types of portable cooking stove, the Lightweight (L) and the Megarange (M). The Megarange is more sophisticated and sells for more than twice as much as the Lightweight which is very popular. Consequently, nine Ls are sold for every M. The selling prices for Ls and Ms respectively are £8.20 and £19.40; their variable costs are £3.70 and £10.90. The budget for next year shows 50,000 stoves sold altogether with fixed overheads costing £150,000 in total.
  For next year, calculate:

1 Profit if sales mix remains L:M = 9:1.
2 Breakeven point if sales mix remains L:M = 9:1.
3 Breakeven point if sales mix becomes L:M = 15:1.
4 Profit if sales mix becomes L:M = 15:1.

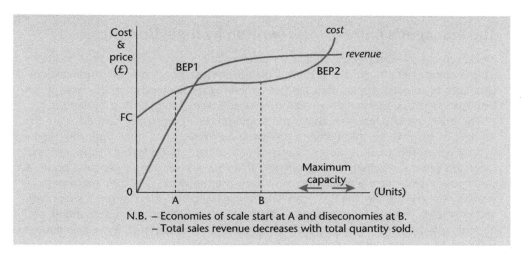

Figure 5.11 Economist's cost–volume chart

Limitations of variable costing

The relationship between sales income and quantity sold may not be linear. Beyond a certain point, it may be necessary to reduce the selling price in order to achieve further sales. The previously straight sales revenue line starts to curve beyond this point. (See Figure 5.11.)

The relationship between total costs and quantity produced may not be linear. The greater the quantity of units produced, the lower may be the price per unit of materials purchased. The straight total cost line also turns into a curve. (See Figure 5.11.)

Contribution analysis can be unreliable outside the relevant range (the range of activity levels for which the curves approximate to straight lines). At very high (close to maximum capacity) and very low activity levels, costs and revenues may not be representative of normal values (see Figure 5.11).

Breakeven analysis is not very useful for multi-product businesses as different breakeven points are produced for different sales mixes. Because different products have different unit contributions, different sales mixes for the same overall activity will have different breakeven points.

It is difficult to measure activity for 'jobbing' businesses, where every item produced is different. Breakeven calculations and charts are applicable to firms which make large volumes of the same product. They are of no use to firms which make only one or a few of each item. This would include civil engineering firms producing public buildings and boatyards producing to customer specification only.

It is assumed that all the items made are sold, i.e. there is no increase or decrease in stock levels over the period. But stock levels may change over a financial period. When this is the case, the production activity will not be the same as the sales activity. Which of these two activity levels should be used for breakeven purposes? As breakeven is based on contribution (sales revenue – variable cost), the sales activity level should be used. 'Variable cost' is the variable cost of the items sold, not the items made.

The manager's point of view (written by Nigel Burton)

Breakeven analysis can provide vital financial information, particularly for small, relatively simple companies. It also has a role to play in larger, more complex organizations, although its potential applications tend to be limited. In all companies, however, it can help managers to understand the cost/price/volume relationships in their businesses.

The main use of breakeven analysis in single-product companies is to calculate the number of items to be sold before a profit can be made. Most small businesses know exactly where this point is, and it becomes one of the driving forces of the business. Once this point is reached, managers know that they are starting to generate profit. A small businessman of my acquaintance reckons that he works on Mondays to pay the taxman, Tuesdays to pay the VAT man, Wednesdays and Thursdays to pay his suppliers, and only starts working for himself on Fridays. He knows nothing about accounting, and his logic may be slightly suspect, but his little joke demonstrates that, even if he doesn't realize it, he has grasped the principles of breakeven analysis!

The same basic technique is employed for various purposes in large companies. It is commonly used, in conjunction with other measurements, in capital appraisals. All formal proposals for capital projects will be accompanied by supporting financial data, which will inevitably demonstrate that a satisfactory rate of return and payback period can be expected. But are the numbers reasonable? It is possible that the underlying assumptions about projected sales, capital expenditure and operating costs are all at their most optimistic limits, and could spell disaster if just one of them failed to materialize. To test the figures, therefore, it is useful to carry out a sensitivity analysis, calculating the impact on the rate of return of, say, a 10% reduction in sales, or a 20% overspend in capital expenditure. One of the key calculations here is the breakeven point, which represents the 'least acceptable' position. What level of inaccuracy in the numbers will bring the project down to its breakeven level? This neatly puts all the alternative scenarios into context and allows management to assess the robustness of the proposed figures.

Some years ago, breakeven principles played an important part in another type of major project, this time the sale of a business. We were instructed by our American parent company to shed a particular product line, and achieve a specified net gain for the company. The matter was greatly complicated when the favoured purchaser decided to buy only the trading assets, i.e. customer lists, product know-how and working capital, but not the fixed assets, i.e. land, buildings and plant. As a result, we were obliged to close down the factory, leading to significant expenditure which had not been envisaged when the sale of the business had first been authorized. This included decommissioning of the plant, building demolition, environmental testing, land remediation, and redundancy, among many others. Against these we had several unforeseen items of revenue, such as sale of plant and the disposal of the land. Our job was to ensure that the ultimate sale of the land covered all the net expenditure, leaving the American parent company with the profit it expected from the sale of the business. We used a breakeven model to monitor progress on this project, initially using estimated figures, and replacing them with the actual numbers as they became confirmed. In this way we were able to monitor constantly the proceeds required from the sale of the land to break even, and keep an eye on the property market to see if this level was achievable. Unfortunately, when we were ready to sell, the property market was in a slump, so we retained the land for a further five years until the market had recovered sufficiently to enable us to reach our breakeven point.

These examples will hopefully illustrate that breakeven principles can be used in a variety of different ways, even if the determination of sales volume, especially in small companies, remains its most common application. However, in large companies, the breakeven point of individual items is rather muddied by the multiplicity of products being sold; if you sell more of Product A than you expected, thus recovering a higher level of overhead, the breakeven point on Product B may go down. That is why we found ourselves concentrating more on the overall level of marginal income being generated by groups of products, and the contribution that they made towards fixed costs. The concept of contribution is a useful way of focusing on profit, and analysing the elements which are causing you to over- or underachieve the profit target. By increasing volume, or by changing the mix of sales towards the higher margin products, more marginal income will be generated. This additional contribution should fall straight through to the bottom line profit, assuming that the fixed costs remain fixed. In practice, of course, they rarely do. There are always spending variances to be managed, but this merely demonstrates another opportunity for effective profit generation. If you can reduce the level of fixed costs, at the same time as increasing marginal income, the gearing effect on the profit line can be significant.

Finally, the concept of contribution can sometimes show expenditure in a startling light. For instance, how big a deal do your American salespeople have to make, in order to pay for the managing director's first-class flight to New York to sign the final contract? The contribution calculation will tell you this, although you may not wish to point it out to the MD! Perhaps a more relevant question is: 'Will the contribution generated by the New York sale cover all the costs associated with it, and still leave a satisfactory profit?' Consider not only the variable costs of materials, labour, variable overhead and freight, but also other related costs, such as warehousing, export documentation, currency risks from $ invoicing, extended credit terms and bank charges, as well as the cost of customer visits and technical support. The MD's visit could be the final straw which pushes this piece of business into loss!

Summary

- Costs can be analysed into variable and fixed.
- Contribution is sales revenue minus variable cost, either per unit or in total.
- Total contribution equals total fixed cost plus profit.
- At breakeven point (profit = 0) total contribution equals total fixed cost.
- There are two types of breakeven charts, traditional and contribution.
- The margin of safety shows how far above breakeven point a firm is operating.
- Operational gearing affects the amount of profit due to changes in sales volume.
- Activity levels can be calculated for target profits.
- The profit–volume chart is an alternative to the breakeven chart.

Further reading

Horngren, C. T. (2004) 'Management accounting: some comments', *Journal of Management Accounting Research*, Vol. 16, 207–211.

Horngren, C., Bhimani, A., Datar, S. and Foster, G. (2002) *Management and Cost Accounting*, 2nd edition, Prentice Hall Europe, Harlow. See Chapter 8, 'Cost–volume–profit relationships'.

Upchurch, A. (2003) *Management Accounting, Principles and Practice*, 2nd edition, Financial Times/Prentice Hall, Harlow. See Chapter 6, 'Cost/volume/profit analysis'.

Weetman, P. (2002) *Management Accounting, an Introduction*, 3rd edition, Financial Times/Prentice Hall, Harlow. See chapter 'Profit measurement and short-term decision making'.

Answers to self-assessment questions

S5.1 Good Health drinks tent

$$
\begin{aligned}
&\text{£}\\
\text{Sales revenue} &= 2.50\text{/unit}\\
\text{Variable costs} &= \underline{1.00}\text{/unit}\\
\text{Unit contribution} &= 1.50\text{/unit}\\
\text{Number of units} &= \underline{4,000}\\
\text{Total contribution} &= 6,000\\
\text{Fixed costs} &= \underline{2,700}\\
\text{Net profit} &= \underline{\underline{3,300}}
\end{aligned}
$$

a) Total contribution = £6,000
b) Net profit = £3,300

S5.2 Good Health drinks tent

Let BEP occur when B drinks have been sold.

$$
\begin{aligned}
\text{Total contribution} &= \text{total fixed costs}\\
B \times \text{unit contribution} &= \text{total fixed costs}\\
B \times (2.50 - 1.00) &= 2,700\\
B &= 2,700/1.50\\
\text{Breakeven point, } B &= 1,800 \text{ drinks}
\end{aligned}
$$

S5.3 Contribution breakeven chart for the drinks tent

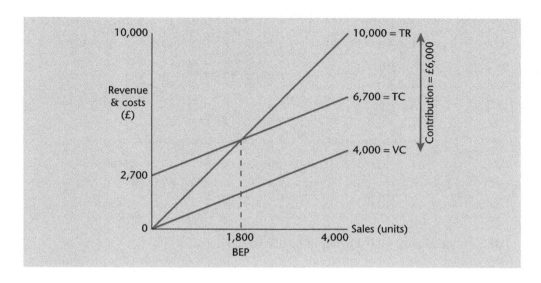

S5.4 For the Good Health drinks tent example

a) Actual number of drinks sold = 4,000
Breakeven level of sales = <u>1,800</u>
Margin of safety = <u>2,200</u> drinks

b) $\dfrac{\text{Margin of safety in units}}{\text{Actual sales in units}} \times 100 = \dfrac{2,200}{4,000} \times 100 = 55\%$

So, sales could fall by 55% before losses occurred.

S5.5 Variable costs

Materials	25	
Labour	30	(2.5×12)
Overheads	<u>5</u>	(2.5×2)
Total	60	
Sales price	<u>160</u>	
Unit contribution	<u>100</u>	

Let the number of items needed = N
Total contribution = total fixed costs + profit
$N \times 100 = (600 \times 12) + 20,000$
$N = 27,200/100$
$N = 272$

So, 272 bass guitars need to be sold to create a net profit of £20,000.

S5.6 Profit–volume chart for the Good Health drinks tent

a) If 1,200 drinks are sold, a **loss** of £900 would occur.

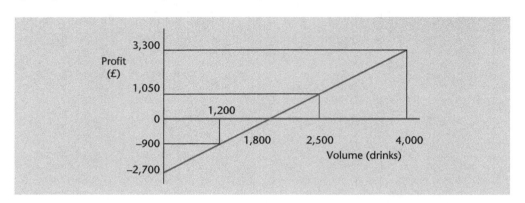

b) If 2,500 drinks are sold, a **profit** of £1,050 would occur.

S5.7 Hoffman Ltd

The current sales mix is 9 Ls are sold for every M (L:M = 9:1).

Product	L	M	Total
Sales price	8.20	19.40	
Variable cost	3.70	10.90	
Unit contribution	4.50	8.50	
Quantities	45,000	5,000	50,000
Total contribution	202,500	42,500	245,000
Total fixed costs			150,000
Profit			95,000

To calculate the breakeven point, let N = number of Bs sold at BEP:

$$\text{Total contribution} = \text{total fixed cost}$$
$$9N(4.50) + N(8.50) = 150,000$$
$$49N = 150,000$$
$$N = 3,061$$
At BEP, 27,549 Ls and 3,062 Ms are sold (30,611 stoves in total)

But if the sales mix changed to 15:1 (= L:M),

$$\text{Total contribution} = \text{total fixed cost}$$
$$15N(4.50) + N(8.50) = 150,000$$
$$76N = 150,000$$
$$N = 1,974$$
At BEP, 29,610 Ls and 1,974 Ms are sold (31,584 stoves in total)

Note that this is 973 stoves more in total than the previous sales mix.

What if the original volume was sold in total (50,000 stoves) but in the new sales mix of 15:1?

Product	L	M	Total
Sales price	8.20	19.40	
Variable cost	3.70	10.90	
Unit contribution	4.50	8.50	
Quantities	46,875	3,125	50,000
Total contribution	210,937	26,563	237,500
Total fixed costs			150,000
Profit			87,500

Note that this is £8,000 less than with the original sales mix.

<table>
<tr><td>CASE
STUDY
1</td><td># The Hutton Vinification Company</td></tr>
</table>

HVC Ltd is based in north Somerset and has a financial year starting on 1 August. It produces wine from bulk grape juice bought from vineyards in southern England. In 2012/13 it made and sold 90,000 litres of wine in standard-sized 750 millilitre bottles to customers located throughout the UK. The maximum annual output of its plant is estimated to be 98,000 litres. Demand has grown steadily over the last 10 years in step with increased interest in, and knowledge of, wine in the UK. Home market production has been encouraged by the recent gradual warming of the climate.

However, the number of complaints received by HVC Ltd has risen sharply over the last two years and, if nothing is done to correct this, sales and profits are expected to fall next year. The directors attribute the complaints to the difficulty in controlling the quality of the 'must' (bought-in grape juice). The managing director has suggested that it would be easier to control the quality of harvested grapes rather than processed must. This means that HVC Ltd would have to acquire wine-pressing equipment to process the purchased grapes. Despite the extra temporary labour involved in pressing the grapes, the resulting self-pressed must is expected to have a variable cost equal to only 60% of bought-in must. The necessary grape-pressing machinery will cost £440,000 and will last 10 years before being scrapped (at zero value).

The managing director's remuneration is £42,000 p.a. and the sales director's is £38,000 p.a. In addition to the two directors, HVC Ltd has five full-time employees, whose pay in 2012/13 totalled £89,000. This included £25,000 annual salary for the production manager and basic annual pay of £10,000 for each of four operatives. This remuneration is considered to be a fixed cost but the remainder, which was earned as overtime by the four operatives, is considered to be a variable cost.

The total cost of must purchased in 2012/13 was £45,000. The average cost of the bottle, cork and label is £0.20 a bottle and delivery costs average £0.10 a bottle. HVC Ltd has a policy of having zero stocks at the end of July (this is also the company's financial year-end). Apart from a negligible amount, it has managed to achieve this for the last few years.

With effect from 1 August 2013 the directors will be entitled to a profit-related bonus dependent on the annual increase in net profit. Naturally, they are both very keen to earn a good bonus. With this in mind, the managing director has analysed the costs for 2012/13 (which was a typical year) as follows:

Fixed costs	£	Variable costs	£
Salaries and wages	145,000	Must	45,000
Depreciation	88,000	Overtime pay	24,000
Production costs	47,000	Bottle, cork and label	24,000
Selling costs	33,000	Delivery	12,000
Administration costs	29,000		£105,000
Interest	8,000		
	£350,000		

The sales director is not entirely convinced that the managing director's idea is the best solution. She thinks it would be better to go further south than at present, into central France, in order to purchase better-quality must. She believes that the effect of this would be to increase the must cost by 25% but this would be more than covered by her proposed 5% increase in the sales price.

HVC Ltd: Profit and loss account for y/e 31 July 2013

	£000	£000
Sales		504
Must	45	
Operatives' wages	64	
Bottles, corks and labels	24	
Production depreciation	53	
Other production costs	47	
Manufacturing costs of goods sold		233
Gross profit		271
Salaries	105	
Depreciation	35	
Selling costs	33	
Delivery costs	12	
Administration costs	29	
Bank interest	8	
Total overheads		222
Net profit		49

Tasks:

1 For 2012/13:
   a) Calculate the breakeven point in litres.
   b) Calculate the net profit if HVC Ltd had made and sold 95,000 litres.
   c) How many litres would have to be sold to increase net profit by 50%?

   (20 marks)

2 If the MD's plan to buy and press grapes (instead of purchasing grape must) is put into operation for 2013/14 and output increases to 95,000 litres and the selling price increases by 5%:
   a) What would the revised breakeven point be?
   b) What would the revised profit be?

   (20 marks)

3 Alternatively, if the sales director's plan to buy better-quality grape must is put into operation for 2013/14 and output increases to 95,000 litres and the selling price increases by 5%:

 a) What would the revised breakeven point be?

 b) What would the revised profit be?

(20 marks)

4 Evaluate the directors' plans and recommend a course of action for 2013/14. You may wish to use chart(s) to illustrate your answer.

(40 marks)

(Total 100 marks)

CASE STUDY 2	The Muesli Company

The Muesli Company (TMC) is a small business which makes and sells muesli. It was started two years ago by Rosemary Helms on the basis of her family's liking for the homemade mixture of cereals, nuts and dried fruits she had created for personal consumption. When a new farm shop opened nearby, she enquired if it would be interested in selling her muesli. The shop agreed to give it a try and found that it sold sufficient quantities to justify a permanent place in the shop. Rosemary now has five outlets and is considering selling her muesli on the Internet.

The business has reached a point where decisions have to be made concerning product type and distribution channel. The original recipe used nine different ingredients which were sourced from supermarkets and local shops. However, in recent months, Rosemary has created a new simplified recipe which uses only organic ingredients. Her idea is to appeal to the growing health food market which is willing to pay premium prices for organic foods. However, she has discovered that, if she wishes to use the word 'organic' on the label, she must register with the Soil Association and pay an annual fee of £440. As the business is just starting up, she is undecided as to whether this cost is worthwhile. She could continue with the current labels (omitting the word 'organic') while still using the organic ingredients to improve the taste.

While searching for organic materials, she discovered a wholesaler based 25 miles (40 km) away which delivers direct to its customers. The minimum quantities purchased are much higher but the prices are significantly lower than local shops. Rosemary now saves time and effort by using this supplier for all her ingredients. The supplier has pointed out that she could get even better prices if she ordered in greater quantities (about five times what she orders now). Although she is tempted by these low prices, she is not sure if she should buy her ingredients in these quantities.

Her son, who is something of a computer expert, has suggested creating a website to sell the muesli over the Internet. She is not too sure about this but is investigating the possibility and thinking about the consequences. How much would it cost to set up? What would the minimum delivery size have to be? How much extra would customers be prepared to pay for postage and packing? Could she cope if demand surged? How much would she need to sell to break even? Are there any 'hidden' costs?

In a two-and-a-half-hour session, she makes 12 kg of muesli. The product is packed in individual 500 g bags and special scales are needed to ensure that the weight is accurate. (To ensure that no bag is underweight, each one is slightly overfilled.) The Internet orders would be for a 'parcel' of seven bags. She thinks the website would last for about five years before a complete overhaul would be necessary. Although it is a few years old, she could use her present computer, but she would need to purchase broadband access.

The current selling price is £2.00 a bag to her retail outlets who sell it to their customers for £3.00 a bag. For the Internet business, direct to the consumer, she thinks she will charge £21.00 a parcel (7 bags @ £3.00).

While doing this exercise, Rosemary realizes that she does not know what her current breakeven point is and decides to calculate it. Also, it will serve as a useful comparison with the proposed Internet business. She does not use a computer for the local farm shop business and she uses her own car to deliver orders. It is difficult to be precise but she estimates that her average delivery is 12 bags, takes one hour and costs her £1.80 in petrol. She has recently purchased scales and a bag-sealing machine. Her costs are shown below.

For all sales:	£
Cereals	0.20/500 g bag
Nuts	0.45/500 g bag
Dried fruits	0.50/500 g bag
Plastic bags and sealing tape	0.01/500 g bag
Labels	0.05/500 g bag
Bag-sealing machine	45.00
Weighing scales	235.00
For Internet sales only:	
Creation of website	250.00
Maintenance of website	50.00 per month
Internet payment company charges	30.00 per month
Broadband access	20.00 per month
Packing materials	0.42/parcel of 3.5 to 4.0 kg
Postage	7.21/parcel of 3.5 to 4.0 kg

At the moment she is only selling about 12 bags a week and wants to expand in order to create more income. Her objective is to make a profit of approximately £10,000 a year by working no more than 20 hours a week for 50 weeks a year on her muesli business.

Tasks:

Without the use of 'organic' labels – Soil Association fee not paid:

1 Calculate the breakeven point of her current 'farm shop' business (in numbers of bags). Assume all sales are through farm shops and Internet sales are zero.

(15 marks)

2 If Internet sales caused the volume to increase sufficiently, the bulk purchase of edible ingredients would be justified, giving a 25% saving on current costs. Calculate the breakeven point (in numbers of bags) if this was so. Assume all sales are over the Internet and farm shop sales are zero.

(15 marks)

3 Assuming the 25% bulk saving was in operation, how many bags would Rosemary need to sell in order to make a profit of £10,000 a year? Assume all sales are over the Internet and farm shop sales are zero.

(15 marks)

With the use of 'organic' labels only – Soil Association fee paid:

4 Repeat task 1.

(5 marks)

5 Repeat task 2.

(5 marks)

6 Repeat task 3.

(5 marks)

General

7 Advise Rosemary about the possible expansion of her business to achieve her desired level of profit.

(40 marks)
(Total 100 marks)

Questions

An asterisk * on a question number indicates that the answer is given at the end of the book. Answers to the other questions are given in the Lecturer's Guide.

Q5.1* Bodgit Ltd

Bodgit Ltd makes 200 wooden kitchen chairs every month and sells them for £50 each. Fixed monthly overheads are £3,000 and the standard cost of one chair is as follows:

	£
Materials	15
Direct labour	8
Variable overheads	7

Tasks:

1 Calculate for one month:
   a) the variable cost of one chair;
   b) the breakeven point;
   c) the profit if 200 chairs are sold;
   d) the number of chairs sold to give a profit of £4,000.
2 In an attempt to boost sales, Bodgit plans to reduce the selling price to £48, improve the quality by spending 20% more on materials and increase its advertising by £1,000 a month.
   Calculate:
   a) the new breakeven point;
   b) the profit if 350 chairs are sold;
   c) the margin of safety (expressed as a % of sales) if 350 chairs are sold;
   d) the number of chairs sold to give a profit of £4,000.
3 Explain why your answers to the above questions should be seen as estimates rather than exact answers.

Q5.2* Concord Toy Company

The Concord Toy Company has two separate strategic business units. A draft plan, incorporating a target return on capital employed (ROCE) of 20% per annum, has been created by the managing director. Aware that the toy industry is a volatile one, the board of directors wishes to review the flexibility of the profit forecast shown by the plan. In preparation for the board meeting to discuss the plan, certain questions have been posed for each operating unit (see below).

Operating Unit 1 – novelty pens

This unit produces novelty pens. Most of these are based on popular cartoon characters. Variable costs are taken as raw materials and royalties. All other costs are assumed to be fixed in the short term. The following forecasts have been made:

Selling price per pen	£2
Variable cost per pen	£1.50
Sales revenue	£800,000
Average capital employed	£300,000

Within the output range 300,000 to the maximum capacity of 450,000 pens, the fixed costs are £150,000.

Operating Unit 2 – dolls' accessories

This unit produces three main products – a doll's buggy, a doll's scooter and a doll's MP3 player. In the past, the company has exported most of its products but, in its drive to develop home sales, it has recently obtained a contract to supply a national chain store. The store's toy buyer has requested the company to supply a doll's convertible car in addition to its existing products.

Forecast accounts

Product	Buggy	Scooter	MP3 player	Total
Selling price	£20	£10	£10	
Unit sales (000)	100	100	100	
Sales (£000)	2,000	1,000	1,000	4,000
Variable costs (£000)	600	200	400	1,200
Contribution (£000)	1,400	800	600	2,800
Fixed costs (£000)	700	700	700	2,100
Profit/loss (£000)	700	100	(100)	700

Fixed costs are apportioned on the basis of unit sales. The average capital employed is estimated at £3.6 million. To make a doll's convertible car would require new plant, financed in full by a bank loan.

Tasks re Unit 1:

1 What is the breakeven point in sales volume and value?
2 What is the margin of safety shown by the forecast?
3 Will the operating unit achieve a 20% return on capital employed?
4 What will be the profit if production output increases to maximum capacity? Qualify your answer.
5 How many pens must be sold to make a profit of £60,000?
6 What actions can be taken to improve profitability?

Tasks re Unit 2:

1 Will this operating unit achieve a 20% return on capital employed on the existing sales forecast?

2 If the sales mix remains at equal volumes of the three products, what is the breakeven point in sales volume and value?
3 What will the operating profit be if the sales volume on each product falls
   a) 10% below forecast?
   b) 20% below forecast?
4 Should Concord stop producing and selling the MP3 player?
5 Should the selling price of the MP3 player be increased to £12 to cover the full costs?
6 What further information is required to decide whether or not to make a doll's convertible car?

Q5.3* Rover's 'last chance saloon'

The following comments were broadcast on a television news programme in the first week of February 1999:

> *Rover's future depends on the success of their latest model, codename R75. They intend to attract buyers away from Audi and Volvo to what they describe as the best car they have ever built. They claim to have paid more attention to detail than ever before on this upmarket saloon car. This may be why the launch has been put back from autumn 1998 to the summer of 1999.*
>
> *Selling prices will be a crucial element in their battle for market share and are expected to range from £18,000 to £26,000. Rover say they need to sell 140,000 cars a year to break even and acknowledge that this is a significant challenge. However, this is one test they cannot afford to fail. It is no coincidence that the R75 has been nicknamed 'the last chance saloon'!*

Investigation

Assume:

The retail selling price is £22,000 (average of £18,000 and £26,000).
The trade selling price is 75% of the retail price.
The total cost is 80% of the trade selling price.
The variable cost is X% of the total cost.

Tasks:

1 Calculate the total fixed costs for the R75 project if X is
   a) 50%
   b) 65%
   c) 80%.
   As well as an annual total, express your answers in £/day.
2 Assuming the variable cost is 65% of total cost, how many R75s need to be sold for profit to be £100 million?
3 If 200,000 R75s were sold in the year, assuming the variable cost is 65% of total cost, how much profit would they make?
4 If the total capital employed on the R75 project is £10,000 million and Rover's owners wanted a 20% return on capital employed (ROCE), how many cars would have to be sold?

Q5.4 SACCUS

SACCUS is a local charity which decides to hold an outdoors fund-raising event in mid-summer. The secretary has a connection with an entertainments company which puts on musical laser light shows for the public. For charities, it charges a reduced rate of £375 all-inclusive. The venue would be provided free of charge by a local farmer. A barbecue would be put on and the food and drink would be included in the ticket price. It is estimated that the food would cost £2 a head and the drink £1 a head. Also, a special licence for the sale of alcohol would be needed at a cost of £25. Based on the experience of similar events, SACCUS expects to sell 500 tickets at £5 each.

However, the treasurer (who has a degree in business studies) is a little concerned about this plan and proposes an alternative. She suggests hiring a nationally known West Indian steel band at the special rate of £100 plus £50 transport costs. The ticket price would remain at £5 and food would be provided as before. However, no drink would be provided, the audience being invited to bring their own. The number of people attending is expected to be half that for the laser show.

Tasks:

1 Advise SACCUS as to which event it should stage.
2 Illustrate your answer by sketching a contribution breakeven chart for each event.

Q5.5 Royal Hotel

Jim Culf is the manager of the Royal Hotel, Bigtown-on-Sea. In anticipation of preparing next year's budget, he has analysed his recent costs and income. His findings are summarized below.

	£/week
Staff salaries	2,000
Head office charge	400
Depreciation of equipment and fittings	875
Heating	425

For each guest the average variable cost of food, drink, linen and sundries totals £100 per week. Jim considers all other overheads to be semi-variable and has produced the following data from his records:

Week no.	Occupancy (no. of guests)	Other overheads (£)
13	75	7,050
14	94	8,200
15	70	6,980
16	61	6,500
17	57	6,350
18	83	7,590
19	85	7,700

The average price charged for a week's stay is £240 per guest. Since it is a seaside hotel, the vast majority of its customers stay for either one or two weeks at a time.

Tasks:

1 Calculate the average number of guests needed each week to avoid making a loss.
2 The hotel can accommodate a maximum of 120 people. How much is the weekly profit if the average occupancy level is:
   a) 70%?
   b) 80%?
   c) 90%?
3 Jim has been invited by an international tour company to quote a competitive price for a group of 20 Japanese tourists who wish to stay in the area for two weeks. They are due to arrive in 10 days' time.
   a) Calculate the lowest price Jim can quote if he is to avoid making a loss on the tour. (Assume that the hotel is currently 70% booked for the two weeks in question.)
   b) If Jim wants to make a profit of £2,000 from this tour, what price should he quote?

Q5.6 Hughes Healthfoods

Hughes Healthfoods makes and sells two types of diet supplement, Slim Quick (SQ) and Healthy Living (HL). It has a single production line on which the two products are made alternately in batches. Some details from next year's budget are shown below:

Product	Unit selling price (£)	Unit variable cost (£)	Annual sales volume (units)
SQ	5.00	2.00	800,000
HL	9.00	4.00	200,000

The annual total fixed cost is £2.9 million and the production facility has an absolute maximum capacity of 1.1 million units a year.

Tasks:

1 Calculate the budgeted profit.
2 Determine the breakeven point. (Assume the budgeted sales mix is stable throughout the year.)
3 Is it possible for the business to double its profit while maintaining the budgeted sales mix?
4 Is it possible for the business to double its profit if the budgeted sales mix changed to two SQs being sold for every HL?

Review questions

1 Define variable and fixed costs.
2 Define contribution.
3 Explain the relationship between contribution, fixed costs and net profit.
4 Define breakeven point.
5 Draw traditional and contribution breakeven charts.
6 Define the margin of safety.
7 Explain operational gearing.
8 Draw a profit–volume chart.
9 Discuss the assumptions and limitations of breakeven analysis.

The answers to all these questions can be found in the text of this chapter.

CHAPTER 6

Short-term decisions using variable costing

Introduction

Suppose you were a director of a well-known international passenger airline whose main route was London–New York. You operate this route with a fleet of several large aircraft, each with a capacity to carry 450 passengers. However, due to the number of competitors flying the same route, there is much surplus capacity and your aircraft often fly with more than 100 of their seats empty. Your standard return fare is £500, which is based on the total cost of £400 per available seat plus a 25% profit margin. The £400 total cost includes items such as depreciation of aircraft, fuel, on-board food and drink for passengers, rent of airport facilities, staff pay, training and administration costs.

Unexpectedly, a well-known holiday company offers to purchase 50 seats on every one of your flights for the next six weeks but is only willing to pay £100 a seat – only one-quarter of the total cost! What would your response be? Would you, politely but firmly, inform the holiday company that its offer is far too low or would you accept gladly and get the contract signed as soon as possible?

To solve this problem, you need to think about how your net income would change if you accepted the offer. Obviously, your revenue would increase by £100 for each of the 50 seats. But what about your costs? Which of the costs listed in the previous paragraph would increase? Most of them would not change at all! Only the cost of the on-board food and drink for passengers would increase. If this costs £10 per person, you would be increasing your net income by £90 a seat or £4,500 per return flight. If there were 100 flights during the six-week period, the net income from the contract would be £450,000. This is the case even though each seat is sold at £300 less than total cost. This is because most of the costs are 'fixed' and only the food and drink are 'variable' (see Chapter 1 on cost behaviour if you do not understand this). Your positive decision to accept the offer is based on your knowledge of variable costing and your company is nearly half a million pounds better off because of it! An understanding of variable costing will enable you to make similar, good, profitable decisions in your business career.

Note that this use of variable costing for short-term decision making is also known as contribution analysis.

Having worked through this chapter you should be able to:

- advise whether or not to cease certain activities;
- advise on the order of production when one of the resources used is scarce;
- advise whether or not to accept one-off contracts;
- advise whether to produce or buy in components used in your products;
- discuss the limitations of decision making using variable costing.

Cessation of activities

The previous chapter dealt with the application of variable costing to breakeven analysis. We will now concentrate on commercial decision making in the short term, i.e. the immediate future. This aspect of variable costing is also known as *contribution analysis*. Four typical situations will be considered.

The first situation is where a financial analysis shows that a product line or profit centre is making a net loss and a proposal is made to close it down. A contribution analysis is performed to confirm or deny this course of action.

Provided the selling price of a product is greater than its variable cost, each sale will create a positive contribution towards the organization's fixed costs. This is so even when the product is making a net loss. Cessation of that product would mean that fewer of the fixed costs were covered **and the loss would be greater than before.** Remember that fixed costs are, by definition, costs which do not change with the level of activity, even if that level falls to zero. In other words, fixed costs cannot be eliminated **in the short term.**

Take the example of the Top Ski Holiday Company, which offers specialist skiing holidays in Norway, Spain and Italy. A financial analysis of last season in which 3,000 holidays were sold (1,000 for each country) shows the following:

	£000			
	Norway	**Italy**	**Spain**	**Total**
Total cost	950	700	450	2,100
Sales revenue	700	650	800	2,150
Net profit	(250)	(50)	350	50

The company would like to increase its selling prices but believes this to be unwise as its competitors are offering very similarly priced holidays in those countries. Alternatively, it has been suggested that if the Norwegian and Italian holidays for next season were withdrawn (starting in the near future) Top Ski would increase its profits from £50,000 to £350,000 by eliminating the losses for those two countries. This is based on the reasonable assumption that 1,000 holidays will continue to be sold for Spain.

A more detailed examination of the financial analysis reveals that the total fixed costs for last season were £600,000. These were for items such as brochures, advertising, directors' salaries and head office administration costs. These fixed costs were spread evenly over all the holidays. As 3,000 holidays had been sold, fixed costs of £200 (£600,000/3,000) were absorbed into each holiday. A contribution analysis of the above figures reveals the following:

		£000			
		Norway	**Italy**	**Spain**	**All**
	Total cost	950	700	450	2,100
Less:	Total fixed costs	200	200	200	600
	Variable cost	750	500	250	1,500
	Sales revenue	700	650	800	2,150
	Contribution	(50)	150	550	650
Less:	Total fixed costs				600
	Net profit				50

If the Norwegian and Italian holidays did cease, the analysis would change as follows:

		£000			
		Norway	**Italy**	**Spain**	**All**
	Contribution	0	0	550	550
Less:	Total fixed costs				600
	Net profit/(Loss)				(50)

So, instead of the profit increasing by £300,000, it would actually decrease by £100,000 to give a net **loss** of £50,000. The situation would be much worse than if no action had been taken and the Norwegian and Italian holidays sold as before.

The contribution analysis shows that, although the Italian holidays are making a loss, they are still making a positive contribution to the company's fixed costs. However, the Norwegian holidays are making a negative rather than positive contribution. Every time one of these is sold the company loses money it otherwise would not lose. Thus, it does seem a good idea to cease the Norwegian holidays.

If this happened and the Italian holidays continued, the analysis would be as follows:

	Norway	Italy	Spain	All
		£000		
Contribution	0	150	550	700
Less: Total fixed costs				600
Net profit				100

The rule is, in order to improve profitability, cease activities with negative contributions. (This assumes that these negative contributions cannot be made positive in the short term.)

Of course, **in the long term**, maybe the fixed costs could be reduced or maybe an alternative holiday venue could be found. In the long term **anything** is possible. However, for short-term decisions, the correct course of action comes from a contribution analysis. Although a sudden cessation of the Norwegian and Italian holidays seemed a reasonable proposition at first sight, it would have been a disaster for Top Ski Holidays if they had both been withdrawn.

From a business point of view, other aspects of the situation should always be taken into account. In particular, are the products interrelated? Consider a company selling three products: a basic food processor, a grating attachment and a coffee grinding attachment. Suppose the company stops making the coffee grinder because the accounting system shows that it is making a loss while the other two items are making a profit. Those potential customers who would have bought the processor and the grinder will not now do so. As the products are interdependent, sales of related items will be lost. Suppose it was the processor making the loss instead of the grinder. Anyone suggesting that production of the processor should cease should be asking themselves if they are in the right job.

Self-assessment question S6.1

Try the following question for yourself (answer at the end of the chapter).

The V&A Group is made up of four operating subsidiaries: A, B, C and D. Its corporate accounting system has produced the following figures which show the group has made a loss of £1,000. Analyse them and state which operations (if any) you would recommend for closure in order to return the group to profitability.

Summarized profit and loss accounts for last year (£000)

	A	B	C	D	Group
Sales	180	420	500	900	2,000
Raw materials	41	95	202	370	708
Direct labour	62	89	37	105	293
Direct cost	103	184	239	475	1,001
Gross profit	77	236	261	425	999
Total overheads	90	210	250	450	1,000
Net profit	(13)	26	11	(25)	(1)

Note: Fixed overheads have been apportioned according to the amount of sales revenue from each operation. Overheads are considered to be 90% variable and 10% fixed.

Tasks:
a) State which operations you recommend closing and why.
b) What would the group's profit be if your recommendations were actioned?
c) What would the group's profit be if A and D were closed?

Scarce resources

The usual factor limiting an organization's activities is the number of products it can sell. However, occasionally, a shortage of something it uses in its operations means that it cannot sell as many items as it otherwise would have. The item in short supply is known as a *scarce resource*. It is usually either a raw material or a particular type of specialized labour. For example, if there were an unforeseen shortage of crude oil due to some international dispute, the refining companies would not be able to make as much petrol as they could normally sell. In this case, in order to maximize profits, they would concentrate on the products which gave them the largest amount of contribution per barrel of oil.

The highest contribution might come from high-octane kerosene for jet engines. When the refining companies had produced all the aviation fuel that they could sell, they would concentrate on the product with the next-highest contribution per barrel, which might be unleaded petrol for cars. If there were any crude oil left after this, they would choose the next-highest-contribution product, and so on. In this way, they would ensure that they made the best use of every barrel of crude oil, i.e. every unit of their scarce resource. Here is a numerical example.

The following information has been extracted from the budget of Lonestar Petroleum:

	Contribution per 000 litres (£)	Barrels of crude per 000 litres	Sales forecast for month 5 (000 litres)	Quantity required (barrels)
Unleaded petrol	15.00	4.0	35,000	140,000
Diesel	12.00	3.0	18,000	54,000
Kerosene	20.00	4.0	8,000	32,000
Paraffin	8.00	5.0	7,000	35,000
				261,000

Due to an unexpected worldwide shortage of oil, the quota of crude oil available to Lonestar for month 5 has been set at 200,000 barrels.

Obviously, Lonestar will not be able to make all it planned to in month 5; it is 61,000 barrels short. One answer is to cut back production of all products pro rata but this would not maximize its profits. As crude oil is scarce, it needs to maximize the profit from each barrel. This is done by producing the highest-contribution-**per-barrel** product first, then the next highest, etc. **Lonestar needs to put its products into order according to their** *contribution per unit of scarce resource* **and produce in this order.**

Care must be exercised here for the contributions shown in the budget information are per thousand litres of finished product, not per unit of scarce resource which is a barrel of crude oil. To solve the problem, the contributions per barrel of crude oil must be calculated for each of the four products.

	Contribution per 000 litres (£)	Order	Barrels of crude per 000 litres	Contribution per barrel (£)	Order
Kerosene	20.00	1	4.0	20/4 = 5.00	1
Unleaded petrol	15.00	2	4.0	15/4 = 3.75	3
Diesel	12.00	3	3.0	12/3 = 4.00	2
Paraffin	8.00	4	5.0	8/5 = 1.60	4

So, the order of production would be kerosene, diesel, unleaded petrol and paraffin, until the quota of crude oil was all used up. Production in this new order gives the following results:

	Order	Quantity required (barrels)	Cumulative quantity (barrels)	Actual quantity (barrels)	Contribution/ barrel (£)	Total contribution (£)
Kerosene	1	32,000	32,000	32,000	5.00	160,000
Diesel	2	54,000	86,000	54,000	4.00	216,000
Unleaded petrol	3	140,000	226,000	114,000	3.75	427,500
Paraffin	4	35,000	261,000	–		–
		261,000		200,000		803,500

It is clear from the cumulative column that not all the unleaded petrol and none of the paraffin will be able to be produced. The total contribution for month 5 is £803,500. After the kerosene has been produced in full, any other order of production will give a smaller total contribution (and so a smaller profit). To prove this, the following table shows the result of producing in the incorrect order of contribution per thousand litres of output:

	Order	Quantity required (barrels)	Cumulative quantity (barrels)	Actual quantity (barrels)	Contribution/ barrel (£)	Total contribution (£)
Kerosene	1	32,000	32,000	32,000	5.00	160,000
Unleaded petrol	2	140,000	172,000	140,000	3.75	525,000
Diesel	3	54,000	226,000	28,000	4.00	112,000
Paraffin	4	35,000	261,000	–		–
		261,000		200,000		797,000

This total contribution is £6,500 lower than before.

The decision-making rule here is to produce in the order of the highest **contribution per unit of scarce resource** until it is used up.

From a business point of view, other aspects of the situation should always be taken into account. Are the sales of the products related? Would the lack of paraffin cause any customers to purchase their petrol or diesel elsewhere? These are not easy questions to answer but in-depth knowledge of the customers should go a long way in arriving at the correct answers.

Try the following question for yourself (answer at the end of the chapter).

Your company manufactures three products, Alpha, Beta and Gamma. The following information refers to next month:

	Alpha	**Beta**	**Gamma**
Sales demand (units)	50	150	200
Raw materials/unit	£100	£150	£80
Direct labour hours/unit	5	10	2
Fixed overheads/unit	£30	£60	£12

Direct labour is paid at £3.00 per hour. Variable overhead is equal to 10% of the cost of materials. Fixed overheads are attached to the products at the rate of 200% of the total direct labour cost. The selling price is calculated by doubling the prime cost (= total direct cost).

Tasks:

1 Calculate the contribution per unit for each product and rank them.
2 Using the ranking from the previous answer, prepare a forecast of the profit for each product and in total for next month if only 1,650 direct labour hours are available.
3 Calculate the contribution per direct labour hour for each product and rank them.
4 Using the ranking from the previous answer, prepare a forecast of the profit for each product and in total for next month if only 1,650 direct labour hours are available.
5 Quantify the difference between the answers to tasks 2 and 4 and comment on your findings.

One-off contracts

Occasionally, in addition to their 'normal' business, organizations are offered work which is of a 'one-off' nature. Take the example of Goodtime Holiday Centre plc (GHC) whose normal business is to provide package holidays in the UK at its custom-built holiday village in Cornwall. All accommodation, meals and entertainment are included in the holiday price, which averages £350 per person per week. The centre can accommodate a maximum of approximately 500 people and holidays are offered between the beginning of May and the end of September. The winter months are taken up with maintenance and new projects. GHC has been approached by an international charity to provide a one-week holiday for 500 refugee children during the last week of April. The charity is willing to pay a total of £50,000 (£100 per child). In deciding whether to accept the offer, GHC must bear in mind its duty to its shareholders to maximize their wealth.

The following information is from GHC's management accounting system and is used to determine its holiday prices.

Annual costs	£000	£000
Marketing and advertising	600	
Depreciation of equipment, vehicles, etc.	538	
Administration staff (permanent)	132	
Insurance	80	
Local rates	90	
		1,440
Holiday season* costs		
Other staff (temporary)	470	
Food and drink	310	
Other holiday running costs	120	
		900
Total		2,340

* The holiday season lasts for 20 weeks.

The total cost of providing one week's holiday = £2,340,000/20 = £117,000
The price for one week's holiday offered by the charity = 500 × £100 = £50,000
It may appear that acceptance of the proposition will lead to a loss of £67,000

However, before a decision is made, GHC should calculate the **contribution** arising from this one-off proposal.
Variable costs of special holiday:

	£000	
Other staff (temporary)	470	
Food and drink	310	
Other holiday running costs	120	
	£000	
Total variable costs for 20 weeks	900	
Total variable costs for 1 week	45	(900/20)
Total sales revenue from the charity	50	
Contribution for the special holiday week	+5	(50 – 45)

GHC should accept the offer because **profit will increase by £5,000.**

This positive contribution means that GHC will not be £67,000 worse off by agreeing to the special holiday but will, in fact, be **£5,000 better off.** This is because the remaining costs of £1,440,000 are **fixed** and will occur whether the special holiday goes ahead or not. If the fixed costs do not affect the financial outcome, they should not be used to make the decision. The fixed costs are absorbed into, and recovered by, the sales revenue from the 'normal holidays'.

The decision-making rule for one-off propositions is that **they should be accepted if they have a positive contribution and rejected if they do not.**

From a business point of view, other aspects of the situation should always be taken into account. For example, if the contract is a trial for a possible much larger order to follow, it should be made clear to the customer that the price is also a one-off and will not be sustainable in the long term. Also, any possible effects on normal sales should be considered. If a regular customer finds out that you have produced and sold a very similar product to the one it purchases from you but at a lower price for someone else, the customer may insist on renegotiating the price. The customer may even place future orders with a competitor.

Self-assessment question S6.3

Try the following question for yourself (answer at the end of the chapter).

a) Abacus Inc. is a small one-product firm which plans to make and sell 1,000 ornamental abacuses a year at a price of $250 each. How much profit does Abacus expect to make in a year if the standard cost of one abacus is as follows?

	$/unit
Materials	100
Direct labour	25
Variable overheads	20
Variable cost	145
Fixed cost (based on a budget of 1,000)	75
Total cost	220

b) An export order is received for 200 abacuses modified by the addition of some semi-precious stones. The effect of this is a 30% increase in the cost of materials and a 40% increase in the cost of direct labour. Also, special export insurance will cost $5 for each modified abacus shipped. However, the customer is not willing to pay more than $44,000 in total for this large order. Should Abacus Inc. accept this order?

Make or buy

Products and services are often made up of several component parts. A CD-player consists of an amplifier, motor, speakers, laser and casing. A holiday may consist of travel, accommodation, courier, food and drink. Businesses have a choice of creating these components themselves or buying them in from outside. Some very successful companies buy a significant proportion of their components from 'outside' companies. For its aero engines, Rolls-Royce buys in about 75% of parts included in its turbine-driven engines, enabling it to concentrate on the technology-critical areas. When reviewing their costs, organizations should compare the cost of making each component with that of buying it in. Sometimes, they are offered the chance of buying a component instead of making it. How should they decide?

Take the example of a meals-on-wheels service run by a local authority. It provides 100,000 meals a year from kitchens also used to prepare school dinners. Its costings for the meals-on-wheels service are as follows:

	£
Depreciation of kitchen equipment*	20,000
Depreciation of delivery vehicles	30,000
Catering staff wages*	30,000
Drivers' wages	90,000
Food and drink	50,000
Vehicle running costs	80,000
Total cost	300,000

* Based on proportion of total time used for meals-on-wheels.

An independent firm of caterers has offered to cook all the meals on its own premises and provide them to the authority for £0.90 each.

The cost of preparing the meals is:

	£
Depreciation of kitchen equipment	20,000
Catering staff wages	30,000
Food and drink	50,000
Total cost	100,000

As 100,000 meals are provided a year, each one costs £1.00 (£100,000/100,000). This is £0.10 more than the price being offered by the outside caterers, whose offer looks very attractive in this light. However, in order to make the best decision, the **variable** costs should be determined as they will be the only ones that change if the offer is accepted.

Assuming the number of part-time catering staff and the hours they work can be easily adjusted, the variable cost of meals-on-wheels is:

	£
Catering staff wages	30,000
Food and drink	50,000
Total variable cost	80,000

As 100,000 meals are provided a year, each one has a variable cost of £0.80 (£80,000/100,000). The fixed cost of kitchen depreciation will now have to be borne in full by the school dinners.

If the authority accepts the offer, it will be £10,000 worse off than before. This is because the offer price is £0.10 greater than the variable cost per meal. So the authority should not accept the offer.

The decision rule for make-or-buy situations is that **a component should be bought in only if its price is below the variable cost of producing it.**

From a business point of view, other aspects of the situation should always be taken into account. Will the supply of components be adequate and reliable? Will the quality of components be satisfactory? Will the price of components escalate in future? How easy would it be to start making the components again if the buying-in arrangement goes wrong?

Self-assessment question S6.4	*Try the following question for yourself (answer at the end of the chapter).*

Vendco manufactures a variety of vending machines which have a number of common components. As part of a cost review, Vendco has found an external supplier who will supply it with one of these parts (which has a standard cost of £90 – see below) for £75.

	£
Direct labour	25
Direct materials	30
Variable overheads	5
Fixed overhead	30
Standard cost	90

Advise Vendco whether it should continue to make this part or to buy it in at £75.

Limitations of short-term decision making using variable costing

All the above decision-making techniques have been used strictly within the confines of the variable costing model. This is the accounting part of decision making. It provides a good basis for solving the problem. However, do not forget that making decisions is essentially a management function. The role of accountancy is to provide good information to help managers make the right decisions. Remember, the reality of the situation being faced is always more complex than the assumptions from which the financial model is constructed.

The next chapter, on relevant costing, builds on what you have learnt in this chapter. It, also, is about making decisions but its context is widened to include any other effects caused by those decisions. For example, your contribution analysis may indicate that you should stop making one of your products. However, this may cause a significant number of redundancies to be made at a cost of hundreds of thousands of pounds. Whereas the variable costing model would not take this into account, relevant costing would include the redundancy costs because its boundary of cause and effect is so much wider. To find out more, have a look at the next chapter.

The manager's point of view (written by Nigel Burton)

Like most manufacturing concerns, my chemical company carried out periodic business reviews to consider withdrawing products which were no longer generating a satisfactory profit. There are many reasons why profitability might be in decline on individual items – perhaps a mature product has reached the end of its natural life, and been superseded by new technology, or fierce competition from Far Eastern suppliers has caused prices to fall to uneconomic levels. Management had to decide whether there was any course of action which would bring these products back into profitability, or whether they should be terminated, to allow the company to concentrate its resources on the newer, more profitable products.

The decision often hinged on the impact of a product's withdrawal on the recovery of fixed overhead. If a product is making a marginal loss (i.e. its variable cost is greater than its selling price) and therefore making no contribution to fixed overhead, the decision is simple. But if the product is making a marginal profit, although not enough to cover all the overheads attributed to it by the costing system, the decision is rather more complicated. If it is terminated, and there is no accompanying reduction in fixed overhead, the contribution will be lost and the company will be worse off. The fixed overhead attributed to the product will simply be reallocated to the next product. This may then become unprofitable as well, and be terminated in its turn, and so it goes on, until the domino effect wipes out the business! In the short term, fixed overheads cannot easily be reduced, so it may well be wise to persevere with the product until longer-term actions can be taken.

In this situation, variable costing is clearly crucial in preventing you from making inappropriate short-term decisions, although you will still have uncovered a problem which needs resolution in the longer term, probably by fixed overhead reductions. The decision to terminate a product is a long-term issue, which will change the future shape of the business. However, variable costing is also valuable in assessing the appropriateness of temporary actions, as a situation in our chemical factory demonstrates.

One of our plants made a high-volume product for use in the paper industry. The plant had been built in the 1970s, and despite one or two capacity improvements, the demand had grown so much by the late 1980s that we were unable to cope, even with continuous shift working. At this point, we were faced with two options: we could increase capacity by building a second plant, or we could concentrate our existing resources on the most profitable pieces of business. An analysis of the business showed that some of the sales generated a relatively low marginal income, and that, by eliminating these and accepting only the higher margin business, the profitability of the group would continue to rise.

This strategy was successful in the short term, and profitability improved. But it was an unsatisfactory way to run a business. Nobody likes to turn away business. It alienates the customer and sends them to the competition. The rejected business may have been at a lower margin, but it was still making a reasonable contribution to profit. The problem was that, at the time, there was insufficient business available to justify the cost of building a new plant. Fortunately, this changed over a period of time, and the growth in demand of both high- and low-margin business reached a point where the numbers started to add up. Accordingly, a new plant was built, doubling the capacity.

Now we had another problem. We had too much capacity for the present demand, and our sales projections showed that we would not be able to fill the plant for several years. At this point we had an enquiry from a large paper company, which needed a volume of product which roughly equated to 30% of our new plant's capacity. The margin on this product was lower than we would normally have accepted, but after much debate, we concluded that it did indeed make a positive contribution towards both fixed overheads and labour, which would otherwise have remained idle. We therefore accepted the business.

Such decisions are not as easy to make as they may seem. There are both quantifiable and unquantifiable issues to take into account. For instance, how fixed is the labour? If we do not accept this business, can we switch the labour on to cheaper single shifts, or is the volume of other business sufficient to require continuous shift working anyway? What is the impact on the cover provided by other departments, such as maintenance, quality control or the canteen? What about the level of raw material and finished goods stocks that will be needed, with the consequent warehousing and interest costs? Are we happy that the product costs on which we are basing this significant decision are sufficiently accurate in the first place? We certainly do not want to discover too late that the new business is actually draining profit from the company. And there are also the less quantifiable issues to consider, such as the extent of management input required, or the impact on the company's ability to accept unexpected, but more profitable, orders that may arise in the near future.

Once you have decided that it is in your company's interests to accept low-margin business, it is imperative that all parties are fully aware of the implications. Our American parent used marginal income percentage as one of the key measurements of our group's performance. The inclusion of a substantial piece of low-margin business naturally caused the marginal income percentage to decline, so it was important to ensure that the parent understood both the rationale and the effect of it, and that, if we chose not to do the business the following year, the parent would understand the reasons for a fluctuating sales line.

Such business should always be regarded as a one-off, separate piece of business which is outside the normal course of the company's activities. The business does not cover its share of the overheads, and is therefore technically unprofitable. We only consider accepting it when the overheads are already covered by other more profitable business. If there were a temptation to repeat this low-margin business year after year, perhaps a more advantageous course of action for the company would be to pursue a reduction in the level of fixed overheads.

There is also a risk in accepting low-margin business, in that it might encourage salespeople to chase more and more of it. After all, isn't any sale with a positive marginal income making a contribution towards overhead? Well, maybe, if you are a supermarket, where high sales volumes may well compensate for low margins and be sufficient to generate a satisfactory return. In manufacturing companies, however, capacity constraints will tend to limit the opportunity for substantial volume increases, so primary concentration on high-margin business is essential.

Summary

- Cease activities only if there is a negative contribution.
- Produce in the order of 'contribution per unit of scarce resource'.
- Decide whether to accept one-off contracts on the basis of their contribution.
- Buy in components if their price is less than the variable cost of manufacturing.
- Do not forget to take into account the factors outside the variable costing model. (The next chapter looks at this in greater depth.)

Further reading

Horngren, C., Bhimani, A., Datar, S. and Foster, G. (2002) *Management and Cost Accounting*, 2nd edition, Prentice Hall Europe, Harlow. See Chapter 8, 'Cost–volume–profit relationships'.

Upchurch, A. (2003) *Management Accounting, Principles and Practice*, 2nd edition, Financial Times/Prentice Hall, Harlow. See chapter 'Cost/volume/profit analysis'.

Weetman, P. (2002) *Management Accounting, an Introduction*, 3rd edition, Financial Times/Prentice Hall, Harlow. See chapter 'Profit measurement and short-term decision making'.

Answers to self-assessment questions

S6.1 V&A Group

	A	B	C	D	Group
Total overheads	90	210	250	450	1,000
Variable overheads (90%)	81	189	225	405	900
Fixed overheads (10%)	9	21	25	45	100
Variable costs					
Raw materials + direct labour	103	184	239	475	1,001
Add: Variable overheads	81	189	225	405	900
Variable costs	184	373	464	880	1,901
Sales income	180	420	500	900	2,000
Contribution	(4)	47	36	20	99

(a) Close factory A only

If A is closed:

	A	B	C	D	Group
Contribution	–	47	36	20	103
Less: Fixed costs					100
(b) Net profit					3

If A and D are closed:

	A	B	C	D	Group
Contribution	–	47	36	–	83
Less: Fixed costs					100
(c) Net loss					(17)

S6.2 Alpha, Beta, Gamma

	Alpha	Beta	Gamma	Total
Direct costs:				
Raw materials	100	150	80	
Direct labour	15	30	6	
Prime cost	115	180	86	
Variable overhead	10	15	8	
Variable cost	125	195	94	
Fixed overhead	30	60	12	
Total cost/unit	155	255	106	
Fixed overhead/unit	30	60	12	
Sales demand (units)	50	150	200	
Total fixed overhead	1,500	9,000	2,400	12,900

1 Selling price

	Alpha	Beta	Gamma	
Selling price	230	360	172 (200% of prime cost)	
Variable cost	125	195	94	
Contribution/unit	105	165	78	
Ranking	2	1	3	

2

	Alpha	Beta	Gamma	Total
Labour hours/unit	5	10	2	
No. of labour hours	150	1,500	–	1,650
No. of units sold	30	150	–	
Contribution/unit	105	165	78	
Total contribution	3,150	24,750	–	27,900
Less: Fixed costs				12,900
Net profit				**£15,000**

3

	Alpha	Beta	Gamma	
Contribution/unit	105	165	78	
Labour hours/unit	5	10	2	
Contribution/labour hour	21.0	16.5	39.0	
Ranking	2	3	1	

4

				Total
Labour hours/unit	5	10	2	
No. of labour hours	250	1,000	400	1,650
No. of units sold	50	100	200	
Contribution/unit	105	165	78	
Total contribution	5,250	16,500	15,600	37,350
Less: Fixed costs				12,900
Net profit				**£24,450**

5 Using the contribution per direct labour hour ranking gives £9,450 more profit than the contribution per unit ranking. So, using the contribution per unit of scarce resource does give the highest profit.

S6.3 Abacus Inc.

(a) Normal activity

	$
Sales price	250
Variable cost	145
Contribution	105/unit

Total contribution = 1,000 × $105 = 105,000
Less: Fixed costs = 1,000 × $75 = 75,000
Net profit = **$30,000**

(b) Export order

	$
Materials	130 ($100 + 30%)
Direct labour	35 ($25 + 40%)
Variable overheads	20
Export insurance	5
Variable cost	190/unit
Sales price	220 ($44,000/200)
Contribution	+30/unit

Total contribution = +$6,000 (200 × $30)

Recommend acceptance of the export order as it has a positive contribution.

S6.4 Vendco

Compare the relevant variable costs of manufacture with the buying-in cost. Remember that fixed overheads will still have to be paid for in the short term so these are irrelevant to the decision.

Variable production costs	£
Direct labour	25
Direct materials	30
Variable overheads	5
Total	60
Buy-in price	75

Therefore, buying in is not recommended (in the short term).

CASE STUDY	Sara Wray Enterprises

Sara Wray lives in the Cotswolds, an area of outstanding natural beauty in central–south-west England. She started her working life as a teacher of French and art but, after several years, she gave this up to have a family. As her children grew older, she went back to work on a part-time basis, not as a teacher but as an administrator of a local art gallery. Her children are now adults with jobs of their own and Sara is the driving force behind a successful business offering language tuition and cultural holidays to non-UK residents.

Her business actually started seven years ago when she decided to gain a Teaching English as a Foreign Language (TEFL) qualification. Having achieved this, she provided English language tuition to foreign students in the summer months. Two students would come to stay in her home at any one time, receiving formal tuition in the morning and going out for visits to local places of interest in the afternoon and evenings with Sara. During her first summer season, she had a total of nine students, eight staying for two weeks and one staying for one month. This was a total of 20 student-weeks' tuition. She established a good reputation and the number of students grew each year.

After a few years, Sara branched out by offering one-week Tours of the Cotswolds for groups of approximately 16 adults without any formal language tuition element. Her success with these tours is based on her organizational ability and her experience of arranging local trips for her language students. As well as general tours, she now offers two specialized ones: English Gardens and Arts and Crafts. Sara still sees her English language courses as the basis of her operations as many of her tours include some people who have been students of hers or have been recommended by them. However, most of her tour customers come from her advertisements in France, the Netherlands, Germany, Italy and Spain.

Current demand for her TEFL courses is such that she now employs seven other qualified teachers, each taking two students at a time. The students live in the teachers' homes and are taught there in the mornings but join together for the visits and eat out together each evening at a different venue. For these outings, Sara hires an 18-seater minibus and driver for her 12-week season (mid-June to mid-September). Her non-tuition tours start in May and finish in October but do not take place every week. These tour customers stay in local hotels which are block-booked in advance by Sara. She hires the same type of minibus and driver for her tour parties and she also hires a guide to accompany them.

Up to now, there has been no difficulty finding guides of the right quality. Unfortunately, her regular garden tour guide, Rose, is about to move to Paris due to her partner's unexpected relocation and will no longer be available to guide these tours. However, one of the TEFL teachers, Mary, is also an expert gardener and has volunteered her services as garden tour guide. As Mary speaks reasonably good French, Spanish and German, she would be an ideal choice for this job. But the two planned garden tours are scheduled to take place during the TEFL season and Sara would have to find a replacement teacher for those weeks. Most of the other good TEFL teachers living in the area have contracted with the many English language schools based in nearby Oxford and Sara is finding it impossible to find a suitable replacement. As the season is just about to start, it looks as though Sara will have to cancel either two teacher-weeks of English tuition or two one-week garden tours. She is unsure whether to use Mary as a TEFL teacher or a garden tour guide.

While she is pondering this dilemma, Sara receives a letter from one of her previous students, Michael, who lives in Munich. Michael wants Sara to arrange a one-week 'Beer and Brewing' tour to include five beer-related visits for himself and 15 of his friends. When he was brushing up his English last year with Sara, he was very impressed with several local beers he tasted in the Cotswold area. He is offering to pay Sara £5,600 (16 @ £350 per person) for local accommodation, food, transport, brewery visit fees and knowledgeable guide. He will organize the travel between Munich and the Cotswolds.

Sara's friend, David, is a member of the Campaign for Real Ale (CamRA) and says that he would be willing to give up a week of his holidays to guide this tour for £500. Sara estimates admission fees at £650 and other costs the same as for a general or gardens tour. She does not see any reason why this tour should not go ahead. The only thing concerning her is that the price offered seems so low that the tour will make a loss. The lowest cost of her other tours is £6,000 (see below). She thinks she will probably have to contact Michael and refuse his offer.

As well as all this, she notices that the financial analysis prepared by her accountant shows that, although the general and gardens tours are profitable, the arts and crafts tours are making a loss (see below). Although they are more costly to run, she is reluctant to drop them but, on the other hand, does not want to run any of her activities at a loss. She is reluctant to increase her prices as she is aware of a firm in nearby Oxford which offers very similar arts tours at the price of £385 per person.

Sara wants to increase her profit next year by at least £3,000 by expanding either the English teaching or the tours but she is unsure what she needs to do to achieve this.

Financial analysis of TEFL activities

Maximum activity for season is 8 teachers for 12 weeks = 96 teacher-weeks
Each teacher has two students each week. Each student pays £400/week
Fixed costs (minibus hire, insurance, advertising, etc.) for TEFL total £19,200

For one teacher-week	£
2 hours' tuition/day for 5 days = 10 h @ £15/h =	150
Agent's commission, 2 students @ £25 =	50
Accommodation, 5 nights @ £20 × 2 students =	200
Evening meals, £5 × 2 students × 5 days =	50
Admission fees, £5 × 2 students × 5 days =	50
Total variable cost =	500
Fixed cost (£19,200/12 weeks/8 teachers) =	200
Total cost =	700
Sales revenue (2 @ £400) =	800
Net profit =	100

Financial analysis of tour activities

Tours planned: 3 general, 2 gardens and 2 arts and crafts
Maximum of 16 per tour, each person paying £400
Fixed costs (administration, insurance, advertising, etc.) for tours total £12,810

Per tour (16 people)	General/Gardens £	Arts and Crafts £
Minibus and driver	800	800
Guide fees	350	500
Hotel, bed, breakfast & evening meal	2,620	2,620
Admission fees	400	800
Total variable costs	4,170	4,720
Fixed costs	1,830	1,830
Total cost	6,000	6,550
Sales revenue (16 × £400)	6,400	6,400
Net profit	400	(150)

Tasks:

Advise Sara on the decisions facing her:

1 Is it better to use Mary as a garden tour guide or English teacher for two weeks?

(25 marks)

2 Should she decline Michael's offer of £5,600 for a Beer and Brewing tour?

(25 marks)

3 Should she stop offering the Arts and Crafts tours?

(25 marks)

4 Next year, should she expand the English teaching or the tours?

(25 marks)
(Total 100 marks)

Questions

An asterisk * on a question number indicates that the answer is given at the end of the book. Answers to the other questions are given in the Lecturer's Guide.

Q6.1* Burgabar Corporation

Burgabar Corporation owns and operates a range of fast food outlets throughout the East End of London. A summary of next year's budget (before head office costs are taken into account) is given below:

Branch	Sales revenue £	Variable costs £	Salaries & wages £	Fixed costs £
West Ham	100,000	20,000	32,000	30,000
Hackney	120,000	24,000	32,000	30,000
Forest Gate	120,000	24,000	34,000	32,000
Mile End	140,000	28,000	34,000	34,000

The administrative head office of Burgabar Corporation is at Epping. Its running costs of £96,000 a year are apportioned to branches on the basis of sales revenue.

Concern is being expressed about the West Ham branch as it is showing a loss (after head office costs have been deducted). One director has suggested that the branch is closed as soon as possible and a new branch opened, possibly in the Ilford area. However, it would take approximately 12 months to open a new branch. The closure of the West Ham branch would reduce head office costs by £10,000 p.a. with immediate effect. Also, although West Ham's salaries and wages bill would disappear immediately, redundancy pay of £8,000 would be payable.

Task:

Advise the directors of Burgabar Corporation.

Q6.2* Profoot Ltd

Profoot currently makes and sells two types of protective shoe, model P1 and model P2.

	P1	P2
Annual sales demand (pairs)	14,000	10,000
Selling price	£40	£40
Variable costs per pair:		
Materials	£15	£15
Labour – Machining (£8/hour)	£2	£2
– Assembly (£7/hour)	£3.50	£3.50
– Packing (£6/hour)	£0.50	£0.50

Annual total fixed costs are currently £300,000.

For the next financial year, Profoot intends to keep model P1 as it is but to upgrade model P2 by the use of better materials. The materials cost for P2 is expected to be £20 a pair (an increase of £5 a pair) and its new selling price will be £50 a pair. Also, the amount of time spent machining P2s will double and the cost of this will increase to £4 a pair.

Also, next year, Profoot intends to introduce the PDL, a top-of-the-range model with a selling price of £65. Labour costs for machining will be £4 a pair, assembly £7 a pair and packing £0.50 a pair. Materials will cost £32.50 a pair.

Demand for the P1, P2 and PDL next year is predicted to be 14,000, 7,000 and 5,000 pairs respectively. Annual fixed costs are expected to increase by 2% next year.

Tasks:

1 Calculate the annual net profit for the current year.
2 Calculate the annual net profit for next year assuming the predicted demand is met in full.
3 If the maximum number of machine hours available next year is 8,500, create a production plan to maximize net profit. (Clearly show the quantity of each model produced and calculate the net profit.)
4 Profoot could purchase an additional machine costing £420,000 which would last for 10 years and have no residual value at the end of that period. This machine could be used for a maximum of 1,750 hours a year. How would the purchase of this machine affect next year's net profit?

Q6.3* King & Co.

The current annual budget for King & Co., makers of baseball caps, is summarized as follows:

	£000
Sales (1 million caps @ £5 each)	5,000
Less manufacturing cost of caps sold	3,000
Gross margin	2,000
Less sales and administration expenses	1,500
Operating income	500

King's fixed manufacturing costs were £2.0 million and its fixed sales and administration costs were £1.0 million. Sales commission of 5% of sales is included in the sales and administration expenses. The company is approaching the end of the current financial year and looks as though it will exceed its budgetary targets.

King's has just been asked by its local First Division football club to make a special order of 50,000 caps in the club colours to celebrate the club's promotion to the Premier League; the club is willing to pay £4 a cap. However, a special badge of the club's emblem would have to be made for each cap.

Even though King & Co. has the necessary capacity to produce the order, the managing director has decided to reject the club's offer of £200,000 for the 50,000 caps. He explained his decision by saying,

> *The club's offer is too low. I know we would save the sales commission but the badges alone will cost twice as much as that, and it costs us £4.50 to make our ordinary caps. I'm willing to cut our usual 10% profit margin to 5%, or even less, to get this order but I'm not prepared to do it for nothing and I'm certainly not prepared to make a loss on the deal.*

Task:

Comment on the managing director's decision.

Q6.4 Parfumier Jean-Paul

Jean-Paul Cie (J-P) is a world-famous haute-couture fashion house based in Paris. It also manufactures a range of perfumes, all made from secret recipes. Only one ingredient called 'maylarnge', a mixing agent, is used in all their products. Maylarnge is obtained from SML Laboratoire in Brussels and the quantity used varies with the particular perfume recipe.

Due to temporary processing difficulties, SML has informed J-P that it can supply only €13,100 worth of maylarnge over the next three months.

The budget below relates to the quarter in question under normal circumstances. The shortage of the mixing agent means that the budget will have to be revised.

Perfume	Passion	Entice	Magique	Exotique
Sales volume (50 ml bottles)	6,000	5,500	6,500	4,500
Variable costs per bottle	€	€	€	€
Maylarnge	1.00	0.80	1.20	0.60
Ingredients (as per recipe)	2.00	3.10	2.60	1.90
Selling price	12.90	15.70	16.10	14.50

Fixed costs for the quarter amount to €133,300 (including all wages and salaries).

Tasks:

1 What would the quarter's profit be if there was no shortage of maylarnge?
2 Calculate the profit for this period of shortage if the perfumes were manufactured in the order of their contribution per bottle until they ran out of maylarnge.
3 Calculate the revised sales budget and profit assuming J-P wishes to maximize its profit for this period of shortage.

Q6.5 MPB Ltd

Marie and Peter Bridge run a business manufacturing and selling sets of the popular French game, boules. The boules are turned from aluminium, packaged in a neat carrying case and sold for £22 a set. The raw materials cost £8 a set and each set takes 20 minutes of turning by skilled operatives who are paid £9.00 an hour. The fixed costs of the business are £480,000 a year. This year, MPB plans to produce 80,000 sets.

Tasks:

1 Calculate:
   a) the variable cost of a set of boules;
   b) the absorption cost of a set of boules;
   c) the breakeven point;
   d) the profit or loss if 80,000 sets are sold.
2 A large French champagne house has asked MPB Ltd if it will produce 5,000 boule sets for a worldwide promotion. Each set has to be engraved with the French company's logo and the carrying case must bear its brand name. The extra work involved in this will cost £2.50 a set. It has offered to pay a total of £75,000 for the order. Should MPB accept this offer?
3 A Chinese company has proposed to MPB that it could manufacture the finished boule sets in China and supply them to MPB for £14 delivered. This price would apply to the first 50,000 sets, but after this it would reduce to £10 a set. MPB appreciates that this would change its function to trading only and it would be able to eliminate its manufacturing facilities, saving £180,000 a year.
   a) Advise MPB whether or not it should accept this proposition.
   b) List the points MPB should consider carefully before accepting this proposition.

Q6.6

BBQ Ltd manufactures two types of barbecue – the Deluxe BBQ and the Standard BBQ. Both undergo similar production processes and use similar materials and types of labour. However, a shortage of direct labour has been identified and this is limiting the company's ability to produce the required number of barbecues for the year ending 31 May 2002. Labour capacity is limited to 235,000 labour hours for the year ending 31 May 2002 and this is insufficient to meet total sales demand.

BBQ Ltd has stated that the standard selling price and standard prime cost for each barbecue for the forthcoming year are as follows:

	Deluxe BBQ	Standard BBQ
Selling price	£100	£50
Direct material	£50	£11
Direct labour (rate £5 per hour)	£25	£20
Estimated sales demand (units)	10,000	50,000

It has been company policy to absorb production overheads on a labour hour basis. The budgeted information for the year ending 31 May 2002 is as follows:

Fixed production overhead	£188,000
Variable production overhead	£2 per direct labour hour

Non-production costs for the year ending 31 May 2002 are estimated to be:

Selling and distribution overhead:
   Variable　　　　　　10% of selling price
   Fixed　　　　　　£35,000
Administrative overhead:
   Fixed　　　　　　£50,000

Required:

a) Calculate the production plan that will maximize profit for the year ending 31 May 2002.

(7 marks)

b) Based on the production plan that you have recommended in part (a), present a profit statement for the year ending 31 May 2002 in a marginal costing format.

(9 marks)

c) Discuss two problems that may arise as a result of your recommended production plan.

(4 marks)

d) Explain why the contribution concept is used in limiting factor decisions.

(5 marks)

(Total = 25 marks)

CIMA Foundation: Management Accounting Fundamentals, May 2001.

Review questions

1 Explain how to tell whether or not to cease certain activities.
2 Explain how to determine the order of production when one of the resources used is scarce.
3 Explain how to tell whether or not to accept one-off contracts.
4 Explain how to tell whether to produce or buy in components used in your products.
5 Discuss the limitations of decision making using variable costing.

The answers to all these questions can be found in the text of this chapter.

CHAPTER 7

Short-term decisions using relevant costing

Introduction

Managers should take decisions that result in maximum benefit for the organization **as a whole**. This means taking into account **indirect** effects as well as the direct ones. Suppose that a lawn mower manufacturer decides to buy in a particular component, e.g. the motor, instead of making it, the justification being that the £15 purchase price of the motor is less than its £17 variable cost of manufacture. If the company uses 10,000 motors a year then the annual saving should be £20,000.

This looks like a good decision. But suppose that one indirect effect of this was to make five jobs redundant in the motor production section. If the average redundancy pay was £12,000, it would take three years before the total redundancy pay of £60,000 was covered by the savings made!

The point is that **all** the known quantifiable effects of a decision should be part of the analysis, not just the obvious ones. Relevant costing is particularly appropriate for managers as they are more likely to be aware of the indirect effects than the accountants. This applies even more so to the consideration of the qualitative factors involved. The voice of the manager should be paramount in these decisions.

Having worked through this chapter you should be able to:

- describe relevant costing;
- distinguish between relevant and irrelevant costs;
- identify avoidable costs, opportunity costs, sunk costs, committed costs, non-cash costs and opportunity benefits;
- quantify the relevant cost of decisions;
- discuss the importance of qualitative factors;
- give good advice based on relevant costing.

Definition of relevant cost/revenue

Relevant costs/revenues have three criteria. They are **always**:

- **avoidable** – they are caused by a positive decision and would not happen if the decision was negative;
- **future** – costs/revenues that have already happened cannot be altered by a decision not yet taken;
- **cash** – the net change in cash (not profit) is used to measure the decision's effects.

All three criteria must be fulfilled. If only one or two criteria are met, the cost/revenue is not relevant.

The topic of 'relevant costing' is really about **relevant cash flows** (which would be a better title due to its descriptive nature). These relevant cash flows can be 'in' (revenues) or 'out' (costs).

Types of relevant cost

The two main types of relevant costs are *avoidable costs* and *opportunity costs*.

Avoidable costs

These will only be incurred if a certain course of action is followed, otherwise they will not occur. If a positive decision means that a new lorry will be purchased for £22,000 then a negative decision means that expenditure of £22,000 will be **avoided**.

Opportunity costs

These are a measure of the net cash **benefit** foregone from the next most desirable alternative course of action. Even though these do not appear on the profit and loss account, they are real and relevant for decision making.

For example, if some **scarce** specialized labour (like a high-level relational database programmer) is reassigned due to a positive decision, the opportunity cost will be the net cash benefit sacrificed due to the discontinuation of the programmer's current assignment. If there are plenty of these programmers in the organization, the opportunity cost will not arise as both projects can be performed at the same time.

Types of irrelevant cost

The three main types of irrelevant costs are sunk costs, committed costs and non-cash costs.

Sunk costs

These relate to the proposal under consideration but are incurred **prior** to the decision being made. A good example is the cost of market research undertaken to help make decisions about a new product. Sunk costs are also known as 'past costs'.

Committed costs

These are costs that have not been paid at the time of making the decision but a legal obligation exists to pay them at some time in the future; for example, lease payments of premises for the project under consideration if that lease is already in existence but the premises are currently unoccupied. As the lease payments must be made whether the decision is positive or negative, these costs are also called 'common costs'. (They are common to both the 'yes' and 'no' decision as to whether the project goes ahead or not.)

Non-cash costs

The most usual example of these is the depreciation charged in the profit and loss account. Depreciation is a legitimate cost; indeed the net profit figure would be incorrect if depreciation had not been deducted from gross profit together with the other overheads. However, depreciation does **not** cause any movement of cash and therefore cannot be a relevant cost.

Relevant costing

Example
7.1

Frank Jeffery Limited is a manufacturer of reproduction antique furniture. Three months ago it tendered for a one-off order from English Heritage to make a copy of a four-poster bed that was once slept in by Queen Elizabeth I. The cost of preparing this tender was estimated to be £250. The specification would use 5 cubic metres ('cubes') of English oak, a timber in regular use in the factory. Its current price is £400 a cube. There are three cubes in stock at the moment, which were bought in at £375 a cube.

Business is good and the factory is working at full capacity. To make the bed would need three skilled craftworkers for two weeks each. The company operates a 40-hour week and pays skilled craftworkers at the rate of £10 per hour. It is estimated that the normal work lost due to this order would produce a net cash contribution for the company totalling £3,000.

The machinery involved would depreciate by £400 in the two weeks and the cost of electricity to run the machines would be £80. The machines would be in continual use whether or not the tender was successful. Fixed production overheads are absorbed at the rate of £25 per direct labour hour.

One month ago, a new advanced type of hand-held router was purchased at the cost of £750 as it would be very useful if the bid was selected by English Heritage. (This was a bargain introductory offer for last month only; its price is now £899.) The company's policy is to write off in full hand tools costing less than £1,000 to the profit and loss account in the year of purchase.

What is the relevant cost to Frank Jeffery Limited of making the four-poster bed?

Solution

Item	Avoidable	Future	Cash	Note	Amount	Relevant
Tender preparation			X	1		–
English oak	X	X	X	2	5 cubes × £400	2,000
Craftworkers' pay		X	X	3		–
Cash contribution lost	X	X	X	4		3,000
Machine depreciation		X		5		–
Machine electricity		X	X	6		–
Fixed production overhead		X		7		–
New router			X	8		–
					Relevant cost	**£5,000**

Notes:
1 Sunk cost.
2 As oak is in regular use, 5 cubes will need to be replaced at the current price.
3 Craftworkers are assumed to be permanent employees paid on a time basis.
4 Opportunity cost of next-best alternative.
5 Depreciation is not a **cash** cost. It is a book entry not causing any cash to flow.
6 Common cost. The machines will be running irrespective of the tender.
7 Overhead absorption is a book entry. It does not change the overheads **incurred**.
8 Sunk cost.

Self-assessment question S7.1

Try the following question for yourself (answer at the end of the chapter).

Welgrow Ltd is a manufacturer of garden seed compost. At the moment, it makes six different types and is considering adding a new basic compost to its range. Initially, it will make a batch of 10,000 kg and has listed the following costs involved:

1 Exclusive use of the company's mixing machine will be needed for one week. The depreciation of this machine is included as a production overhead at £520 per year.
2 The trial batch will need 7,000 kg of vermiculite. Welgrow does not use this material and does not have any of it in stock at present; its market price is £1.00 per kg.
3 Several years ago Welgrow bought a large quantity of black sand at £0.10 per kg for a special project. A left-over surplus of 3,000 kg is currently in stock as it has proved impossible to resell. Welgrow has no alternative use for this surplus other than as an ingredient in the new compost.
4 To ensure successful marketing of this new product at the right time, a contract for advertising space with a total cost of £500 has been signed. A deposit of 20% has been paid and the balance is due one month before launch next spring.
5 An aluminium storage bin, which was due to have been offered for sale at the realistic price of £100, will be used for the new compost.

Consider each item and state why you think it is relevant or not. Calculate the relevant cost to Welgrow of the decision to go ahead. Also, calculate the breakeven selling price of the new compost.

Opportunity benefits

These benefits, or savings, may be created by taking a positive decision to go ahead with a project. For example, some redundancy costs which were about to be incurred may be avoided by going ahead.

The avoidance or prevention of a cash cost is equivalent to cash income.

Opportunity benefits are relevant to the decision and must be taken into account.

Relevant cost of materials

The relevant cost of a material is not what it cost to buy it in the first place, i.e. a sunk or committed cost. If a material is in regular use, its relevant cost is its **replacement** cost. This is the **future, avoidable, cash flow** caused by the decision to use it.

But if the material was already owned and would not be replaced if used (i.e. it was not in regular use) its relevant cost is the **greater** of:

a) its current realizable value (i.e. the amount received from selling it); and
b) the value obtained from alternative uses.

You should recognize this as its opportunity cost.

Relevant cost of materials

Example
7.2

Birch Brothers is a low-volume, high-specification bicycle manufacturer based in South Yorkshire. It has been requested to quote for producing a special pedal-powered vehicle for promoting bicycle use in the UK. The vehicle has four pedalling positions at the front and four at the rear. In between these is a three-dimensional platform structure for advertising the various benefits of cycling. It is approximately the size of a small lorry.

Birch Brothers is currently short of work and is operating at well below its maximum capacity. Unfounded rumours of possible redundancies are circulating among the 20-strong workforce and morale is not good. No additional labour or overtime would be needed to build this 'promotional platform'. This order would provide some very welcome work for the business.

However, the contract would need the following materials:

a) New materials not normally used, e.g. a trailer chassis for the central advertising platform. These would total £5,000.
b) Materials currently in regular use and in stock, e.g. wheels, pedals, etc. These have a book value of £1,780 but would cost £2,000 to buy now.
c) 80 metres of stainless steel tube: Birch Brothers has 60 metres of this disused item in stock left over from a discontinued model. This stock has a resale value of £500 but it is planned to use it all for an export order commencing in four months' time in place of a very similar specification tube which would cost £12.50 a metre. The current price of stainless steel tube is £20 a metre.
d) 95 square metres of aluminium sheet: it has just this amount in stock. It was left over from the manufacture of a batch of bike-trailers, a product that was unsuccessful for the company. Birch Brothers has tried reselling these sheets but not a single buyer was found. The sheeting is taking up a lot of workshop space and it was decided last week to pay £200 to have it removed in the near future.
e) 8 sets of brakes: the company has 20 sets of old-fashioned brakes that are perfectly functional although there is no demand for them. The original cost of these was £12 a set. Whatever is left of this stock item will be thrown in the bin at the financial year-end stocktake.

Solution

Item	Avoidable	Future	Cash	Note	Amount	Relevant
a) New materials	X	X	X	1	£5,000	5,000
b) Regular materials	X	X	X	2	£2,000	2,000
c) 60 m st. steel tube	X	X	X	3	60 m × £12.50	750
d) 20 m st. steel tube	X	X	X	4	20 m × £20	400
e) Aluminium sheet	X	X	X	5	£200	(200)
f) Old-fashioned brakes				6	–	
					Relevant cost	**£7,950**

Notes:
1 At current buying-in market price (= replacement cost).
2 At replacement cost.
3 First 60 metres at opportunity cost (= cost saved by use for export order).
4 Next 20 metres need to be bought in (at current replacement price).
5 This is an opportunity **benefit**. By using the sheeting, the company is saving the cost of its disposal.
6 No cash flows of any sort are caused by using these brakes.

Note also that there are no relevant labour costs. The labour force would be paid whether the contract is obtained or not. This is a common cost.

Self-assessment question S7.2

Try the following question for yourself (answer at the end of the chapter).

Tilly Ltd has been approached by a customer who wants a special job done and is willing to pay £20,000 for it. The job would require the following materials:

Material	Total units required	Units in stock	Book value of units in stock (£/unit)	Realizable value (£/unit)	Replacement cost (£/unit)
A	1,000	0	–	–	6
B	1,000	600	2	2.5	5
C	1,000	700	3	2.5	4
D	200	200	4	6	9
E	500	500	5	–	–

Material B is regularly used by Tilly Ltd in the manufacture of its standard products.
   Materials C and D are specialist materials, in stock due to previous overbuying. No other use can be found for material C. However, the stock of material D could be used in another job as a substitute for 300 units of material M. Tilly has no stock of material M at present but it can be purchased locally at £5 a unit.

Since the stock of material E was acquired, its sale has been banned by the government (although previously acquired stocks are allowed to be used up). It is a toxic chemical and Tilly is expecting to pay £500 in the near future for its safe disposal as it has no other use for it.

Task:

To help Tilly Ltd decide whether or not to accept the job, calculate the relevant cost of materials needed.

Qualitative factors

Although relevant costing is a numerical or quantitative analysis technique, only a poor manager would ignore the non-numerical or qualitative factors involved in a decision. These are just as important, if not more so, and should be given serious consideration before the decision is made.

Take the case of an advertising agency that currently handles the Mars UK account being offered the chance to pitch for the business of Cadbury's Chocolate. Before doing so, it should think very carefully about the reaction of Mars UK to its acting for a major competitor. Would Mars UK see it as a conflict of interests and take its business elsewhere?

Although no **definite** numerical answers are attainable in such cases, organizations should be aware of the possible risks involved and act accordingly.

Limitations of decision making using relevant costing

The context of relevant costing is broader than that of variable costing (discussed in the previous chapter). This lack of artificial boundaries makes it much more realistic. It also makes it more useful, as decisions usually have indirect consequences which should be included in the decision-making process. The main limitation of relevant costing is the difficulty in foreseeing all the indirect consequences arising from the decision in question.

Take the example used in the 'Limitations' section of the previous chapter on variable costing. This described the decision, based on an analysis of product contributions, to cease manufacturing one of several products. The indirect consequence of multiple redundancies and associated payments occurring had been foreseen and taken into account in the cessation decision. However, it may be that the dropping of that particular product would enhance the market's perception of the company as the product was considered to be outmoded and unattractive. Cessation may improve the 'positioning' of the company in the eyes of its customers and sales may increase accordingly. This particular indirect effect is much more difficult to foresee than the ensuing redundancies but its consequences are just as real.

This emphasizes the point that making decisions is essentially a management, rather than an accounting, function. The role of accountancy is to provide good information to assist managers make the right decisions. But the manager always has a limited time frame in which to make the decision. During that short time, it is impossible to foresee **all** the consequences of the decision. Even when you have made the best decision you possibly could, events may yet overtake you. Being aware of this will make you a wiser and better manager.

The manager's point of view (written by Nigel Burton)

Business decisions need to be taken in the round, giving thought to all the relevant factors and potential consequences of any actions taken. The decisions based on variable costing, as discussed in Chapter 6, would in practice never be taken on the arithmetic alone, but on their total impact on the business. While some of this will be quantifiable, much of it will not, and will require the input of judgement, inspiration and informed guesswork. Nevertheless, the starting point for most decisions remains the arithmetic. The way in which the quantifiable factors are handled in practice is perhaps best illustrated by the Capital Investment Appraisal procedures adopted by our company.

In every capital investment decision, the fundamental issue is: What is the total impact on my business of making this investment? To answer this question from a financial standpoint, we have to compare the consequences of making the investment with the consequences of not making it. Our capital appraisal model required a 'Before Case', which consisted of a 10-year income statement showing the results which would be expected if no capital investment was made, and an 'After Case', which showed the forecast position after the investment had been made. The 'Before Case' might, for example, see a flat sales line due to capacity constraints, or perhaps a declining sales line if perseverance with the old plant results in increased downtime for maintenance. Perhaps the old plant has been condemned for environmental reasons, so without the investment sales will be reduced to nil, and redundancies will ensue. All the costs and quantifiable implications of refusing the investment are considered here, including committed costs and opportunity costs, the latter being opportunities which would have been seized but for the project.

The 'After Case', on the other hand, might reflect continued sales growth arising from increased capacity, or reduced marginal costs due to more process automation, larger batch sizes or higher yields. Also shown here are the expected fixed overheads following the investment, including any changes to areas such as selling and administration. In producing these two sets of figures, the principles of relevant costing are regularly utilized. Is a particular cost directly attributable to the project, or would we have incurred it anyway? Many costs will be incurred regardless of the project, and therefore will appear in both cases.

Then, by deducting the 'Before Case' numbers from the 'After Case' numbers, we arrive at the 'Incremental Case'. This represents exactly the expected impact of the initial investment on each line of the income statement for each of the next 10 years, i.e. the net increase in sales, the net reduction in marginal costs, the additional selling expenses, and so on. From this basic data, we can calculate both the rate of return and the number of years needed to pay back the initial investment, two of the key indicators used by management to assess the viability of the project.

This Capital Investment Appraisal procedure neatly captures and displays the quantifiable elements of an investment decision. These elements may tell a good financial story, but it may well be non-quantifiable issues which cause management ultimately to approve or reject the investment proposal. Another example from my chemical business illustrates the kinds of issues which may have an influence on the decision.

One of our products had been used for many years by both the petroleum and plastics industries. It had always been profitable, not least because none of our competitors had quite managed to duplicate it, despite the fact that the patents had expired many years previously. Cheaper, but inferior, alternatives had become available on the market, but our business maintained its competitive edge.

The plant, and the technology on which it was based, was some 40 years old. Over the years, there had been many repairs and part replacements, but eventually the time came when a number of considerations, among them environmental concerns, brought us to the point when substantial changes were necessary. Failure to improve the environmental performance was ultimately likely to result in the plant's closure, although the timescales involved in this were indeterminate. We were also aware that the demand for the product from the petroleum companies might decline at some stage in the future as alternative technologies became available, although sales to the plastics industry were likely to continue. The timing of any decline was again largely a matter of guesswork.

Our options were: (a) to do nothing, and subcontract manufacturing when the plant was closed; (b) to patch up the plant once again, with a view to temporarily satisfying the environmental concerns, until such time as the petroleum business died a natural death, then sub-contract; or (c) to build a new plant, incorporating state-of-the-art technology. The financial implications of each of these scenarios were reasonably easy to establish. The 'Before Case' represented option (a), and included the costs of closing down and decommissioning the plant, as well as the redundancy costs of surplus staff. It also reflected the additional cost of buying in the material from a sub-contractor, for which role the most likely candidates were in India and China. Our first 'After Case' scenario (option (b)) was clearly the cheapest, but would provide us with only a short-term solution to our environmental problems. If the petroleum business did not decline within five years, a further patching-up project would almost certainly be required. Moreover, if the product turned out to have a much longer life than we anticipated, we might end up putting up a new plant anyway. Our second 'After Case' scenario (option (c)) was a high-cost, high-risk strategy, because if the petroleum demand turned out to be short term, we could find ourselves left with a relatively new but largely redundant plant. It would, however, solve all our environmental issues at a stroke.

Interestingly, neither of the capital investment scenarios (options (b) and (c)) produced a satisfactory 'Incremental Case' when compared against option (a). This was not because either of the proposals themselves were non-viable, but because the cost of contracting out manufacture turned out, rather unexpectedly, to be much less than expected. The additional cost of buying in from a sub-contractor was substantially offset by overhead and labour savings, so a satisfactory level of profitability could more or less be maintained without any capital investment. The financial advantages offered by the two 'After Case' scenarios were therefore relatively small, and did not appear to justify the capital outlays. The financial arguments clearly pointed towards sub-contracting as a solution to our plant problem, but here the non-quantifiable aspects came into play. Did we really want to divulge our company secrets to a third party? Could we trust any confidentiality agreement signed by the sub-contractor? Was it worth the risk? After all, the product might yet have many years of life left with the petroleum industry and would anyway still be in demand from the plastics companies.

So we had to balance the risks of losing control of our know-how, and then possibly finding our business under threat from our own product coming in cheaply from the East, against the possibility of a white elephant of a plant if the petroleum companies converted in the near future. After much deliberation, we decided to carry out the full plant renewal (option (c)). Our 'Before Case' was changed to reflect our new assumption that we would lose business to the Eastern threat, and on this basis the figures showed an acceptable return and payback period. Now, several years later, the petroleum companies are still using the product, the capital outlay has already been paid back and the environmental problems are a thing of the past. There is still talk that the petroleum companies may soon discontinue their use of the product, but the new plant has already justified its existence.

So our gamble has paid off, but we hit upon the right solution not because we followed the direction pointed out by the financial information, but because we took our decision in the light of wider business considerations. The financials, however, built up on relevant costing principles, provided an essential basis for further decision making. Sound financials, plus informed judgement, experience, and a little bit of luck, can minimize risk, and bring you to the correct conclusion.

Summary

- Relevant costing is a financial model to aid managers with decision making.
- Its objective is to maximize future net cash inflows to the business.
- It considers the indirect, as well as direct, effects of decisions.
- Its method is to identify the relevant costs and benefits **caused by** the decision.
- Relevant costs are avoidable **and** future **and** cash.
- The two types of relevant cost are *avoidable* and *opportunity* costs.
- The three types of irrelevant cost are *sunk, committed* and *non-cash* costs.
- Opportunity benefits must be taken into account.
- Qualitative factors are important and should be seriously considered.
- Relevant costing is more realistic than variable costing but it is not perfect.

Further reading

Balakrishnan, R. and Sivaramakrishnan, K. (2002) 'A critical overview of the use of full-cost data for planning and pricing', *Journal of Management Accounting Research*, Vol. 14, 3–31.

Drury, C. (2004) *Management and Cost Accounting*, 6th edition, Thomson Learning, London. See chapter 'Measuring relevant costs and revenues for decision making'.

Horngren, C., Bhimani, A., Datar, S. and Foster, G. (2002) *Management and Cost Accounting*, 2nd edition, Prentice Hall Europe, Harlow. See chapter 'Revenues, costs and the decision process'.

Upchurch, A. (2003) *Management Accounting, Principles and Practice*, 2nd edition, Financial Times/Prentice Hall, Harlow. See chapter 'Relevant costs and benefits for decision making'.

Answers to self-assessment questions

S7.1 Welgrow Ltd

Item	Avoidable	Future	Cash	Note	Amount	Relevant
1 Mixing machine		X		1		–
2 Vermiculite	X	X	X	2	7,000 @ £1	7,000
3 Black sand				3		–
4 Advertising space			X	4		–
5 Storage bin	X	X	X	5		100
					Relevant cost	**£7,100**

Notes:
1 Depreciation is a non-cash expense.
2 Vermiculite needs to be bought in at replacement cost.
3 Sunk cost with no alternative use.
4 The 20% deposit is sunk and the 80% remainder is committed.
5 Opportunity cost.

For the batch of 10,000 kg, the breakeven selling price is **£0.71 per kg.**

S7.2 Tilly Ltd

Item	Avoidable	Future	Cash	Note	Amount	Relevant
Material A	X	X	X	1	1,000 × £6	6,000
Material B	X	X	X	2	1,000 × £5	5,000
Material C	X	X	X	3	700 × £2.50	1,750
Material C	X	X	X	4	300 × £4	1,200
Material D (200 units)	X	X	X	5	300 × £5	1,500
Material E	X	X	X	6	£500	(500)
					Relevant cost	**£14,950**

Notes:
1 All 1,000 units need buying in at replacement cost.
2 600 units from stock need replacing and 400 need buying at replacement cost.
3 Opportunity cost = resale value.
4 Remaining 300 units bought in at replacement cost.
5 Opportunity cost is greatest of resale value of £1,200 (200 × 6) and saving the purchase of 300 units of M, £1,500 (300 × £5).
6 Opportunity **benefit**: using the stock of E in production avoids disposal costs of £500.

CASE STUDY	Roverco

Roverco plc manufactures and markets a house-cleaning robot. At present, it is in the middle of a project to develop a voice-controlled robot from a laboratory prototype. The prototype was built from a patent which the company acquired for £50,000. The inventor agreed to accept payment in five equal instalments, three of which have now been paid.

At a recent board meeting, it was revealed that sales of Roverco's standard product had taken an unforeseen downturn and that this would have a knock-on effect on profitability and liquidity. This situation is partly due to increased competition from Housemouse Ltd, a dynamic new entrant to the market which specializes in the application of the very latest technology to its products. Also, Roverco's two long-established rivals, Cleanbot plc and Nomess plc, have been competing on price for the last year or so. Roverco decided against joining in the price war, hoping that it would soon be over. However, the market has responded positively to the price reductions, with increased orders going to Cleanbot and Nomess, causing Roverco to lose market share.

During the meeting, there was a heated discussion concerning the voice-controlled robot project. The project manager presented a financial statement (shown below) and reported that progress was slower than expected due to snags with the voice-recognition system. In connection with this, he recommends that a specialist electronic engineer be employed for the duration of the project, which he estimates will now continue for the next 18 months. The salary would be £28,000 p.a. on a fixed-term contract basis. Without this additional appointment, it is very doubtful that the project will be completed.

Project manager's financial statement

		£
Costs to date		42,000
Estimated costs for completion of project:		
Final payment for patent	20,000	
Gross salaries of two development engineers	75,000	
Gross salary of new engineer	42,000	
Materials and equipment (including M4411)	19,000	
Overheads	65,000	
		221,000
Total cost of project		263,000
Budgeted cost of project		218,000
Requested increase in budget		45,000

Following this, the finance director shocked the meeting into silence by proposing that the project be abandoned. She justified this course of action by pointing out that Roverco's share price had been falling slowly but steadily for the last three months and that in her regular meeting with share analysts from the big City firms, scheduled for next month, she feels it would be wise to issue a profits warning. The effect of this would be a steeper fall in the share price which, in turn, would make the company more vulnerable to a takeover bid. However, to avoid this, she believes the downward profit trend can be quickly reversed by abandoning the voice-controlled project and putting the savings of £191,000 into price cuts on the existing product range.

The chairman is not sure what to do. He postpones the discussion for one week and asks you for advice. You ascertain the following information:

1 Market research costing £35,000 was commissioned for the project. This predicted that the optimum price/volume relationship was a selling price of £999, creating sales of 6,000 robots a year. The product life cycle was estimated as four years, at which point a major redesign would be needed to remain competitive.

2 Roverco's accountant has estimated that the new production facility fixed assets for the voice-controlled robot will cost £900,000 and will have a resale value of £400,000 after four years. Other fixed overhead costs of £340,000 p.a. will be incurred; these are caused solely by this product and include depreciation of £90,000 p.a. for the production facility. The variable cost of producing each robot will be £917.

3 A special miniature hydraulic mechanism will be used in the robot's production. Roverco has a stock of 9,000 of these left over from a previous product. They were originally bought at a 'bargain price' of £9 each (the current market price is £15 which is included in the £917 total variable cost). They could probably be sold as a job lot for £45,000. Roverco has no other use for these items.

4 If the project is abandoned, two development engineers will have to be made redundant at a cost to Roverco of £18,000 each.

5 Some specialized voice-control testing equipment could be sold for £8,500 in its present condition, or for £2,500 at the end of the project. The rest of the equipment has no resale value.

6 A £6,000 order (order no. M4411) for bespoke electronic components was placed last month for delivery in two months' time; three months' credit is normally allowed by the supplier. A legal contract was signed for this order which Roverco is not able to cancel.

7 The project overheads of £65,000 include £15,000 for depreciation of the buildings used for product development and a general administration charge of £3,000 (nominally for services from the rest of the company). They also include £17,000 as a proportion of the project manager's pay.

Task:

Identify the relevant cash flows and advise the chairman whether, on purely financial grounds, the project should continue or be abandoned. Support your calculations with clear statements as to why particular items have been included or excluded and state any assumptions that you make.

Questions

An asterisk * on a question number indicates that the answer is given at the end of the book. Answers to the other questions are given in the Lecturer's Guide.

Q7.1* Burton Brothers

Burton Brothers manufactures machine tools for metal-based industries. One of its customers, Wey Ltd, has placed a £590,000 order for a machine, including £10,000 for delivery and installation. Wey paid a deposit of £180,000 and has since paid instalments totalling £150,000. Unfortunately, Burton Brothers has received a letter from a solicitor informing it that Wey Ltd has gone into liquidation and is unlikely to be able to pay any of its debts. This project has incurred the following costs to date:

	£
Engineering design	70,000
Materials	129,000
Direct labour (760 hours @ £10/h)	7,600
Production overheads (760 hours @ £88/dlh)	66,880
	273,480

The production overheads are all fixed costs and it is company policy to absorb them on the basis of direct labour hours (dlh).

Another customer, Bridge & Co., has expressed an interest in the machine, provided some additions are made to the specification, and is willing to pay a price of £400,000. To complete the machine to the original specification, it is estimated that a further 2,000 direct labour hours (at £10/hour) and a further £204,000 of materials will be needed. Contracts for £24,000 of these materials have already been signed but no money has yet been paid. The contract provides for a cancellation fee of £6,000 provided cancellation is confirmed in the next 11 days. These materials are components made especially to order for this machine and have no other use or value. The rest of the materials are in regular use by Burton Brothers. Twenty-five per cent of the £204,000 of materials are currently in the stores.

The additions requested by Bridge & Co. will need a further £45,000 of materials and 400 hours of direct labour. Some of these additional materials, which have an estimated purchase price of £13,500, could be replaced by similar material currently in the stores. This was left over from a previous contract and has no other use. It originally cost £9,500, which is its current stock valuation, but if it were to be sold on the open market it would fetch £12,000.

Burton Brothers is itself in a precarious position as it has no new orders on its books. If this job is abandoned, its direct workforce will be put on standby, which means they will be sent home and paid a rate of £4 an hour to retain their services. However, if this were to happen, the directors believe that some of these skilled workers would find permanent work elsewhere and would leave the company.

If no customer is found for the machine, it will be sent for scrap; this is expected to produce £6,000 income.

Task:

Burton Brothers is unsure whether or not to accept the offer from Bridge & Co. Consider each of the above items and advise the company accordingly.

Q7.2* Eezikum

Eezikum is a duo of rap artists currently touring the UK. They still have 11 venues remaining when they are asked to fill in at short notice on a tour of the USA, starting in two days' time. They will be the first act on stage to warm up the audience in preparation for the big American star whose tour it is. They know that this could establish them in the lucrative North American market but are not sure of the financial implications. There is a cancellation fee of £10,000 for each abandoned concert. Each time they perform in the UK they are paid a fee of £15,000 and their out-of-pocket expenses amount to £2,500. At present, they have no future work commitments once the UK tour is over.

If they join the tour of the USA, they will need to buy new equipment compatible with the US electricity supply and safety standards. The cost of this is estimated at £100,000 but it could be sold for £40,000 at the end of the nine-month tour, on their return to the UK. The money is not a problem as they currently have more than £1 million in a deposit account earning interest of 12% a year.

The US tour consists of 125 performances, each paying fees of £10,000 and having associated out-of-pocket expenses of £2,000. The airfare for the whole entourage, including a considerable amount of luggage, is £14,500 each way. Additional health insurance will cost £6,000 for the duration of the tour. Travel insurance is £9,000 (three-quarters of their existing annual worldwide policy, which carries a premium of £12,000).

Task:

Calculate the relevant benefit/cost of accepting the US tour.

Q7.3* Carbotest Corporation

Carbotest Corporation manufactures equipment to test for the presence of carbon monoxide in confined spaces. It has just been offered a contract to build some specialized monitoring equipment to test for the presence of carbon dioxide in the freight containers of lorries and railway wagons. The contract offers to pay £152,000 for 1,000 sets of testing equipment, which must be delivered in six months' time. Carbotest has looked into this opportunity and has produced the following information.

Materials

The contract will need 40,000 components which Carbotest does not currently use; these cost £3 each. However, it could use up old stock of 5,000 components that it recently tried to sell without success. But £1 will need to be spent on each of them to make them into suitable replacements for 5,000 of the 40,000 components needed. This old stock originally cost £20,000 but now has a scrap value of only £1,000. Each testing set also needs a carrying harness identical to those used for the carbon monoxide testing equipment. Carbotest has 600 of these currently in stock, valued at their cost price of £8 each. The suppliers of this harness have just increased their price to £9, which Carbotest will have to pay for future orders.

Labour

The contract will use five skilled operatives full time for six months. These operatives are paid £1,400 a month gross and are presently employed on the carbon-monoxide-testing production. They will have to be redeployed from this work to the new contract. Their combined output for the six-month period is estimated to have a sales revenue of £60,000, a variable cost of £48,000 and to absorb £8,000 of fixed overheads. It is thought that one of the factory supervisors (currently with a light workload) could manage the project for 50% of his time. His annual gross pay is £24,000. Carbotest is working at full capacity and has enough orders to keep it busy for 15 months.

Machinery

Three years ago, Carbotest bought a machine for a similar project, which had to be abandoned after two years. It cost £25,000 and was estimated to have a useful life of five years, with a zero residual value. (Carbotest uses the straight-line method of depreciation for all its fixed assets.) The machine has been 'mothballed' for the last 12 months and has been stored out of the way. Carbotest was just about to advertise it for sale at the very reasonable price of £5,000. It is thought that this intensive contract will effectively wear it out. To meet the six-month deadline, Carbotest plans to lease an identical machine for six months at a cost of £500 a month.

Accommodation

Employees have to park their cars on the road outside the factory. As the company is located in a busy area, this is often difficult, with cars having to be parked some distance away. Carbotest is just about to convert a rough piece of land in one corner of its site into an employees' car park. It hired a professional firm of surveyors to obtain planning permission for this and their invoice for £2,200 has recently been received but not yet paid. The cost of building the car park is £28,000. But if the contract is accepted, this land will have to be used for a temporary building to house the necessary machinery. The construction of this building will cost £8,000 and when the contract is completed, it will be demolished at a cost of £2,000. The car park will then go ahead.

Fixed overheads

Carbotest's absorption costing system attaches fixed overheads to production on a machine hour basis. The contract is expected to absorb £10,000 of fixed overhead.

Tasks:

State whether each of the above items is relevant or irrelevant to Carbotest's acceptance of the contract and explain your reasoning. Advise it whether or not to accept the contract. Discuss any other factors the company should take into consideration when making this decision.

Q7.4 Murray Polls

Murray Polls Limited recently contracted to conduct an opinion poll concerning global warming and its causes. Its costing for this job is shown below:

		£
Planning	100 hours @ £12	1,200
Questioning	800 hours @ £7	5,600
Travel and subsistence		4,800
Telephone	30,000 minutes @ £0.02/min	600
Analysis of results & report	60 hours @ £12	720
Fixed overheads	800 hours @ £25	20,000
Total cost		32,920
Profit @ 20% mark-up		6,584
Price to client		£39,504

(Overheads are absorbed on the basis of questioning hours.)

The client paid a deposit of £5,000 and contracted to pay the remainder within one month of receiving the report. Unfortunately, Murray has just been informed that its client has gone into liquidation and is not expected to be able to meet any of its debts.

At this point, Murray has completed all the planning and 75% of the questioning; travel and subsistence so far total £3,700 and 50% of the telephoning has been completed. No analysis has yet been done. If the poll is abandoned, two of the ten researchers involved will have to be paid a cancellation fee of £200 each.

The managing director of Murray immediately suspends all work on the contract and decides to attend an international conference on the environment, taking place in Stockholm next week. He is hopeful of finding another client for this project as he will be able to offer the completed poll and report at a greatly reduced price. His airfares, hotel bills and out-of-pocket expenses for the five-day Stockholm trip are expected to be £2,200. His rate of pay works out at £400 a day.

Task:

Calculate the lowest price the managing director can quote without making his firm worse off and advise him accordingly. State your reasons for including or excluding the above factors in your calculation.

Q7.5 Eldave Advertising Agency

The Eldave Advertising Agency has been working on a campaign for Greenpoint Leisure Limited for the last four months. The campaign is for Greenpoint's eco-friendly holidays in South America and uses both TV and Sunday-paper magazines. The adverts have almost been completed and the campaign launch date is in six weeks' time. The estimated cost of completion is £2,400 (two people @ £400/week for three weeks). Greenpoint has signed a contract to pay Eldave £50,000 (for advert production) plus media space at cost.

Eldave has just received a letter from a firm of solicitors stating that Greenpoint has ceased trading with immediate effect and that its creditors are unlikely to receive any of the money they are owed. Fortunately, Eldave has received a non-returnable deposit of £25,000 (50% of the production fee) from Greenpoint but a summary of its account reveals an overall balance owing of £61,000 for work to date. This includes a general fixed overheads charge of £6,000 apportioned on the basis of total direct cost.

In order to minimize Eldave's losses, Eloise Thompson, the partner in charge of the Greenpoint account, has contacted three other travel firms specializing in the South American market. She has shown them the adverts and tried to persuade them to take over the work-in-progress for the special price of £25,000. One of these three, Trek Hols Limited, has offered £12,000 for the appropriately modified and completed adverts on condition that the campaign starts in two weeks' time.

Eldave has provisionally booked advertising space for eight consecutive weeks starting in six weeks' time. The cost of this is £30,000 a week, for which it has paid £12,000 (a 5% non-returnable deposit included in the £61,000). It has also booked a one-quarter-page colour space in the *Independent on Sunday* magazine for the same eight weeks. Each of these spaces costs £9,000 but, although a contract has been signed, no money has yet been paid (not included in the £61,000). The contract allows for a 50% reduction if cancellation occurs less than four weeks before publication. This reduction increases to 75% if cancellation occurs more than four weeks before publication. Although Trek Hols is happy to take over Greenpoint's media slots, it also wants the same weekly coverage for the four weeks immediately prior to the original launch date. Trek Hols insists the campaign must start in two weeks' time and agrees to pay for all the media space in full, at cost.

In order to complete the adverts for launch in two weeks' time, Eldave will have to redeploy two of its employees (gross pay £400 a week each) for one and a half weeks, at the end of which the adverts will be delivered to the media. As a result of this, the job these two are currently doing will be one and a half weeks late and Eldave will incur a financial penalty of '£1,000 a week or part-week'.

Tasks:

Identify the **relevant costs and income** and advise Eldave as to whether it should accept Trek Hols' offer. Your calculations must clearly show the reasons why each of the above items has been included or excluded. State any assumptions that you make.

Q7.6 MOV plc

MOV plc produces custom-built sensors. Each sensor has a standard circuit board (SCB) in it. The current average contribution from a sensor is £400. MOV plc's business is steadily expanding and in the year just ending (2001/2002), the company will have produced 55,000 sensors. The demand for MOV plc's sensors is predicted to grow over the next 3 years:

Year	Units
2002/03	58,000
2003/04	62,000
2004/05	65,000

The production of sensors is limited by the number of SCBs the company can produce. The present production level of 55,000 SCBs is the maximum that can be produced without overtime working. Overtime could increase annual output to 60,500, allowing production of sensors to also increase to 60,500. However, the variable cost of SCBs produced in overtime would increase by £75 per unit.

Because of the pressure on capacity, the company is considering having the SCBs manufactured by another company, CIR plc. This company is very reliable and produces products of good quality. CIR plc has quoted a price of £116 per SCB, for orders greater than 50,000 units a year.

MOV plc's own costs per SCB are predicted to be:

	£	
Direct material	28	
Direct labour	40	
Variable overhead	20	(based on labour cost)
Fixed overhead	24	(based on labour cost and output of 55,000 units)
Total cost	112	

The fixed overheads directly attributable to SCBs are £250,000 a year; these costs will be avoided if SCBs are not produced. If more than 59,000 units are produced, SCBs' fixed overheads will increase by £130,000.

In addition to the above overheads, MOV plc's fixed overheads are predicted to be:

Sensor production in units:	54,001 to 59,000	59,001 to 64,000	64,001 to 70,000
Fixed overhead:	£2,600,000	£2,900,000	£3,100,000

MOV plc currently holds a stock of 3,500 SCBs but the production manager feels that a stock of 8,000 should be held if they are bought in; this would increase stockholding costs by £10,000 a year. A purchasing officer, who is paid £20,000 a year, spends 50% of her time on SCB duties. If the SCBs are bought in, a liaison officer will have to be employed at a salary of £30,000 in order to liaise with CIR plc and monitor the quality and supply of SCBs. At present, 88 staff are involved in the production of SCBs at an average salary of £25,000 a year: if the SCBs were purchased, 72 of these staff would be made redundant at an average cost of £4,000 per employee.

The SCB department, which occupies an area of 240 × 120 square metres at the far end of the factory, could be rented out, at a rent of £45 per square metre a year. However, if the SCBs were to be bought in, for the first year only MOV plc would need the space to store the increased stock caused by outsourcing, until the main stockroom had been reorganized and refurbished. From 2003/04, the space could be rented out; this would limit the annual production of sensors to 60,500 units. Alternatively the space could be used for the production of sensors, allowing annual output to increase to 70,000 units if required.

Required:

a) Critically discuss the validity of the following statement. It was produced by Jim Elliot, the company's accountant, to show the gain for the coming year (2002/03) if the SCBs were to be bought in.

Saving in:	£
Manufacturing staff – salaries saved: 72 staff × £25,000	1,800,000
Purchasing officer – time saved	10,000
Placing orders for SCB materials: 1,000 orders × £20 per order	20,000
Transport costs for raw materials for SCBs	45,000
Cost saved	1,875,000
Additional cost per SCB: (£116 – £112) × 58,000 units	232,000
Net gain if SCBs purchased	1,643,000

(10 marks)

b) i)   Produce detailed calculations that show which course of action is the best financial option for the three years under consideration. (Ignore the time value of money.)

(12 marks)

ii) Advise the company of the long-term advantages and disadvantages of buying in SCBs.

(3 marks)

(Total = 25 marks)

CIMA Intermediate: Management Accounting – Decision Making, May 2002

Review questions

1 Describe relevant costing.
2 Distinguish between relevant and irrelevant costs.
3 Explain the terms: avoidable costs, opportunity costs, sunk costs, committed costs, non-cash costs and opportunity benefits.
4 Discuss the importance of qualitative factors.

The answers to all these questions can be found in the text of this chapter.

CHAPTER 9

Product costs using absorption costing

Introduction

At some stage in your career, you may find yourself responsible for controlling costs. The object of this exercise is to minimize the costs of your products, which should enable you to keep their selling prices competitive. Hopefully, the result of this will be increased numbers of items sold and good levels of profit. Cost control is an important activity for all organizations. So how is it achieved?

The first step is fundamental. In order to control a cost, you have to have an accurate measurement of it, i.e. you need to know exactly how much the cost is. Without this information your task is impossible.

Another good reason for determining product costs is that, from time to time, you may be required to make decisions concerning your products. For example, if you do not know the cost of a product when setting its selling price, you may unknowingly set the price lower than cost. The obvious consequence of this is that you will trade at a loss rather than at a profit.

A further important reason for knowing your product costs is that they are used to value the cost of sales and stock in the periodic accounts of organizations. Indeed, the second international accounting standard (IAS 2) prescribes that production and stock must be valued at the 'absorption' production cost for accounts which are accessible to owners and other interested people **outside** the organization. In effect, if this is not done, the Companies Act is breached and the company is acting illegally and should expect to suffer the adverse consequences.

Note that this chapter applies to those organizations which perform work on their raw materials to convert them into finished products. It does not apply to merchanting or trading companies which buy at one price and sell for a higher price without changing the products in any way.

Learning objectives

Having worked through this chapter you should be able to:

- explain the difference between direct and indirect costs;
- list the constituent parts of an absorption cost;
- allocate and apportion overheads to cost centres;
- calculate overhead absorption rates using a variety of different bases;
- use overhead absorption rates to attach overheads to products.

Direct and indirect costs

(This section first appears in Chapter 1 but is repeated here for your convenience.) The absorption cost of a product is based on the assumption that costs can be analysed into their 'direct' and 'indirect' components which are defined as follows.

Direct cost

This is expenditure which can be economically identified with, and specifically measured in respect to, a relevant cost object or product. Consider an advertising agency specializing in the production of television adverts. The cost of hiring a celebrity to appear in one such advert is a measurable direct cost of that advert. Similarly, if the company is a furniture manufacturer, the cost of materials used to make a chair and the pay of the operative assembling it are measurable direct costs of that chair.

Indirect cost (or overhead)

This is expenditure on labour, materials or services which cannot be economically identified with a specific saleable cost unit or product. There are many, many different overheads, including supervisors' pay, depreciation of fixed assets, business rates and insurance. Remember,

$$\text{Total absorption cost} = \text{direct cost} + \text{indirect cost}$$

Self-assessment question S9.1

Try the following question for yourself (answer at the end of the chapter).

Macframe Ltd makes photograph frames and sells them to national retail chains. The following costs are incurred in connection with its manufacturing process. Decide whether each cost is direct or indirect and give your reasons.

1 Picture frame moulding.
2 Pay of assembly department's supervisor.
3 Heating oil used for cutting department.
4 Pay of employees assembling frames.
5 Dab of glue put in each corner joint of frame.

The absorption cost of products

The way the product cost is determined in absorption costing is illustrated in Figure 9.1. This shows that as well as the total of direct costs (prime cost) the production overheads

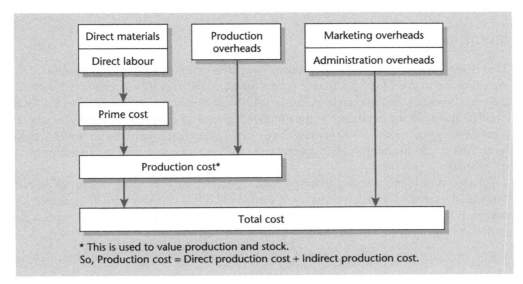

* This is used to value production and stock.
So, Production cost = Direct production cost + Indirect production cost.

Figure 9.1 **Outline of the absorption costing system**

are included in the production cost (in accordance with IAS 2). Stock of finished goods is unsold production so it is logical to value it at production cost. Note that all other overheads, although part of the total cost, are excluded from the production cost. These other overheads are treated as 'period' costs and are listed in the profit and loss account as deductions from the gross profit.

The objective of absorption costing is to ensure that both the direct and indirect costs of production are included in the production cost. The CIMA *Management Accounting Official Terminology* (2000) describes absorption costing as 'a method of costing that, in addition to direct costs, assigns . . . production overhead costs to cost units by means of . . . overhead absorption rates'.

Determining the direct production costs is relatively simple as the amount of them in each product can be measured. But how do we know how much of the production director's pay, depreciation of equipment, etc., to include in the cost of a specific product or service? These indirect costs cannot be measured so there has to be some other mechanism for attaching them to products. This is achieved by allocation, apportionment and absorption of overheads.

Attaching overheads to products

Allocation

This is the assigning of **whole** items of cost, or revenue, to a single cost unit or centre. For example, in a company making furniture, an invoice for 50 kilograms of sausage meat can be safely allocated **in total** to the canteen cost centre. However, if the company produced processed foods, further investigation would be necessary. If the sausage meat was an ingredient of one of the company's products, it would be a direct cost and not an overhead.

Apportionment

This is the spreading of costs or revenues over two or more cost centres or units. For example, the invoice total for flu injections for all employees should be spread over all the cost centres in the organization. But how is this done? In this particular case, the total could be spread in the same ratio as the number of people in each cost centre. For example, if the invoice was £500 for 500 people, the dispatch cost centre with 12 employees would receive twice the amount (£12) apportioned to the site security cost centre employing six people (£6).

An apportionment base should have a logical connection to the nature of the overhead concerned. It should have a rationality of some kind but it need not give as 'accurate' an answer as the flu injection example above. Costs can be apportioned in a 'fair' way to cost centres by means of physical or financial units. For example,

Costs	Basis of apportionment
Personnel department	Number of employees
Business rates	Area
Heating and lighting	Area **or** volume
Insurance	Net book value **or** cost of assets
Maintenance	Number of machines
Central stores	Value of production **or** number of stores issues
Production planning	Value of production

Absorption

This is the attaching of overheads to products or services by means of overhead absorption rates (OARs) using some measure of activity. For example,

£/direct labour hour	% of total labour cost
£/machine hour	% of prime cost

Overhead attachment procedure (illustrated in Figure 9.2)

Step 1

Allocate or apportion the overheads to the production and service cost centres (by reasonable bases of apportionment).

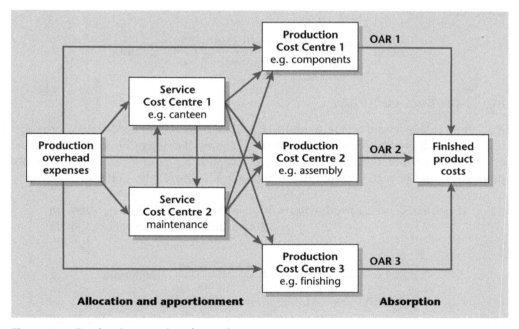

Figure 9.2 **Production overhead attachment**

Step 2

The total cost of the service centres is apportioned first to other service centres which use their service, and second to the production centres so that all overheads end up in production centres.

Step 3

The total amount of each production centre is divided by some measure of activity (e.g. machine hours) to derive the overhead absorption rate (OAR).

Note that production overheads are absorbed only from production cost centres or departments. All service centre overheads must be transferred into production cost centres. Where service cost centres service each other, the easiest way of dealing with this is to determine the order in which it happens and transfer the costs in that order. It may not exactly reflect reality but, unless the overheads involved are a very large proportion of total overheads, it will do the job. Remember that the nature of apportionment leads to estimates rather than perfect 'accuracy'.

Single- and multi-product companies

To illustrate these two alternative scenarios, a fork-lift truck driver's pay of £200/week is used as an example of a production overhead.

Single-product company

If a factory makes only one product, and makes 40 of them each week, the overhead absorption rate is

$$OAR = \frac{\text{estimated pay for period}}{\text{number of items made}} = \frac{200}{40} = £5/\text{unit}$$

Multi-product company

If a factory makes several different products, a different method is needed to absorb overheads into each product on an equitable basis. One way of doing this is to use the number of direct labour hours (dlh) for each type of product. Suppose a company makes two products, G and K, each G taking 10 dlh and each K taking 25 dlh to make.

If estimated weekly production = 30 × product G @ 10 dlh each = 300 dlh
4 × product K @ 25 dlh each = 100 dlh
400 dlh

$$OAR = \frac{\text{estimated pay for period}}{\text{output in dlh}} = \frac{£200}{400 \text{ dlh}} = £0.50/\text{dlh}$$

Each G would have £5 (10 dlh × £0.50/dlh) and each K would have £12.50 (25 dlh × £0.50/dlh) of the fork-lift truck driver's pay attached to it.

This approach is then extended to include all overheads. If these totalled £6,000 a week, then

$$\text{OAR} = \frac{\text{estimated total overhead cost for period}}{\text{output in dlh}} = \frac{£6,000}{400} = £15/\text{dlh}$$

In a machine-intensive, automated manufacturing environment, machine hours would probably be used instead of direct labour hours. (Remember that other factors may be used for OARs, such as multiples of the material cost or wages cost.)

Overhead attachment

Example 9.1

Maykit Ltd manufactures plastic chairs. It has two production departments (Moulding and Assembly) and one service department (Canteen). The following information is taken from this year's budget:

	Moulding	Assembly	Canteen
Direct labour hours	10,000	50,000	–
Machine hours	15,000	5,000	–
Direct labour pay (£)	100,000	200,000	–
Indirect labour pay (£)	3,030	5,220	4,000

Fixed factory overheads (per year)

	£
Rent and rates	15,000
Depreciation of machinery (straight line)	7,200
Heat and light	4,800
Protective clothing	6,500

Other information

	Moulding	Assembly	Canteen
Number of employees	2	8	3
Area (square metres)	3,000	5,000	2,000
Cost of machinery (£)	60,000	36,000	24,000

Tasks:

1 Calculate the total overhead cost for each department.
2 Attach the service department overhead to the production departments.
3 Calculate the most appropriate overhead absorption rate for each production department.
4 What value of production overheads would be absorbed by a batch of chairs taking two machine hours to mould and three direct labour hours to assemble?

Solution

Apportionment of rent and rates (total cost £15,000):

Most rational basis of apportionment is 'area'. Total area 10,000 sq. m.

	Moulding	Assembly	Canteen	Total
Proportion	$\frac{3,000}{10,000}$	$\frac{5,000}{10,000}$	$\frac{2,000}{10,000}$	$\frac{10,000}{10,000}$
	= 3/10	= 5/10	= 2/10	= 10/10
Overhead cost	£15,000	£15,000	£15,000	£15,000
Apportionment	**£4,500**	**£7,500**	**£3,000**	**£15,000**

Apportionment of protective clothing (total cost £6,500):

Most rational basis of apportionment is 'number of employees' = 13.

	Moulding	Assembly	Canteen	Total
Proportion	2/13	8/13	3/13	13/13
Overhead cost	£6,500	£6,500	£6,500	£6,500
Apportionment	**£1,000**	**£4,000**	**£1,500**	**£6,500**

1	Moulding	Assembly	Canteen	Total
Indirect pay	3,030	5,220	4,000	12,250
Rent and rates (area)	4,500	7,500	3,000	15,000
Depreciation of machinery (cost)	3,600	2,160	1,440	7,200
Heat and light (area)	1,440	2,400	960	4,800
Protective clothing (employees)	1,000	4,000	1,500	6,500
Total overhead cost	**13,570**	**21,280**	**10,900**	**45,750**

2				
Canteen overheads (employees)	2,180	8,720	(10,900)	–
Service overhead attachment	**15,750**	**30,000**	–	**45,750**

3	Moulding	Assembly
Machine hours	15,000	–
Direct labour hours	–	50,000
OAR	$\frac{15,750}{15,000}$	$\frac{3,000}{50,000}$
	= £1.05/mh	= £0.60/dlh

4			
Batch of chairs	2 mh	3 dlh	
Batch overhead	**£2.10**	**£1.80**	Total £3.90

Try the following question for yourself (answer at the end of the chapter).

Cayten Ltd produces domestic robots to perform household chores. Its manufacturing facilities consist of three production departments and two service departments. The following information is taken from the company's current annual budget.

	Production cost centres			**Service cost centres**	
	PA	**PB**	**PC**	**SD**	**SE**
Indirect labour (£)	80,850	87,750	36,600	45,900	42,400
Direct labour (£)	100,000	110,000	140,000		
Direct labour hours (dlh)	90,000	120,000	90,000		
Machine hours (mh)	80,000	90,000	75,000		

Production overheads   **£**

Business rates	8,000
Electricity to run machines	6,000
Heating and lighting	4,800
Insurance for machinery ('like for like' policy)	2,700
Depreciation of machinery (straight line over 10 years)	19,000
Total	40,500

The following information relates to the cost centres:

	PA	**PB**	**PC**	**SD**	**SE**
Number of employees	20	35	25	12	8
Original cost of machinery (£)	60,000	70,000	40,000	20,000	–
Machinery written-down value (£)	20,000	40,000	25,000	5,000	–
Machinery power rating (joules)	350	450	250	150	–
Floor area (square metres)	12,000	8,000	5,000	3,000	4,000

Required:

a) Calculate the total overhead for each cost centre.

b) Reassign service cost centre overheads to production cost centres on the following basis:

	PA	**PB**	**PC**
SD	30%	50%	20%
SE	25%	40%	35%

c) Calculate an overhead absorption rate for each production cost centre using the following bases:

PA	machine hour basis
PB	direct labour hour basis
PC	percentage of direct pay

d) Calculate the total of production overheads absorbed by an order requiring the following resources:

	PA	**PB**	**PC**
Machine hours	7,000	2,100	900
Direct labour hours	600	9,800	2,000
Direct wages (£)	2,700	45,000	11,600

Limitations of absorption costing

Absorption costing is approximately a hundred years old. It was devised for a manufacturing era whose products relied upon direct labour much more than they do today. Volume production in the twenty-first century is based on computer-controlled automatic machinery. Compare a car production line from the 1930s with one 70 years later and the difference is quite astonishing. From a distance, the old line would look something like an ant's nest, with men scurrying about doing all kinds of job. The machinery used by them consisted to a great extent of hand-tools such as screwdrivers and spanners. The latest lines are often quite devoid of people apart from the occasional machine minder. The robotic machinery being overseen probably cost millions of pounds, which causes a commensurately large amount of depreciation (a production overhead). The trend over the last 50 years has been an increase in the importance of overheads. The proportion of overheads in the total production cost is far greater now than it was in the past.

Absorption costing was not designed for the modern automated technological environment. Overhead absorption rates are a crude device for attaching overheads to products. The absorption costing system is mathematically sound and ensures that all the production overheads are absorbed by all the production. In the days when overheads were only a small part of the total costs, it did not matter if they were not particularly accurate. Today, when overheads often represent well over 50% of total costs, it does matter. Fortunately, activity-based costing now exists to fill that gap. Having said all this, many businesses still use absorption costing. Like many aspects of business life, there is a reluctance to change from a tried-and-tested system to something new. However, the pressures of competitive marketplaces will drive the change. Absorption costing will be used less and less as time passes.

The manager's point of view (written by Nigel Burton)

No single costing system is ever likely to provide the perfect answer to a company's costing requirements. However, all systems, by providing views of the business from different angles, will produce some information of greater or lesser value to management. In certain circumstances, absorption costing may indeed prove to be the best available solution, although its inherent drawbacks will render it inappropriate for many companies.

Absorption costing is essentially simple and is therefore best suited to companies with simple processes. Consider, for example, a paint blending operation, consisting of a wide range of end products being produced on a number of standard blending machines. The blending process is simple, identical for each product, and unlikely to require significant levels of overhead. In this case, the simple spreading of overhead across all products, on a volume (i.e. number of units produced) or machine hours basis, may be perfectly adequate, particularly as overhead is likely to be a relatively small component of the overall product cost.

As companies become more complex, the simple principles of absorption costing may give a distorted picture of product costs. If our paint blender were to decide to backward-integrate into paint manufacture, and, at the same time, diversify into paint can production, its previous practice of spreading overhead simply across products would clearly no longer be valid. It would need to introduce more sophistication into its costing system to match the needs of the more complicated business. As complexity grows, the problems with absorption costing become more apparent.

Imagine a large manufacturing company, with multiple production cost centres, each producing a range of products, by differing processes, on various items of plant. The absorption costing system first requires the allocation of expenses to cost centres. Consider electricity. How many companies can accurately attribute electricity usage to individual production areas, as opposed to equipment in the maintenance department, or heating in the offices, or lighting in the factory yard? Larger companies may have it all metered, but most will need to determine some kind of apportionment. This may apply not only to utilities like electricity, but also to other items such as supervisors' salaries where the supervisors work in more than one cost centre. This is a general problem, and not necessarily specific to the absorption costing method, but it does introduce a measure of inaccuracy which absorption costing compounds.

Then the service centre costs have to be reapportioned to production cost centres. These costs, which may include maintenance, quality control, waste treatment, general factory expenses, etc., can be relatively high, so the basis of apportionment is critical. Take the cost of maintaining machinery: 'number of machines' or 'machine hours' may be a reasonable basis, but the likelihood is that Machine A is continually breaking down, while Machine B runs perfectly smoothly. Some processes place much greater physical demands on the equipment than others. For example, a very corrosive process will wear out the equipment much more quickly than a non-corrosive process. So, perhaps actual time spent on these machines by the maintenance department in the past may be a better basis for reapportioning service centre costs – though not of course if the attention given to Machine A has finally fixed a long-running problem! Similar issues surround the allocation of all service departments, and have the potential to cause major distortions.

Finally, a basis is needed to attribute production cost centres to products. These cost centres now include the reapportioned service department costs, so the numbers are significant. The use of direct labour hours as a basis is very common, but this too can be troublesome. For instance, it does not take proper account of Product C, which requires a large amount of machine time (e.g. for cooling, drying or processing) but with minimum labour input. The use of direct labour hours will seriously undercost this product. On the other hand, using machine hours may substantially undercost Product D, which requires constant supervision throughout its production cycle and consequently uses a disproportionate amount of departmental resource.

A great deal of care is required in identifying the most appropriate bases of apportionment, but a similar amount of attention needs to be given to the flaws inherent in these bases. In arriving at the final cost of our products, we have had to resort to apportionments at every level. This raises some awkward questions. First, does the final product cost contain the correct overall charge for electricity? Answer: We have no idea! Second, is the product cost correct? Answer: We do not know! Third, what level of confidence do we have in the accuracy of the product cost? Answer: We are not sure!

The key to cost apportionment is to ensure that the bases are agreed and accepted as valid by all sides. For organizational reasons, many companies divide their products into logical groupings, or product lines, each with its own business manager. Each product line has its own sales department and production cost centre, but factory management and general administration remain centralized. The apportionment of overheads will have a direct impact on the profitability of individual product lines. And in a competitive world, where demands from senior management for higher returns grow ever louder, the two options available to the business manager are either to increase sales or to cut costs. The easiest way for a business manager to increase profits at a stroke is to convince the accountant that the overhead apportionments are unfair, and that some of the costs should consequently be transferred to other product lines. In my experience, this has proved to be a recurring cause of irritation, argument and management time consumption. For this reason it is essential that the cost apportionment bases are defensible. However, this is not an easy position to achieve in a conventional absorption costing environment.

Finally, while considering the impact of overhead apportionments on the profits of individual business groups, there is another area of legitimate concern for managers. In a single-business-group company, indirect expenses, such as the factory manager's salary, security and business rates, are genuinely fixed costs which do not change as sales levels grow. In a two-business-group company, these expenses will be apportioned between the businesses on the basis of, say, direct labour hours. Similarly, non-production expenses, such as general administration, will also have an arbitrary basis, perhaps sales or volume. If the two businesses grow at the same rate, the proportion of costs assigned to each will remain the same from year to year. But suppose one business ran into trouble, and its sales halved. This would result in a switch of overhead from the failing business to the successful business. Through no fault of its own, and without any increase in the overall level of expenses, the successful business will suffer a substantial increase in its fixed costs. Is this fair? I think not. It seems to me that the failing group should suffer the full impact on profits of its reduced income.

The same situation exists if the sales of the successful business forge ahead. If its apportionment of overhead were to go up proportionately, it would be tantamount to treating fixed costs as variable! Some reapportionment may well be desirable over time, but this could perhaps best be achieved by small changes over a number of years. Business group managers, and indeed all other users of financial information, are looking for consistency, fairness and clarity. Nothing is more frustrating than finding the impact of one's sales achievements being eroded by the blind application of accounting principles, which may be mathematically correct, but logically flawed. Senior managers judge businesses on their ability to produce consistent profit growth over a number of years, and the accounting principles adopted should serve to support this objective. Absorption accounting may do the job for you, but always be aware of its limitations, and treat the results with a due measure of caution.

My purpose here is not to devalue absorption costing as a valid accounting tool, but merely to highlight the potential pitfalls. These difficulties are evident in any accounting system which requires a measure of apportionment. But absorption costing can compound the margin of error through its broadbrush approach, to the point that the information provided is so inaccurate that it risks leading management into making erroneous decisions.

Summary

- The absorption cost is the sum of the direct and indirect costs.
- Absorption costing treats production overheads as product costs.
- Overheads are assigned to cost centres via allocation and apportionment.
- Apportionment uses bases which are rational but not necessarily accurate.
- Service cost centre totals are reapportioned to production cost centres.
- Overheads are absorbed into production costs via overhead absorption rates.
- Overhead absorption rates are usually different for each production cost centre.
- Absorption costing is becoming less relevant to advanced technological production.

Further reading

Atkinson, A., Banker, R., Kaplan, R. and Young, S. (2001) *Management Accounting*, 3rd edition, Prentice Hall, Harlow. See chapter 'Traditional cost management systems'.

Drury, C. and Tayles, M. (2005) 'Explicating the design of overhead absorption procedures in UK organizations', *British Accounting Review*, Vol. 37, Issue 1, March.

Johnson, H. and Kaplan, R. (1987) *Relevance Lost, the Rise and Fall of Management Accounting*, Harvard Business School Press, Boston, MA. This provides a fascinating history of traditional cost accounting and states the case for a new direction.

Lucas, M. (2000) 'The reality of product costing', *Management Accounting*, February.

Upchurch, A. (2003) *Management Accounting, Principles and Practice*, 2nd edition, Financial Times/Prentice Hall, Harlow. See chapter 'Absorption of overheads'.

Weetman, P. (2002) *Management Accounting, an Introduction*, 3rd edition, Financial Times/Prentice Hall, Harlow. See chapter 'Accounting for materials, labour and overheads'.

Answers to self-assessment questions

S9.1 Macframe Ltd

1 Picture frame moulding is a direct cost – identifiable and measurable.

2 Pay of assembly department's supervisor is an indirect cost – not specifically identifiable in product.

3 Heating oil used for cutting department is an indirect cost – not specifically identifiable in product.

4 Pay of employees assembling frames is a direct cost – identifiable and measurable.

5 Dab of glue put in each corner joint of frame is, in theory, a direct cost as it is identifiable and measurable. However, in practice, this would be treated as an indirect cost as the cost of measuring and valuing the dab of glue would be far greater than the value of the information gained. Accounting activities should always be carried out in a commercially sensible manner.

S9.2 Cayten Ltd

	PA	PB	PC	SD	SE	Total
Indirect labour	80,850	87,750	36,600	45,900	42,400	293,500
Business rates (area)	3,000	2,000	1,250	750	1,000	8,000
Power (joules)	1,750	2,250	1,250	750	–	6,000
Light and heat (area)	1,800	1,200	750	450	600	4,800
Insurance (WDV)	600	1,200	750	150	–	2,700
Depreciation (orig. cost)	6,000	7,000	4,000	2,000	–	19,000
Sub-totals	**94,000**	**101,400**	**44,600**	**50,000**	**44,000**	**334,000**
Adj. SD	15,000	25,000	10,000	(50,000)	–	–
Adj. SE	11,000	17,600	15,400	–	(44,000)	–
Total overheads	**120,000**	**144,000**	**70,000**	–	–	**334,000**

PA   PB   PC

$$\frac{120,000}{80,000} \qquad \frac{144,000}{120,000} \qquad \frac{70,000}{140,000} \times 100$$

$= £1.50/\text{mh} \times 7,000 \text{ mh} \quad = £1.20/\text{dlh} \times 9,800 \text{ dlh} \quad = 50\% \text{ of direct labour cost} \times £11,600$
$= £10,500 \qquad\qquad\qquad = £11,760 \qquad\qquad\qquad = £5,800$

Total absorbed $= £28,060 \ (10,500 + 11,760 + 5,800)$

<table><tr><td>CASE
STUDY</td><td>Travelsound</td></tr></table>

Travelsound Ltd was started five years ago by three friends who had just graduated from university. They had lived in the same house for two years and were all passionate about music. During their many late-night discussions they talked much about music and, as two of them were electronic engineers, they often discussed the latest equipment for sound reproduction and how it could be improved. The third person had a joint degree in finance and marketing and saw the opportunity for a business venture involving state-of-the-art sound systems.

They started out in a garage at the home of one of their parents and soon found that ideas alone were not enough to run a business. Most of their work in the first two years consisted of upgrading and constructing personal computers and laptops. Through their contacts, they also gained from their old university several one-off contracts concerned with upgrading software and hardware (a perennial occupation for universities). At this stage in their development they employed five assistants.

Towards the end of their second year they bid for a contract to manufacture small quantities of an experimental mobile phone for a European electronics group. To their delight, they were awarded the contract and have produced several versions of this phone over the last few years. By the start of their fourth year they had 27 employees. In that year they gained the right to produce, under licence, mini-disc players for a Japanese company. This contract has gone very well despite the very tight profit margins involved. In fact, the sales price was slightly below the original estimated absorption production cost. They decided to go ahead on the assumption that they would be able to reduce their costs as they gained experience of manufacturing this product. (Although they were not aware of it, this was the reason they were awarded the contract, as other more established firms had turned it down as they believed it was not profitable.) Fortunately, Travelsound had made the right decision and this work currently has a positive net profit margin of around 3%.

However, in recent months, relations with this company have deteriorated, mainly due to a change in the pound/yen exchange rate. In fact, the three Travelsound directors believe that their licence will be revoked at the next renewal date in two months' time unless they are willing to trade in euros instead of UK pounds. They are apprehensive about this as the euro/pound exchange rate has been falling consistently for over a year. It would not be difficult for this work to be moved to mainland Europe where a significant amount of overcapacity exists.

Throughout their five-year history, they maintained an active interest in the improvement of sound systems. What little spare time the two engineering directors had was spent on developing a new method of sound reproduction. They are now at the point where, with the help of an agent, they have applied for a patent on their invention. They currently employ 88 people and made a net profit last year of £45,000. Their annual production rate is now 10,000 phones and 38,000 mini-disc players. They wish to grow in size and profitability but are unsure of how to do it. As an organization, they are now approaching a crisis point. One alternative is for them to replace the mini-disc player production with a new product using their own new technology.

This product has been named the MNP, short for Music Net Phone. It combines a WAP phone with their own miniaturized sound reproduction system which is also able to play mini-discs. They have tentatively approached the European electronics group for whom they manufacture mobile phones, with a view to its marketing the MNP. The European company is very interested but needs some indication of price before taking the idea any further.

Travelsound now needs to cost the MNP using the absorption costing system. The directors decide to do this using next year's budget, which is based on continuing production of mobile phones and mini-disc players. They assume the overheads will be the same if the mini-disc player is replaced by the MNP. The following information comes from this budget.

Travelsound has three production cost centres and three service cost centres. The former are electronic components, plastic cases and assembly. The latter are the canteen, material stores and quality control. The quality controllers inspect goods received into the stores as well as the output of each production cost centre. The assembly shop uses the manufactured components, plastic cases and items from material stores to produce the finished items ready for delivery. The estimated cost for one MNP is £12.20 for materials and £9.80 for direct labour. A single materials store serves only the three production departments. The canteen is situated just inside the factory entrance.

The production overheads are shown as:

	£
Factory rent and rates	150,000
Depreciation of machinery (straight line)	89,250
Machinery insurance (like-for-like basis)	53,000
Cost centre managers' pay	80,000
Materials storekeepers' pay	19,125
Quality controllers' pay	32,000
Heating and lighting	14,000
Canteen costs	29,920
Factory security	25,000
	492,295

The managers of the components, cases and assembly cost centres earn salaries of £30,000, £25,000 and £25,000 respectively. Factory security is provided by a local firm patrolling inside and outside the factory at intervals throughout the night. One quality controller earns £20,000 p.a., spending 30% of his time on stores materials and 70% on components. The other quality controller, who works part time, earns £12,000 p.a. and divides her time equally between cases and assembly. Any quality control costs other than pay should be considered proportional to the amounts of quality controllers' pay incurred by each cost centre. All employees eat in the canteen.

Other information:

	Canteen	Stores	Quality control	Assembly	Cases	Components
Area (sq. metres)	550	600	25	1,900	795	1,130
Employees	6	3	2	36	12	29
Number of stores issues	–	–	–	51,000	10,200	2,550
Direct labour hours	–	–	–	120,309	33,410	99,281
Direct labour cost (£)	–	–	–	611,404	148,596	450,000
Machine hours	–	–	–	100,973	51,236	453,791
Machinery cost (£000)	–	–	–	340	510	1,700
Machinery WDV (£000)	–	–	–	250	350	1,400

Tasks:

1 Calculate the overhead absorption rate (OAR) for each production cost centre. The bases used should be direct labour hours for assembly, machine hours for components and a percentage of direct labour cost for cases.

(40 marks)

2 Calculate the absorption production cost for one MNP if a batch of 100 MNPs takes 9,000 machine hours in the component shop, 667 direct labour hours in the assembly shop and has a direct labour cost of £1,100 in the case shop.

(10 marks)

3 Discuss the situation and advise Travelsound Ltd on its future course of action.

(50 marks)

(Total 100 marks)

Questions

An asterisk * on a question number indicates that the answer is given at the end of the book. Answers to the other questions are given in the Lecturer's Guide.

Q9.1* Lewington Ltd

Lewington Ltd makes a variety of kitchen fittings and equipment. It uses a three-stage process involving cutting, assembly and finishing. The following figures are extracted from its budget for the current year:

	Cutting	Assembly	Finishing
Production overheads (£000)	1,600	2,000	1,400
Machine hours	40,000	25,000	14,000
Direct labour hours	10,000	40,000	20,000

The company uses an absorption costing system for calculating its costs.

A batch of 300 'DX' workstations has just been produced using £3,300 of materials, £4,500 of direct labour and the following quantities of time:

	Cutting	Assembly	Finishing
Machine hours	50	25	10
Direct labour hours	20	45	20

Tasks:

Calculate the unit production cost and the total production cost of the batch of 'DX' workstations using the following three alternative bases:

1 Departmental overhead absorption rates are calculated on a machine hour basis.
2 Departmental overhead absorption rates are calculated on a direct labour hour basis.
3 The Cutting overhead absorption rate is calculated on a machine hour basis but the Assembly and Finishing rates are calculated on a direct labour hour basis.

Comment on your findings.

Q9.2* Graham and Sara

Graham and Sara are partners in a clothes manufacturing firm. Graham manages menswear and Sara controls ladies fashions. They have just received last year's accounts which are summarized below.

	Mens £000	Womens £000	Total £000
Materials	78	26	104
Direct labour	18	30	48
Variable overheads	4	4	8
Variable production cost	100	60	160
Fixed production overheads	10	6	16
Total production cost	110	66	176
Increase in stock	2	1	3
Cost of sales	108	65	173
Marketing overheads	8	4	12
Administration overheads	4	4	8
Total cost	120	73	193
Sales revenue	118	78	196
Profit/(loss)	(2)	5	3

Naturally, Sara is pleased with the results but Graham is not so happy. On questioning their accountant he finds that the fixed production overheads have been apportioned on the basis of variable production costs. He wonders how the results would change if they were apportioned on different bases.

Tasks:

1 Redraft the above statement if the fixed production overheads were apportioned on the basis of:
   a) direct material cost;
   b) direct labour cost;
   c) variable overhead cost.
2 What do your answers tell you about the absorption costing system?

Q9.3* Stellar Showers

Stellar Showers Co. Ltd manufactures domestic electric showers. It moulds its own plastic casings but buys in the other components from a variety of sources. In addition to 54 production operatives, it employs two quality controllers and four stores operatives. The company's production facility consists of three production cost centres (moulding, assembly and packaging) and two service cost centres (quality control and material stores). Quality control inspects work in the three production centres as well as goods received into the materials store. The store services the three production centres only.

Stellar's annual budget lists the following production overheads:

	£
Electricity to run machines and equipment	40,000
Material stores running costs	80,000
Heating (oil-fired boiler)	13,000
Lighting	4,000
Supervision	65,000
Production manager	35,000
Business rates	16,000
Fire insurance	10,000
Quality controllers' pay	30,000
Depreciation (straight line)	18,000

The supervision overhead consists of an assembly supervisor (£25,000 p.a.), a moulding supervisor (£20,000 p.a.) and a packaging supervisor (£20,000 p.a.).

The following information is also available:

	Moulding	Assembly	Packaging	Quality control	Stores
Head count	12	36	6	2	4
Machine wattage	4,500	1,200	300	–	–
Stores issue notes	2,000	14,500	3,500	–	–
Area (sq. metres)	300	800	500	50	350
Volume (cu. metres)	1,200	2,100	2,000	100	1,100
Fixed assets – cost	50,000	40,000	20,000	–	10,000
Fixed assets – WDV	22,000	18,000	9,000	–	1,000
Added value (£000)	800	5,700	500	–	–
Machine hours	34,967	24,080	3,944	–	–
Direct labour hours	20,016	63,986	10,998	–	–
Quality control (hrs/wk)	6	18	6	4	6

Tasks:

1 Calculate the most appropriate overhead absorption rate for each production cost centre.
2 Calculate the unit production cost of an SS40T shower if a batch of 800 uses the following resources:

Direct materials	£16,000
Direct labour	£8,800
Machine hours in moulding	1,500
Machine hours in assembly	900
Machine hours in packaging	170
Direct labour hours in moulding	1,200
Direct labour hours in assembly	3,500
Direct labour hours in packaging	1,000

Q9.4 Medley Ltd

Medley Ltd makes dishwashers. There are three production departments: machining, assembly and finishing; and two service departments: maintenance and stores.
   Costs are as follows:

	Machining	Assembly	Finishing	Maintenance	Stores
Direct materials	£240,000	£160,000	£40,000	–	–
Direct wages	£200,000	£150,000	£100,000	–	–
Indirect wages	£9,000	£8,000	£8,000	£11,000	£8,000
Indirectmaterials	–	–	–	£4,000	–

Factory overheads are:

Business rates	£30,000
Factory manager's salary	£30,000
Heat and light	£20,000
Depreciation of machinery	£40,000

Production statistics are:

	Machining	Assembly	Finishing	Maintenance	Stores
Personnel	20	15	10	4	1
Area (sq. metres)	8,000	4,000	4,000	1,000	3,000
Kilowatt hours (000)	100	40	30	10	20
Machinery cost (£000)	100	50	50	–	–
Direct labour hours (000)	40	30	20	–	–
Machine maintenance hours	850	600	200	–	–
Material issue notes	1,800	1,000	500	100	–

Tasks:

1 Calculate an overhead absorption rate based on direct labour hours for each production department.
2 A standard dishwasher uses 4, 3 and 2 direct labour hours in machining, assembly and finishing respectively. If all direct labour is paid £5.00/hour and the cost of materials for one dishwasher is £48, what is the production cost of one dishwasher?

Q9.5 Ugur Ltd

Ugur Ltd makes three different types of marine compass: Type A, Type D and Type N. Each compass passes through two production departments: assembling and finishing. Ugur absorbs its overheads on the basis of direct labour hours.

Production overheads for the next 12 months are expected to be

	£
Factory power	80,000
Depreciation	60,000
Fixed asset insurance	3,600
Supervisors' pay	40,000
Factory rent	70,400
	254,000

The following information for next year is also available:

	Assembly	Finishing
Number of direct operatives	30	20
Floor space (sq. metres)	16,000	9,000
Book value of fixed assets (£000)	60	30
Machine hours	15,000	30,000
Power (kilowatt hours used)	30,000	20,000
Supervisory staff	1	1

Times per product (hours):

	Assembly		Finishing	
	Labour	Machine	Labour	Machine
Type A	1.0	0.75	0.75	0.50
Type D	1.5	0.50	1.00	0.40
Type N	2.5	0.25	1.50	0.30

Each operative is expected to work 36 hours a week for 46 weeks a year.

Tasks:

1 Calculate the total overheads for each department.
2 Calculate the overhead absorption rate for each department (to three decimal places).
3 Calculate the overhead cost attached to each type of compass.
4 Recalculate your answers to tasks 2 and 3 if overheads were absorbed on a machine hour basis and comment on your findings.

Review questions

1 Explain the difference between direct and indirect costs.
2 List the constituent parts of an absorption cost.
3 Explain the difference between allocating and apportioning overheads to cost centres.
4 Explain the different bases that can be used by overhead absorption rates.

The answers to all these questions can be found in the text of this chapter.

CHAPTER 11

Comparison of profits under absorption and variable costing

Introduction

Because the annual profit figure is such an important piece of information ('the bottom line') it is advisable to monitor profit throughout the year. Knowing how things are progressing enables you to take corrective action when necessary and avoid unpleasant surprises at the financial year-end. Most organizations do this by producing monthly or quarterly management accounts.

As the idea is to help meet the annual profit target, it seems sensible to use the same rules by which the annual profit is calculated. One of these is that fixed production overheads must be treated as **product** costs and not as **period** costs (see IAS 2). In other words, annual accounts intended for public circulation are based on absorption costing. This works well for monthly accounting, provided that the pattern of trading is reasonably predictable over the year. However, for businesses whose trading pattern is difficult to predict, profits may be distorted. This also applies, to some extent, to seasonal businesses.

Distortions of profit do not help these businesses to monitor their real performance. So, it is not surprising that they sometimes decide to use a system which avoids this distortion. This alternative approach uses variable (also known as marginal) costing. Variable costing treats fixed production overheads as period costs rather than product costs. This is opposite to absorption costing used in the audited accounts **and will produce a different profit total**. However, at the end of the year, the internally reported 'variable profits' can be reconciled to the externally reported 'absorption profits'.

These two alternative financial models can be applied to a single set of commercial transactions, resulting in two different profit figures. This chapter shows you how to calculate the profits for a trading period in two different ways and how to reconcile them to each other.

Having worked through this chapter you should be able to:

- explain the difference between a product cost and a period cost;
- use budget information to predetermine an overhead absorption rate;
- explain why predetermined OARs are used in preference to actual OARs;
- explain how under- and overabsorption of overheads occur;
- adjust profit and loss accounts for under- and overabsorption of overheads;
- calculate 'absorption' profit and 'variable' profit;
- reconcile 'absorption' profit to 'variable' profit;
- explain the limitations of both systems.

Learning objectives

Treatment of fixed production overheads

As stated above, absorption costing treats fixed production overheads as production costs and variable costing treats them as period costs. A production cost is the total direct cost (prime cost) plus absorbed production overhead (see Figure 11.1a). A period cost is one which relates to a time period rather than to the output of products or services (see Figure 11.1b).

Predetermination of overhead absorption rates

The previous chapter showed how overhead absorption rates (OARs) are calculated via allocation, apportionment and an appropriate choice of the base. These OARs are used to determine the production cost and stock valuations for period-end accounts.

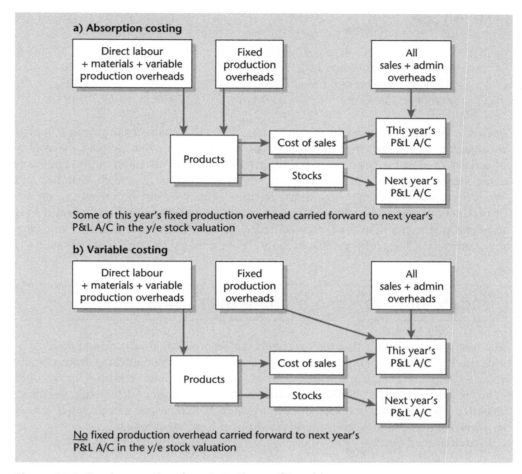

a) Absorption costing

Some of this year's fixed production overhead carried forward to next year's P&L A/C in the y/e stock valuation

b) Variable costing

No fixed production overhead carried forward to next year's P&L A/C in the y/e stock valuation

Figure 11.1 **Tracing overhead costs to the profit and loss account**

The practice is to use predetermined rates rather than actual rates. After all, the actual rates could only be determined after the period has ended, so selling prices could not be based on actual absorption costs. One possibility is to use the actual rates of the last-but-one month so that rates were fairly up to date. However, this would cause monthly fluctuations in the product cost figures (see below). If selling prices were based directly on costs, they would be changed every month. Prices going up and down at each month-end would give the impression of instability and incompetence in the eyes of customers.

Annual basis:

Estimated annual fixed production overheads = £36,000
Estimated annual volume of activity = 12,000 machine hours
OAR = £36,000/12,000 mh = £3.00/mh

Monthly basis:

	Month 1	Month 2	Month 3
Actual overheads incurred	3,000	3,520	2,500
Actual machine hours	1,000	1,100	909
Monthly actual OAR	£3.00/mh	£3.20/mh	£2.75/mh

For these reasons it is normal to calculate the OAR at the start of the year and apply it throughout. This means that the current year's production overhead cost and volume of activity used in the calculation are estimates rather than actual amounts. The major consequence of this is that the total amount of production overheads absorbed into product costs during the year is almost certainly going to be different from the amount of production overheads actually incurred. However, the profit and loss account must use the actual rather than the estimated figure. So an adjustment is necessary to change the overheads in the profit and loss account from estimated to actual amounts.

Under- and overabsorption of overheads

The first thing to note is that the overheads are absorbed by production and are in no way affected by sales volumes. Thus, if actual production volumes differ from planned volumes, either too much or too little overhead will end up in the profit and loss account. (The greater the volume of production, the greater the amount of production overheads absorbed.) If actual sales volumes differ from planned volumes, no change will be caused to the amount of production overheads in the profit and loss account.

Predetermined OAR:

Estimated annual fixed production overheads = £500,000
Estimated annual volume of activity = 100,000 direct labour hours
OAR = £500,000/100,000 dlh = £5.00/dlh

If either of these estimates is incorrect (as they almost certainly will be) the amount of production overheads in the profit and loss account will be inaccurate:

i) Actual annual fixed production overheads = £525,000
Actual annual volume of activity = 100,000 direct labour hours
Overhead absorbed by production = 100,000 × £5.00
= £500,000
Underabsorption of overheads = £25,000 (500,000 − 525,000)
Unless this adjustment is made, profit will be overstated by £25,000.
ii) Actual annual fixed production overheads = £500,000
Actual annual volume of activity = 112,000 direct labour hours
Overhead absorbed by production = 112,000 × £5.00
= £560,000
Overabsorption of overheads = £60,000 (560,000 − 500,000)
Unless this adjustment is made, profit will be understated by £60,000.

Example
11.1

The Jinasy Umbrella Company

The Jinasy Umbrella Company makes an up-market all-purpose umbrella. It produces management accounts for internal use on a quarterly basis. Its fixed production overheads are budgeted at £20,000 a quarter (£80,000 a year) and its marketing and administration overheads at £19,000 a quarter (£76,000 a year). The production plan is for 4,000 umbrellas each quarter (16,000 a year). The selling price is £20 and the variable cost of each umbrella is £8. There are 1,000 umbrellas in stock at the start of the first quarter. The actual results for last year, expressed in numbers of umbrellas, are as follows:

	Q1	Q2	Q3	Q4	Year
Sales	4,000	2,000	1,000	8,000	15,000
Production	4,000	4,000	3,000	6,000	17,000

Calculate the quarterly and annual profits (i) using absorption costing, and (ii) using variable costing. (iii) Explain why the profits differ. (Assume the total of actual overheads incurred was as forecast.)

Under both systems, stocks of finished umbrellas are valued at production cost.

Production cost:	Variable costing variable cost £8	Absorption costing variable cost + fixed production overhead £8 + (£20,000/4,000 units) = £13

Physical stock changes (number of umbrellas):

	Q1	Q2	Q3	Q4	Year
Opening stock	1,000	1,000	3,000	5,000	1,000
Actual production	4,000	4,000	3,000	6,000	17,000
Actual sales	4,000	2,000	1,000	8,000	15,000
Closing stock	1,000	3,000	5,000	3,000	3,000

i) Absorption costing (£000)

	Q1	Q2	Q3	Q4	Year
Opening stock	13	13	39	65	13
Add: Production cost	52	52	39	78	221
Less: Closing stock	(13)	(39)	(65)	(39)	(39)
Under-/(over)absorption	–	–	5	(10)	(5)
Cost of sales	52	26	18	94	190
Sales revenue	80	40	20	160	300
Gross profit	28	14	2	66	110
Non-production overhead	19	19	19	19	76
Net profit	9	(5)	(17)	47	34

ii) Variable costing (£000)

	Q1	Q2	Q3	Q4	Year
Opening stock	8	8	24	40	8
Add: Production cost	32	32	24	48	136
Less: Closing stock	(8)	(24)	(40)	(24)	(24)
Cost of sales	32	16	8	64	120
Sales revenue	80	40	20	160	300
Gross profit	48	24	12	96	180
Production overheads	20	20	20	20	80
Non-production overhead	19	19	19	19	76
Total fixed overheads	39	39	39	39	156
Net profit	9	(15)	(27)	57	24

iii) Reconciliation of profits (£000)

	Q1	Q2	Q3	Q4	Year
Absorption net profit	9	(5)	(17)	47	34
Variable net profit	9	(15)	(27)	57	24
Difference	–	10	10	(10)	10
Increase in stock (units)	–	2,000	2,000	(2,000)	2,000
Production overheads in stock increase (@ £5 a unit)	–	10	(10)	10	10

Annual results

The total of fixed production overheads charged in this year's 'variable' profit and loss account is the total incurred in this period, £80,000 (see Figure 11.1b). Variable profits are £24,000.

On the other hand, the net effect in this year's 'absorption' profit and loss account is that the amount of production overheads is reduced by £10,000, as follows:

> **Production overheads brought forward from last year**
> **(in opening stock) into this year = 1,000 units @ £5 = £5,000**
> **Production overheads carried forward from this year**
> **(in closing stock) into next year = 3,000 units @ £5 = £15,000**

The total of fixed production overheads charged in this year's 'absorption' profit and loss account is £70,000 (see Figure 11.2a).

The net reduction of £10,000 in production overhead charged will increase net profit from £24,000 (variable) to £34,000 (absorption).

Similar explanations and profit reconciliations can be made for each quarter (the process is summarized by Figure 11.3 below).

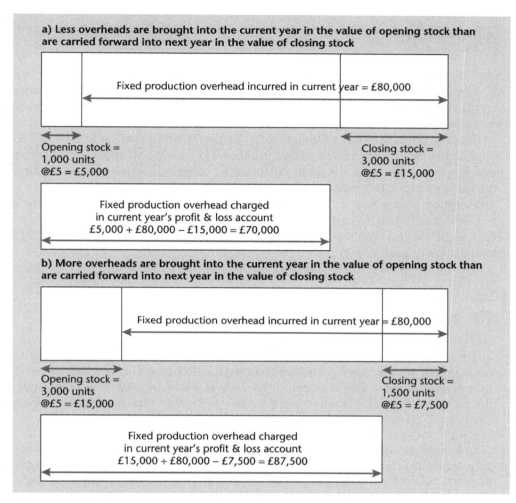

Figure 11.2 **Production overhead charged to the profit and loss account**

Try the following question for yourself (answer at the end of the chapter).

Hiphoptop Ltd produces music CDs. Internal management accounts are drawn up on a quarterly basis. The company plans to produce and sell 12,000 CDs each quarter and have a stock of 2,000 CDs at the start of quarter 1. The selling price is £6 and the variable cost of each CD is £1. The production and non-production overheads are estimated at £24,000 and £30,000 a quarter respectively. The actual results for the year, expressed in numbers of CDs, are as follows:

	Q1	Q2	Q3	Q4	Year
Sales	9,000	16,000	6,000	13,000	44,000
Production	14,000	12,000	11,000	10,000	47,000

Calculate the quarterly and annual profits (a) using absorption costing, and (b) using variable costing. (c) Explain why the profits differ. (Assume the total of actual overheads incurred was as forecast.)

Limitations

Absorption profits make the realistic assumption that, in most years, most businesses will sell most of their stock. However, if the stock of finished goods brought forward into the current year proves to be unsaleable, absorption costing will bring forward overheads which should have been charged in last year's accounts.

When a seasonal business builds up stocks for next period's sales (as in quarter 3 for Jinasy) it can be argued that absorption profits avoid creating 'fictitious' losses for the build-up period. However, the greater the number of periods between production and sales (as in quarter 2 for Jinasy), the less convincing this argument becomes.

Absorption profits may be increased by producing extra units in order to increase stock levels rather than to enable sales. In certain cases, absorption profits may decrease even though the sales volume has increased. This creates some scope for the short-term manipulation of profits.

The manager's point of view (written by Nigel Burton)

Senior managers tend to be busy people who, if not financially orientated, want to spend as little time as possible poring over interim statements of account. In practice, most managers will already have a gut feeling about the current period's performance, or alternatively will have been able to obtain an indication of it from data readily available from the computer. Periodic accounts often serve only to confirm what they already know. Once again, the need for consistency, clarity and accuracy in the accounts is paramount, in order to minimize any time-consuming queries arising from them.

Unfortunately, the application of IAS 2 principles may not help in this regard. The standard requires, quite rightly, that the valuation of products in inventory should include all production costs, including overheads incurred in bringing those products to their current condition. As this is the required basis for year-end accounts, it is logical that the same basis should be used for interim internal accounts. We have already seen how absorption costing and variable costing can generate significantly different profits, and the last thing management want to see is a substantial year-end adjustment as the inventory valuation is switched from one accounting basis to the other.

But the adoption of IAS 2 in interim accounts can itself lead to confusion, particularly for periods as short as one month. Absorption costing may be precisely correct in principle, in that it matches costs to sales by transferring cost into inventory when the product goes into stock, and releasing it back into the profit and loss account when the product is sold. (This results directly from the application of the accruals or matching-up principle of accounting.) But this also means that a simple increase or decrease in the level of production will have a direct impact on the level of profitability, which is especially significant in view of that all-important yardstick, the budget.

In the vast majority of companies, the budget is the principal tool used by management to set targets and monitor performance. The budget predicts not only the levels of sales and costs, but also how these will be phased throughout the year. Unless there are special factors to consider, such as seasonal influences, it would be a reasonable assumption that, in any given month, production will match sales volumes, thus keeping inventory at a constant level. But life rarely turns out as planned. In some months, sales will exceed production, causing a net transfer of period cost out of inventory into the profit and loss account. Conversely, when production exceeds sales, there will be a net transfer of period costs out of the profit and loss account into inventory. And in an exceptionally poor sales month, profitability can apparently be improved by increasing production levels and transferring more overhead into inventory; this is probably the exact reverse of management's correct course of action, which should be to reduce production to reflect the lower demand. I stress that there is nothing wrong with these period cost transfers, which accurately reflect the movements of stock in and out of inventory. But when these movements take place against a fixed overhead monthly budget, the value of this budget as a control tool is diminished.

A solution to this problem is to use a combination of absorption and variable costing. The production overheads are fixed costs, incurred over a period of time, and it would be fair to argue that they should be written off in that period, in exactly the same way as non-production expenses such as marketing or administration. The marginal income generated by sales in the period (i.e. sales less variable costs) can then be set against the total period costs relating to that period, producing an easily understandable 'variable' net profit. The requirements of IAS 2 can be satisfied by a 'below-the-line' adjustment, transferring the necessary amount to or from inventory, before striking a final reportable 'absorption' net profit for the month. In this way, we are structuring a set of figures which achieve all our objectives: they provide data of sufficient clarity for management purposes, meet the requirements of the standard, and also highlight separately the 'accountants' adjustment', which need concern only those who understand it!

The following example relates to the Jinasy Umbrella Company illustration earlier in the chapter.

Variable costing statement:

	Q1	Q2	Q3	Q4	Year
Opening stock	8	8	24	40	8
Add: Production cost	32	32	24	48	136
Less: Closing stock	(8)	(24)	(40)	(24)	(24)
Cost of sales	32	16	8	64	120
Sales revenue	80	40	20	160	300
Gross profit	48	24	12	96	180
Production overheads	20	20	20	20	80
Non-production overhead	19	19	19	19	76
Total fixed overheads	39	39	39	39	156
Variable net profit	9	(15)	(27)	57	24
'Below-the-line' adjustment:					
Adjustment for production overheads in stock increase	–	10	10	(10)	10
Absorption net profit	9	(5)	(17)	47	34

This monthly adjustment for period cost in inventory needs to be carefully monitored. In most systems, the use of budgeted expenditure and budgeted levels of production to calculate overhead recovery rates will be quite adequate for the purposes of internal monthly accounts. But for final audited accounts, the period costs held in inventory must be valued on actual experience, rather than budget. In a normal year, where expenditure and production run close to budget, the adjustment to actual may be minimal, but, in an abnormal year, the company could be in for a nasty surprise. For instance, if the year had been going extremely well, and production had exceeded budget by 25%, the actual overhead rate would be recalculated at 20% (= 25/125) below the budgeted rate. If, at the same time, the production overhead budget was underspent by 10%, the overhead rate would decrease in total by nearly 30%. This would result in a substantial reduction of total overhead in inventory, and a corresponding increase in the charge written off in the profit and loss account. The accountants would not be popular unless this situation had been foreseen and communicated to management well in advance!

In practice, auditors will accept that the valuation of period costs in inventory should be based on normal levels of production and normal levels of expenditure. This will eliminate, or at least diminish, the impact of unusual or non-recurring events. For instance, if production had been halved in the last quarter as a result of serious plant failure, it would be wrong to double the period costs on products manufactured in that period as the situation was abnormal. The impact of such an event should be a write-off of any unrecovered overhead directly to the profit and loss account. Acceptable norms can perhaps best be established by looking at production and expenditure over a longer period of time. In my company, we used the average production over the last three years, which had the effect of smoothing out any anomalies, without discarding them altogether. We also used actual expenditure in the year, as this was usually fairly constant. The most appropriate method of establishing norms is a matter for agreement with the auditors, and may vary from company to company. But, once agreed, it will be expected that this method will be applied consistently in future years.

There is one final point to mention in connection with period cost in inventory. As one moves across a year-end into a new financial year, the overhead absorption rates will be recalculated on the basis of the new budget. Unless your system is such that you can identify the overhead costs attributed to each individual item held in stock, you will have to revalue the whole of the inventory on to the new cost basis. Otherwise you will have some products going into stock at last year's cost, and coming out at this year's higher cost, resulting in an undervaluation of inventory. The revaluation of the period cost in inventory will produce a surplus (or deficit) which will have to be written off to future profit and loss accounts, complicating the period cost in inventory adjustment line still further. In my view, therefore, it is highly desirable to isolate the adjustment below the line, where it will not confuse non-financial users of the interim accounts.

Summary

- The choice between absorption profits and variable profits only exists for internal reporting (external reporting must use absorption profits).
- No change in stock level (P = S): absorption profit equals variable profit.
- Increase in stock level (P > S): absorption profit greater than variable profit.
- Decrease in stock level (P < S): absorption profit less than variable profit.
- (where P = production volume and S = sales volume)
- The more volatile the business, the more suitable are variable profits for internal reporting.
- The less volatile the business, the more suitable are absorption profits for internal reporting.

The process by which the absorption profit is reconciled to the variable profit is shown in Figure 11.3.

It is important to note that variable profit depends solely on sales volume, but absorption profit depends on both sales volume **and** production volume. The implication of this is that absorption profits can be improved by increasing production! The effect of increasing production is to increase closing stock. Remember that absorption profits are the ones that must be used for external reporting. In the short term, profits can be manipulated upwards by this strategy **without breaking any accounting rules.** In the medium/long term, high stock levels due to excess production will return to normal and the effect on profit will be downwards.

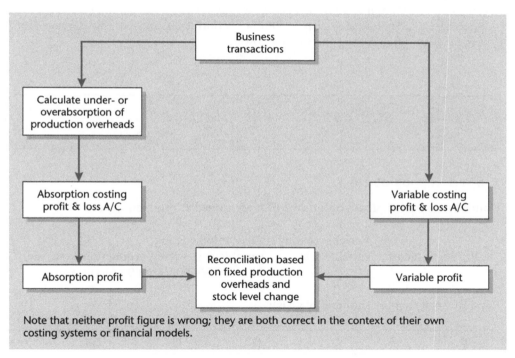

Note that neither profit figure is wrong; they are both correct in the context of their own costing systems or financial models.

Figure 11.3 **Reconciliation of absorption and variable costing profits**

Further reading

Baxter, W. T. (2005) 'Direct versus absorption costing: a comment', *Accounting, Business & Financial History*, Vol. 15, Issue 1, March.

Dugdale, D. and Jones, T. C. (2003) 'Battles in the costing war: UK debates, 1950–75', *Accounting, Business & Financial History*, Vol. 13, Issue 3, November.

Dugdale, D. and Jones, T. C. (2005) 'Direct versus absorption costing: a reply', *Accounting, Business & Financial History*, Vol. 15, Issue 1, March.

Horngren, C., Bhimani, A., Datar, S. and Foster, G. (2002) *Management and Cost Accounting*, 2nd edition, Prentice Hall Europe, Harlow. See Chapter 7, 'Income effects of alternative stock costing methods'.

Upchurch, A. (2003) *Management Accounting, Principles and Practice*, 2nd edition, Financial Times/Prentice Hall, Harlow. See chapter 'Absorption costing and marginal costing'.

Weetman, P. (2002) *Management Accounting, An Introduction*, 3rd edition, Financial Times/ Prentice Hall, Harlow. See chapter 'Profit, performance and current developments', *section*: 'Absorption costing and variable costing'.

Answer to self-assessment question

1. S11.1 Hiphoptop Ltd

Under both systems, stocks of finished CDs are valued at production cost.

	Variable costing	Absorption costing
Production cost:	variable cost	variable cost + fixed production overhead
	£1	£1 + £2 (£24,000/12,000 units) = £3

Physical stock changes (number of CDs):

	Q1	Q2	Q3	Q4	Year
Opening stock	2,000	7,000	3,000	8,000	2,000
Actual production	14,000	12,000	11,000	10,000	47,000
Actual sales	9,000	16,000	6,000	13,000	44,000
Closing stock	7,000	3,000	8,000	5,000	5,000

Under-/(over)absorption of overheads:

	Q1	Q2	Q3	Q4	Year
Planned production level	12,000	12,000	12,000	12,000	48,000
Actual production level	14,000	12,000	11,000	10,000	47,000
Under-/(over)absorption in units	(2,000)	0	1,000	2,000	1,000
Under-/(over)absorption @ £2/unit	(4,000)	0	2,000	4,000	2,000

a) Absorption costing (£000)

	Q1	Q2	Q3	Q4	Year
Opening stock	6,000	21,000	9,000	24,000	6,000
Add: Production cost	42,000	36,000	33,000	30,000	141,000
Less: Closing stock	(21,000)	(9,000)	(24,000)	(15,000)	(15,000)
Under-/(over)absorption	(4,000)	–	2,000	4,000	2,000
Cost of sales	23,000	48,000	20,000	43,000	134,000
Sales revenue	54,000	96,000	36,000	78,000	264,000
Gross profit	31,000	48,000	16,000	35,000	130,000
Non-production overhead	30,000	30,000	30,000	30,000	120,000
Net profit	1,000	18,000	(14,000)	5,000	10,000

b) Variable costing (£000)

	Q1	Q2	Q3	Q4	Year
Opening stock	2,000	7,000	3,000	8,000	2,000
Add: Production cost	14,000	12,000	11,000	10,000	47,000
Less: Closing stock	(7,000)	(3,000)	(8,000)	(5,000)	(5,000)
Cost of sales	9,000	16,000	6,000	13,000	44,000
Sales revenue	54,000	96,000	36,000	78,000	264,000
Gross profit	45,000	80,000	30,000	65,000	220,000
Production overheads	24,000	24,000	24,000	24,000	96,000
Non-production overhead	30,000	30,000	30,000	30,000	120,000
Total fixed overheads	54,000	54,000	54,000	54,000	216,000
Net profit	(9,000)	26,000	(24,000)	11,000	4,000

c) Reconciliation of profits (£000)

	Q1	Q2	Q3	Q4	Year
Absorption net profit	1,000	18,000	(14,000)	5,000	10,000
Variable net profit	(9,000)	26,000	(24,000)	11,000	4,000
Difference	**10,000**	**(8,000)**	**10,000**	**(6,000)**	**6,000**
Increase in stock (units)	5,000	(4,000)	5,000	(3,000)	3,000
Production overheads in stock					
increase (@ £2 a unit)	**10,000**	**(8,000)**	**10,000**	**(6,000)**	**6,000**

CASE STUDY | Canco Foods

Canco Foods specializes in the preparation and canning of three different products: new potatoes, mincemeat and ham. The company has three divisions (one for each product), each with its own production and sales facilities. It so happens that each division has the same cost structure for manufacturing and marketing its product. For each division, the annual fixed production overheads are £200,000 and the annual fixed administration and sales overheads combined are £80,000. These are incurred evenly over the year. Also, each division has an annual budget of 20,000 cases bought and sold; all stocks are zero on 1 January. The selling price is £50 a case and the delivery costs are £2.50 a case.

The preparation and canning of new potatoes starts in February and is completed by mid-June, but sales are evenly spread over the year. Mincemeat is produced at the same rate throughout the year but sales only occur between September and December, mainly for the Christmas mince pie market. Ham is produced and sold at a steady rate with very little variation from month to month. (Stocks of all three products are zero at 1 January.)

Costs per case for each product are:	£
Direct material and direct labour	21
Variable production overhead	3
Variable production cost	24

Activity (number of cases):

		January–June	July–December	Year
Potatoes	Production	20,000	–	20,000
	Sales	10,000	10,000	20,000
Mincemeat	Production	10,000	10,000	20,000
	Sales	–	20,000	20,000
Ham	Production	10,000	10,000	20,000
	Sales	10,000	10,000	20,000

Tasks:

1 Prepare summarized profit and loss accounts for each half-year and the whole year for each division using absorption costing.

(25 marks)

2 Prepare summarized profit and loss accounts for each half-year and the whole year for each division using variable costing.

(25 marks)

3 Reconcile the profits for each of the three periods by producing a statement involving a 'below-the-line' adjustment as shown in 'The manager's point of view' section of this chapter.

(10 marks)

4 **On no more than two sides of A4,** discuss the use of absorption costing and variable costing for the periodic, internal reporting of profitability.

(40 marks)

(Total 100 marks)

Questions

An asterisk * on a question number indicates that the answer is given at the end of the book. Answers to the other questions are given in the Lecturer's Guide.

Q11.1* Clamco

Clamco makes car clamps. The following information is from January's budget, which is based on a production volume of 6,000 clamps:

	£
Opening stock of clamps	0
Fixed manufacturing overhead	72,000
Variable manufacturing overhead	18,000
Selling and administrative expenses (all fixed)	25,000
Direct labour	120,000
Direct materials used	90,000
Selling price (per unit)	64

The actual production and sales volumes for the first three months of the year were as follows:

Number of clamps	January	February	March	Quarter
Production level	6,000	5,000	7,000	18,000
Sales	4,000	6,000	7,000	17,000

Actual variable costs per unit and total fixed overheads incurred were exactly as forecast.

Tasks:

1 Calculate the profit for each month and for the quarter
   a) using absorption costing;
   b) using variable costing.
2 Reconcile the profits for each month and for the quarter. Explain why they differ.

Q11.2* Rivilin plc

Rivilin is a uni-product firm with the following budgeted amounts:

	£
Unit selling price	60
Unit variable cost	20
Fixed production overhead per month	9,600

Rivilin's planned level of production is 800 units a month. However, actual activity was as follows:

	April	May	June
Units produced	800	750	820
Units sold	800	700	850

There was no opening stock at 1 April.

The actual fixed production overhead incurred was accurately predicted at £9,600 a month.

The non-production fixed overheads are £10,000 a month.

Required:

1 A variable costing profit statement for each month.
2 An absorption costing profit statement for each month.
3 An explanation of the difference in profits between the two statements.

Q11.3* The Valley Fireworks Corporation

The Valley Fireworks Corporation manufactures special firework display kits to sell to responsible organizations only. The following information is taken from its budget for 2002:

Opening stock of kits = closing stock of kits = 20 kits
Quarterly production = 300 kits and annual sales = 1,200 kits

	£ per unit	£ per year
Selling price	500	
Direct materials	60	
Direct labour	180	
Variable production overhead	10	
Variable distribution overhead	20	
Fixed production overhead		96,000
Fixed non-production overhead		144,000

The actual production and sales volumes for 2002 were:

(Units)	Q1	Q2	Q3	Q4	Year
Opening stock	10	290	550	690	10
Production	300	300	200	300	1,100
Sales	20	40	60	980	1,100
Closing stock	290	550	690	10	10

The variable costs per kit and the total fixed costs were as forecast.

Tasks:

1 Prepare profit statements for each of the four quarters and the year,
    a) using absorption costing;
    b) using variable costing.

2 Reconcile the two profit figures for each quarter and prepare a summary statement in the following format:

	Qtr 1	Qtr 2	Qtr 3	Qtr 4	Year
Net profit using variable costing					
Adjustment for fixed production overheads in stock change					
Net profit using absorption costing					

3 Explain how both sets of profit figures can be useful to the management of The Valley Fireworks Corporation.

Q11.4 Nalpo Ltd

Nalpo Ltd manufactures and markets a small table that attaches to ladders. The following annual budget is based on 75,000 units made and sold:

	Per unit		Total	
	£	£	£	£
Sales revenue		5		375,000
Sales				
Production cost of sales:				
Variable	3		225,000	
Fixed	1		75,000	
		4		300,000
Gross profit		1		75,000
Selling and admin costs:				
Variable (10% of sales)		0.5	37,500	
Fixed			30,000	
				67,500
				7,500

Actual production figures for year 1 and year 2 were as follows:

	Year 1	Year 2
Opening stock	0	15,000
Production	85,000	70,000
Sales	70,000	80,000
Closing stock	15,000	5,000

Tasks:

You are required to:

1 Prepare budgeted statements of profitability on the basis of:
   a) absorption costing;
   b) variable costing.
2 Reconcile the difference in profit in the two statements produced for part 1.

Q11.5 Brafire Ltd

Brafire manufactures small, portable electric fires. It has operated an absorption costing system since it started many years ago. However, the new managing director (who is studying part time for an MBA) has recently learned of the possibility of using a variable costing system as an alternative to the company's usual approach. He decides to investigate this further by applying both systems to next quarter's budget (shown below). To provide a good comparison, the output will be shown at both a constant level and a fluctuating one.

Budget for quarter 3 (units):

	July	August	September	Total
Sales volume	3,000	3,000	6,500	12,500
Constant output	4,500	4,500	4,500	13,500
Fluctuating output	4,500	4,000	5,000	13,500

There will be 500 fires in stock on 1 July. The selling price is £30 and the cost structure is as follows:

	£/unit
Direct materials	4.00
Direct labour	1.50
Variable production overheads	0.50
Fixed production overheads*	6.00
Fixed marketing overheads*	4.00
Total cost	16.00

* These figures are based on a constant monthly production level of 4,500 fires.

Tasks:

Produce a budgeted profit and loss account for internal management reporting using the following four bases:

1 Absorption costing and constant output levels.
2 Variable costing and constant output levels.
3 Absorption costing and fluctuating output levels.
4 Variable costing and fluctuating output levels.

Comment on your findings.

Q11.6 P Ltd

P Ltd manufactures a specialist photocopier. Increased competition from a new manufacturer has meant that P Ltd has been operating below full capacity for the last two years.

The *budgeted information* for the last two years was as follows:

	Year 1	Year 2
Annual sales demand (units)	70	70
Annual production (units)	70	70
Selling price (for each photocopier)	£50,000	£50,000
Direct costs (for each photocopier)	£20,000	£20,000
Variable production overheads (for each photocopier)	£11,000	£12,000
Fixed production overheads	£525,000	£525,000

Actual results for the last two years were as follows:

	Year 1	Year 2
Annual sales demand (units)	30	60
Annual production (units)	40	60
Selling price (for each photocopier)	£50,000	£50,000
Direct costs (for each photocopier)	£20,000	£20,000
Variable production overheads (for each photocopier)	£11,000	£12,000
Fixed production overheads	£500,000	£530,000

There was no opening stock at the beginning of year 1.

Required:

(a) Prepare the actual profit and loss statements for each of the two years using:
- absorption costing;
- marginal costing

(14 marks)

(b) Calculate the budgeted breakeven point in units and the budgeted margin of safety as a percentage of sales for year 1 and then again for year 2.

(6 marks)

(c) Explain how the change in cost structure (as detailed in the budgeted information) has affected the values you have calculated in your answer to part (b).

(5 marks)
(Total = 25 marks)

CIMA Foundation: Management Accounting Fundamentals, November 2001

Review questions

1 Explain the difference between a product cost and a period cost.
2 Explain why predetermined OARs are used in preference to actual OARs.
3 Explain how under- and overabsorption of overheads occurs.
4 Explain how to reconcile 'absorption' profit to 'variable' profit.
5 Discuss the limitations of profits based on variable costs.
6 Discuss the limitations of profits based on absorption costs.

The answers to all these questions can be found in the text of this chapter.

CHAPTER
14 | Budgets and their creation

Introduction

If you were one of the top managers in an organization, e.g. a director of a company, you would be expected to have a vision of where the organization should be a few years from now. Knowing where you are going is one important aspect of leadership. However, although having a vision is very important, it is not sufficient in itself. You need to know how to go about realizing that vision. First, you need to be able to **make the plans** which will get you to where you want to be. Second, you need to know the best way to **use those plans**. Armed with this knowledge you stand a fair chance of achieving your goals. Without it, you are much less likely to succeed. This chapter is all about how to make those plans, how to create a budget.

Note that although budgets are just as important to service industries as they are to manufacturing industries, their preparation is illustrated in this chapter using examples of manufacturing. Budgets for service organizations are prepared in just the same way but, obviously, without the manufacturing schedules.

Learning objectives

Having worked through this chapter you should be able to:

- explain what a budget is;
- explain how it fits into the corporate planning context;
- list the positive attributes of budgetary control systems;
- differentiate between fixed and flexible budgets;
- differentiate between incremental and zero-based budgeting;
- create functional budgets;
- create a budgeted profit and loss account, balance sheet and cash flow forecast;
- create flexible budgets;
- define standard cost;
- discuss the issues about the setting of standards;
- discuss the limitations of budgets.

Budgets and their context

A budget is a predictive model of organizational activity, quantitatively expressed, for a set time period. In plain English, a budget is a plan of operations and activities for the next year (or month, etc.), stated in monetary values.

The organization's strategic plan, not the annual budget, is the master plan of the organization. This strategic plan should state the long-term organizational objectives and

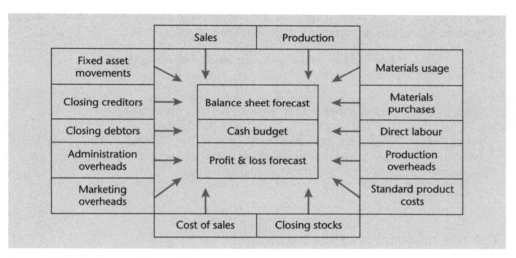

STRATEGIC CORPORATE PLAN
– long-term organizational objectives
– policies through which goals are to be achieved

ANNUAL BUDGET
Master budget – profit and loss account, balance sheet and cash flow forecast,
Functional budgets – for departments or processes,
e.g. purchasing, marketing, material usage, etc.

Figure 14.1 **The budget in context**

Figure 14.2 **Budget relationships**

the policies through which these goals are to be achieved. The annual budget is created within the context of the strategic plan (see Figure 14.1).

The relationships between the various constituent budgets are illustrated in Figure 14.2.

Functional budgets

The primary budget

Where to start? Does it matter which budget is created first? The answer to this last question is 'yes'. Start with the activity that determines all the other activities. In the vast majority of businesses, this is sales. The amount of goods or services that it is realistically considered can be sold in the budget period will influence all the other activities. This primary budget can be thought of as a limiting factor. (However, if titanium components were being manufactured for jet engines and there was a sudden unforeseen shortage of this material, then the limiting factor might be the availability of titanium. In this unusual case, the raw material budget would have to be the first one prepared.)

The sales forecast is the responsibility of the sales and marketing section and, because it is so crucial, it would have to be approved at the highest level in the organization. The management accountant would have little, or no, input into this primary budget.

The production volume budget

To plan the production volume for a period it is necessary to know the stock levels of finished goods at the beginning and end of that period. These may be determined by a policy such as 'opening stock is to be equal to one-half of the next month's sales'. So, if it is planned to sell 100 items in March and 120 items in April, the stock will be 50 items on 1 March and 60 items on 1 April. As the sales volume is already known, the number of items to be made is determined by the following formula:

$$\text{Production} = \text{sales} + \text{closing stock} - \text{opening stock}$$

Self-assessment question S14.1

Try the following question for yourself (answer at the end of the chapter).

The sales of Minnow Ltd are planned to be: April 100, May 140, June 120 and July 160 items. Stock levels are planned to be one-quarter of the next month's sales. What are the planned production budgets for April, May and June?

The raw material purchasing budget

To calculate this, it is necessary to know how much raw material will be used as well as knowing the policy on raw material stock levels. It may be that, due to the unreliability of supplies, the policy of a particular firm is to have sufficient stock at the start of a month for that month's production. The production volume budget will determine the amount of raw material usage and raw material purchases are therefore calculated as follows:

$$\text{Purchases} = \text{usage} + \text{closing stock} - \text{opening stock}$$

(This formula applies to both quantities and values.)

Self-assessment question S14.2

Try the following question for yourself (answer at the end of the chapter).

Minnow Ltd plans to spread its production of 1,800 items evenly throughout the year. Each item uses five units of raw material. Minnow expects to start the year with 80 units of raw material in stock but to reduce this by 25% by the end of the year. If each unit of stock costs £6 to buy in, what is the company's raw material purchasing budget for the year?

The cost of sales budget

For a manufacturing organization, the cost of sales is calculated by the following formula:

$$\text{Cost of sales} = \text{opening stock} + \text{production cost} - \text{closing stock}$$

(All the items in this equation relate to finished goods only.)

Try the following question for yourself (answer at the end of the chapter). **Self-assessment question S14.3** If Minnow Ltd's stock of finished goods is valued at £30,000 on 1 January and £27,000 at 31 March and the cost of production is £20,000 a month, what is the cost of sales for the quarter?

The cash receipts budget

In order to prepare the cash budget, it is essential to know the amount of money planned to be received in each period. For sales made on 'cash terms' (i.e. transfer of goods and payment for them take place at the same time), the total receipts equal the total sales revenue. For sales made on 'credit terms' (i.e. payment takes place at a later time than the transfer of the goods), the picture is more complicated. The total of receipts in a period depends on the amount of debtors at the start and finish of the period as well as the amount sold on credit terms during that period. Thus

$$\text{Receipts} = \text{opening debtors} + \text{credit sales} - \text{closing debtors}$$

Try the following question for yourself (answer at the end of the chapter). **Self-assessment question S14.4** Minnow Ltd plans to sell 2,400 items for £10 each evenly through the year, half on cash terms and half on credit terms of one month. If its opening debtors were £1,300, what would be the planned total of receipts from all sales during the year? (Assume all debtors pay on the due dates.)

The cash payments budget

In order to prepare the cash budget, it is also essential to know the amount of money planned to be paid out in each period. When goods and services are paid for immediately they are received, the total of payments equals the total of purchases. However, when purchases are made on credit terms, the total of purchases must be adjusted by the amount of creditors at the start and finish of the period to give the total amount of payments. Thus

$$\text{Payments} = \text{opening creditors} + \text{credit purchases} - \text{closing creditors}$$

	Self-assessment question S14.5

Try the following question for yourself (answer at the end of the chapter).

Minnow Ltd buys 1,600 items at £5 each evenly through the year, one-quarter on cash terms and three-quarters on two months' credit. If the company's opening creditors were £750, what would be the total of its payments for the year?
(Assume all creditors are paid on the due dates.)

Master budgets

The cash budget or cash flow forecast

This budget is of particular importance to all organizations. If there is insufficient cash to pay all the bills due at a certain time, then the organization may be forced out of business even though it is trading profitably (see Chapter 2).

The summary cash budget for the period is simply

$$\text{Opening balance} + \text{receipts} - \text{payments} = \text{closing balance}$$

However, it is normal to create a detailed cash budget for each month in order to monitor and control the organization's cash resources. It is also useful to know the net result of monthly cash flows. Is more money coming in than going out (i.e. a net inflow) or is more going out than coming in (i.e. a net outflow)? Once this is known, the net cash flow can be combined with the opening balance to give the closing balance:

	Cash in
Less:	Cash out
	Net cash flow
Add:	Opening balance
	Closing balance

It is conventional to give net inflows a positive sign and net outflows a negative sign (shown below by the use of brackets).

The following is an example of a simple cash budget in summary terms:

		Jan	Feb	Mar	Total
	Cash in	45	49	54	148
Less:	Cash out	37	53	41	131
	Net cash flow	8	(4)	13	17
Add:	Opening balance	850	858	854	850
	Closing balance	858	854	867	867

Note that the opening balance for a month must be the same as the closing balance for the previous month. This is only to be expected as exactly the same money is being referred to by each of the two balances.

The illustration below shows these summary figures in bold type together with some of the detailed items that help to make them up.

	Jan	Feb	Mar	Quarter
Receipts:				
Credit sales	32	37	41	110
Cash sales	11	12	12	35
Other	2	–	1	3
Total	**45**	**49**	**54**	**148**
Payments:				
Purchases of materials	25	27	25	77
Wages	8	8	8	24
Expenses	4	4	5	13
Other	–	14	3	17
Total	**37**	**53**	**41**	**131**
Net in/(out)flow	**8**	**(4)**	**13**	**17**
Opening bank balance	**850**	**858**	**854**	*850*
Closing bank balance	**858**	**854**	**867**	*867*

Be careful of the two numbers (in italics) at the bottom right-hand corner. They are **not** found by adding across (like all those above them) but by **copying** the opening balance for the quarter (850) and then working down the 'Quarter' column. The resulting number (867) in the extreme bottom right-hand corner should be exactly the same as that on its immediate left. After all, they should both show the balance on 31 March.

The figures above show the months when the cash actually moves, i.e. comes in or goes out. For sales and purchases made on credit terms, this date will always be later than the point of sale or purchase. The cash budget may be dangerously misleading if these timing differences are not taken into account.

Note that the balances on the bottom two lines of the cash budget can be negative as well as positive. This shows that the organization has a bank overdraft rather than a positive balance, a very common business situation.

When referring to cash budgets, use the terms *net inflow*, *net outflow*, *surplus* or *deficit* but **never** *profit* or *loss*.

The cash flow forecast is a very important management tool. It is used to:

- ensure that sufficient cash will be available to carry out planned activities;
- give a warning of the size of overdraft or loan needed;
- plan for investment of surplus cash.

Try the following question for yourself (answer at the end of the chapter).

Self-assessment question S14.6

Using the pro forma below, create (in pencil?) a cash budget from the following information: Opening balance is £150 *overdrawn*; credit receipts are £100 per month, cash receipts are £30 per month and other receipts are £70 in Feb.; purchases are £100 per month, wages £25 per month, expenses £35 per month and other payments are £15 in Jan.

Cash budget for quarter ended 31 March				
	Jan	**Feb**	**Mar**	**Quarter**
Receipts:				
Credit sales				
Cash sales				
Other				
Total				
Payments:				
Purchases of materials				
Wages				
Expenses				
Other				
Total				
Net in/(out)flow				
Opening bank balance				
Closing bank balance				

The budgeted profit and loss account and balance sheet

These budgets are compiled from information on the functional budgets or provided from elsewhere in the organization. This is best appreciated by working through the case study at the end of this chapter.

Types of budget and budgeting methods

Fixed budget

This is a budget based on one predetermined level of activity. Its main function is to act as a master plan for the following year.

Flexible budget

This is a budget which, by recognizing different cost behaviour patterns, is designed to change as the volume of activity changes. It can be thought of as several fixed budgets, each at a different level of activity, shown side by side.

Incremental budgeting

This approach to budget creation assumes that there will be little change in activity for next year compared with the current year. So, the numerical amounts (known as *allowances*) are arrived at by taking last year's amount and adding an increment for any known changes and for inflation.

Zero-based budgeting

This is a method of budgeting which requires each cost element to be specifically justified, as though the activities were being undertaken for the first time. Without approval, the budget allowance is zero.

Flexible budgets

Shown below is a flexible budget for a firm which expects to sell about 1,400 items a year. However, its market tends to fluctuate year to year and so it also produces budgets for sales of 1,200 and 1,600 items. These are its estimates of the minimum and maximum annual sales.

Flexible budgeted profit and loss account for y/e 31 December

Sales (units)	1,200	1,400	1,600
Sales revenue (£000)	600	700	800
Materials	300	350	400
Labour	120	140	170
Factory overhead	20	21	27
Total	440	511	597
Gross profit	160	189	203
Marketing costs	16	18	20
Admin costs	30	30	30
Total	46	48	50
Net profit	114	141	153

This shows that net profit does not increase in direct proportion to sales volume. At maximum sales the net profit increases by only £12,000 for the extra 200 units sold over the expected number. But at minimum sales (200 units less than expected) net profit decreases by £27,000. This type of situation arises due to the way in which costs behave (see Chapter 2). Remember that many costs have both fixed and variable elements. For example, the marketing costs above have a fixed component of £4,000 and a variable component of £10 a unit. Sometimes, fixed costs step up. Weekend working had to be introduced to produce the extra 200 items needed for maximum sales. This caused extra labour costs at an overtime premium of 50% and additional factory overheads.

Understanding cost structures is essential for the creation of flexible budgets. If you are asked to create one involving stepped fixed costs you will have to be told both the activity level at which the step happened and the size of the step. But you would probably be expected to calculate the semi-variable costs (such as marketing in the above example) for yourself. One way of going about this is known as the 'high–low method' (also covered in Chapter 1, on cost behaviour).

Example
14.1

Illustration using the semi-variable cost of water supplies

For the first six months of the year the monthly invoices for the use of water by the business were:

Month	Usage	Total cost (£)
1	520	12,080
2	570	12,310
3	600	12,400
4	510	12,040
5	540	12,160
6	500	12,000

Using only the highest- and lowest-usage months, the cost structure can be determined as follows:

Highest (month 3)	600 units	£12,400
Lowest (month 6)	500 units	£12,000
Difference	100 units	£400

Variable cost per unit produced = £400/100 = £4
Variable cost of 500 units   = 500 × £4 = £2,000
Fixed cost (at 500 units)   = total cost − variable cost
                        = £12,000 − £2,000
                        = £10,000

This can be checked by substituting these values in the other month. In month 3:

	£
Variable cost = 600 × £4 =	2,400
Fixed cost =	10,000
Total cost =	12,400

When performing this check, be sure to use **only** the other occurrence used in the original calculation (month 3 in this case). Note that many costs do not behave as predictably as water bills.

As this method uses the two extreme values of the variable, it is advisable to check that these are representative of the normal cost behaviour. This can be done by sketching a scattergraph which will show up any 'outliers' or unrepresentative values.

Try the following question for yourself (answer at the end of the chapter).

The monthly costs of machine maintenance have been recorded during the past few months as follows. (During July the machine maintenance team were redeployed to assist on emergency repairs to the factory building.)

Month	Machine Maintenance hours	Total cost
October	155	2,013
September	122	1,723
August	135	1,902
July	69	280
June	157	2,073
May	149	1,937

If the machine maintenance hours for November are planned to be 180, estimate the machine maintenance cost for that month.

Standards and how they are set

A *standard* is the physical and financial plan for **one unit** of output.

> *The* standard cost *is the planned unit cost of the products, components or services produced in a period.*
>
> *(CIMA, Management Accounting Official Terminology)*

Example standard cost data for one plastic wheel (type KR2)

Category	Item	Quantity	Price	Cost
Materials:	Plastic beads	1.2 kg	£2.00/kg	2.40
Labour:	Type A	0.25 h	£4.00/h	1.00
	Type D	0.10 h	£5.00/h	0.50
Variable overhead		0.35 h	£2.00/h	0.70
Variable cost				4.60
Fixed overhead (@ 900 wheels/week)		0.35 h	£4.60/h	1.61
Standard cost				£6.21

Bases for setting standards

There are three common sources for setting standards:

1 Performance levels of a prior period – these are based on recent experience.

2 Estimates of expected performance – these are based on recent experience and knowledge of any imminent changes.

3 Performance levels to meet organizational objectives – these are calculated from set targets; particularly useful if 'target costing' is used.

Approaches to standard setting

Standards are usually set at either *ideal* or *attainable* levels:

- *Ideal standards* make no allowances for any inefficiencies. They are achievable only under the most favourable conditions and represent the theoretical maximum outcomes. It is not possible for actual performance to exceed ideal standards and their use may demotivate many employees.
- *Attainable standards* are set at high but achievable levels; they represent a challenge. They make allowances for normal working conditions and are achievable by operating efficiently. They are capable of being exceeded and, therefore, can be used to motivate the workforce.

However, it is worth considering who decides what is the attainable level of performance. This decision is normally, at least partially, subjective. Top managers may have a different viewpoint from the budget holders charged with executing the budget.

This potential conflict of interests has led to *participative budgeting* where budget holders are involved in creating their own budgets. Management accounting staff help them to create their budgets, which then have to be agreed at a higher level of management. Two important points arise from this.

First, budget holders gain 'psychological ownership' from being involved in creating their own budget. It becomes 'their' budget rather than someone else's imposed upon them. They have a greater commitment to the success of their budget, which leads to improved performance. Non-involvement leads to a lack of interest in its success.

Second, as budget holders know they will ultimately be held responsible for meeting the budget, they have a natural tendency not to set their own targets too high. The technical term for these 'safety' or 'buffer' factors is *budgetary slack*. This is defined as 'the intentional overestimation of expenses and/or underestimation of revenues in the budgeting process' (CIMA *Management Accounting Official Terminology*).

The final decision on the contents of the budget belongs to senior management. However, this form of centralized control is potentially demotivating. To counteract this, the budget holder is usually given a high degree of responsibility for **how** the budget is achieved. He or she makes the day-to-day operating decisions and decides the tactics for meeting the corporate objectives. This bipartite approach effectively defuses the potential conflict between delegation and centralized control.

Importance of accurate standards

Badly set standards cause misleading variances whose investigation wastes both time and resources. Variances caused by poor standards are known as *planning variances*. One way to avoid these is by the systematic reviewing and updating of all standards.

Another aspect of accuracy is the question of how the budget allowance is arrived at for discretionary costs. How do you set the budget for items such as advertising or training? This type of cost may vary significantly from year to year. There is no easy answer to this question but managers should be aware of the problems posed by this type of cost.

Limitations of budgets as plans

In the 1970s, most large UK companies had a planning department employing a significant number of people. The wisdom of that era was that good planning for the next 5 to 10 years would enable the business to operate efficiently by anticipating and being prepared for future changes. Some also had outline plans for the next 15, 20 or 25 years. Many resources were tied up in the planning process. Forty years later, at the beginning of the twenty-first century, the proportion of resources allocated to this process is far smaller.

The main reason is that the rate of change in the business environment has greatly accelerated during those years and shows no sign of slowing down. To plan in detail for the next 10 years is considered to be a waste of time. The organization may be supplying different products and services in different markets by then. It may have been taken over or it may have acquired other organizations to take it in new directions. The stock markets of the world operate globally and faster than ever before. The amount of uncertainty in the business environment is much greater than it was before. Long-term planning is not seen as an effective use of resources. It is common to produce detailed plans only for the next year, and outline plans for the next three years only.

The manager's point of view (written by Nigel Burton)

Almost every field of human endeavour can be improved by a little advance planning. This is particularly true of businesses, which are complicated operations consisting of numerous disparate activities and disciplines. Planning is crucial to ensure that all these disciplines are moving forward in the most efficient way for the enterprise as a whole.

In the vast majority of businesses, the most important driving force is the strategic sales plan. The sales department, with its close knowledge of the market in general and of individual customers' needs in particular, is best placed both to determine the growth potential of existing products and to identify marketing opportunities for new products. Its view of what can be achieved, given the right products and supported by the right infrastructure, will provide the pattern of the company's direction for the foreseeable future.

The activities of all other departments in the company will be directed towards supporting the strategic sales plan. The technical department will develop new products to meet the customer requirements specified by the salesforce. Production will gear themselves up, through new equipment or plant modifications, to meet the sales forecast. Purchasing will identify reliable sources for any new materials required. Even Personnel and Administration will provide an infrastructure designed to support the overall plan.

It is then helpful to pull together the plans of all the departments into a long-range company plan. This should not be a detailed document, but should give an outline of the way the company might look over the next few years. In particular, it should ensure that the timing of any specific initiative is properly co-ordinated. For instance, is the development work for new products being started early enough? How long will it take to get approval for the capacity expansion project? Are we developing our people quickly enough to support the expanding business? All this will also lead to profit and cash forecasts, allowing the viability of the overall plan to be established at an early stage.

This should only be an outline document because the circumstances surrounding it will be constantly changing. Such is the pace of change in all fields now, in production and product technology, in IT and information flow, in increasing competition from all corners of the world, that plans can no longer be rigid. Ideally, they would change as every new circumstance emerged. It may not be practical to keep the company plan regularly updated, but the fact remains that managers must constantly be aware of the impact of external factors on their businesses, in both the short and long term.

The annual budget, however, is quite different. It is a working document, full of important detail, which enables the business to be controlled on a day-to-day basis. In my chemicals company, the establishment of the budget was always the biggest exercise of the year. Although everyone traditionally complained about the amount of time it consumed, there is no doubt that the examination of the detail meant that all managers developed a profound understanding of the dynamics of the business. It was the only time in the year that the elements of the profit and loss account were closely examined, allowing cost/benefit issues to be questioned and cost-saving opportunities to be identified. For the rest of the year, the detailed budget became a yardstick against which actual performance could be confidently and easily measured.

If your company has a relatively stable customer base, it is highly desirable to set up a detailed sales budget by customer and product. A computerized sales reporting system will then be able to highlight with ease the areas where targets are not being met, so that early corrective action can be taken by the sales department. If your business consists of one-off contracts, it is clearly less easy to set up such a monitoring procedure, but it is still important to set up some appropriate measurement to provide an early warning of sales shortfalls.

The same principle applies to both direct costs of production and overheads. The budgeting process provides the opportunity to re-evaluate every aspect of cost. Are the standards used in product costing still accurate? Can we justify the level of expenditure we are proposing for, say, travel or advertising? Are there any new or one-off items we want to budget for in the current year? Or any items incurred last year which we do not expect to be repeated next year? This is why, in my view, zero-based budgeting should be used wherever possible.

In my company, managers were required to justify the whole of their budgeted expenditure each year. Travelling expenses, for instance, were always frighteningly large, as our salesforce used to travel all over the world, but, by breaking this lump sum down into individual trips for each salesperson, it was possible to carry out a realistic review. Is it really necessary to have three trips to the Far East, or will two be enough? The sales manager has to provide a convincing justification. However, not all expense headings lend themselves easily to this type of analysis. Repairs to plant, for instance, was another large sum, which consisted of a mass of generally small items. The problem here is that, despite the use of sophisticated maintenance planning systems, there will always be a large number of unforeseeable repair costs. Moreover, the piece of equipment which incurred costly repairs last year is perhaps unlikely to break down again next year, so there is never an identifiable pattern to repairs. For this type of expense, therefore, we were obliged to adopt the incremental approach, taking average expenditure levels in recent years, and adding or subtracting amounts for known changes. In doing this, however, we accepted that we would be unable to exercise the same level of control as in many other areas of expenditure.

Incremental budgeting is a crude tool which allows inaccuracies and inefficiencies to be built into the system. Take salaries as an example. The actual salaries bill for last year is not the sum of the annual salaries of your employees. Staff turnover will inevitably mean that there are unfilled vacancies at times during the year. Replacement staff may have higher or lower salaries than the previous incumbents. There may have been promotions during the year, with accompanying salary increases. Temporary staff may also have been employed, at a much higher cost than permanent staff. Will overtime patterns be the same next year? As you can see, there are many occurrences which can have an impact on the total salary costs. When you come to budget for the following year, you have two options. You can assume that the same situations will occur again next year, so simply take last year's cost and add on a percentage for inflation. Alternatively, you can construct a detailed budget based on actual salaries and projected overtime levels, perhaps ignoring the impact of staff turnover, as it is impossible to forecast where in the company this will occur. Any savings arising from staff turnover can then be taken as favourable variances next year. My preference would always tend towards the latter option. If the managing director asks you why your department's salaries are over budget, you will be able to give a precise answer if you have a firm, detailed budget. If you have to answer 'Well, I think it's because we were understaffed last year', your credibility will undoubtedly suffer!

A detailed, well-constructed budget will also enable you to understand where there is some slack in the system. This is important for the inevitable moment when you receive an instruction from senior management to find more profit. It is a feature of budgeting that, when the proposals of all the departmental managers are put together, the resulting profit figure is never high enough! You will be asked to find more sales volumes, increase prices, or cut down costs, so it would be an unwise manager who did not leave a little slack in his or her initial numbers. If you work for a large corporation with multiple sub-sidiaries, the same phenomenon will occur at the higher level, when the budgets of all the businesses are added together. The profit is never high enough to meet the share-holders' expectations, and the instruction will come down to increase your local profit by a further factor. With a detailed budget, you can reflect these amendments by specific changes to your plans, e.g. by deferring the recruitment of new staff till later in the year. With a poorly constructed budget, however, this reiterative process will further distance your numbers from reality, and render the budget even less useful as a yardstick.

Summary

- Budgets are medium-term organizational plans expressed in monetary terms.
- They are intended to help the achievement of corporate, strategic long-term goals.
- Detailed functional or departmental budgets are prepared first.
- The summary master budget is prepared last; the process is bottom up.
- Budgets can be fixed or flexible.
- They are usually created incrementally, sometimes by a zero-based approach.
- Standards can be set in different ways and are subjective.
- Their main limitation is that they cannot be easily adjusted for unforeseen changes.

Further reading

Horngren, C., Bhimani, A., Datar, S. and Foster, G. (2002) *Management and Cost Accounting*, 2nd edition, Prentice Hall Europe, Harlow. See chapter 'Motivation, budgets and responsibility accounting'.

Langford, B. N. (2000) 'Production budgets, simplified', *Folio: The Magazine for Magazine Management*, Vol. 30, Issue 1, 1 January.

Otley, D. (1987) *Accounting Control and Organisational Behaviour*, Heinemann Professional Publishing, Oxford. See Chapter 7, 'Budgetary systems design'.

Upchurch, A. (2003) *Management Accounting, Principles and Practice*, 2nd edition, Financial Times/Prentice Hall, Harlow. See chapter 'Budgetary planning'.

Weetman, P. (2002) *Management Accounting, an Introduction*, 3rd edition, Financial Times/Prentice Hall, Harlow. See chapter 'Preparing a budget'.

Answers to self-assessment questions

S14.1

		April	May	June	July
	Sales	100	140	120	160
Add:	Closing stock	35	30	40	
Less:	Opening stock	25	35	30	40
	Production	**110**	**135**	**130**	

S14.2

$$\text{Purchases} = \text{usage} + \text{closing stock} - \text{opening stock}$$
$$= 9{,}000 + 60 - 80$$
$$= 8{,}980 \text{ units of raw material @ £6}$$
$$= £53{,}880$$

S14.3

		£
	Opening stock	30,000
Add:	Production	60,000
Less:	Closing stock	27,000
	Cost of sales	**63,000**

S14.4

		£	
	Opening debtors	1,300	
Add:	Credit sales	12,000	(2,400 × 10 × 0.5)
Less:	Closing debtors	1,000	
		£	
	Receipts from debtors	12,300	
	Receipts from cash sales	12,000	(2,400 × 10 × 0.5)
	Total receipts for year	**24,300**	

S14.5

		£	
	Opening creditors	750	
Add:	Credit purchases	6,000	(1,600 × 0.75 × £5)
Less:	Closing creditors	1,000	(200 @ £5)
	Payments to creditors	5,750	
	Payments on cash terms	2,000	(1,600 × 0.25 × £5)
	Total payments for year	**7,750**	

S14.6

Cash budget for quarter ended 31 March

	Jan	Feb	Mar	Total
Receipts:				
Credit sales	100	100	100	300
Cash sales	30	30	30	90
Other	–	70	–	70
Total	130	200	130	460
Payments:				
Purchases of materials	100	100	100	300
Wages	25	25	25	75
Expenses	35	35	35	105
Other	15	–	–	15
Total	175	160	160	495
Net in/(out)flow	(45)	40	(30)	(35)
Opening bank balance	(150)	(195)	(155)	(150)
Closing bank balance	(195)	(155)	(185)	(185)

S14.7

It is obvious from the question that July is not a representative month and it should be excluded from your calculations. The scattergraph below confirms this:

High month:	June	157	2,073
Low month:	September	122	1,723
		35	350

Variable cost per hour = 350/35 = £10

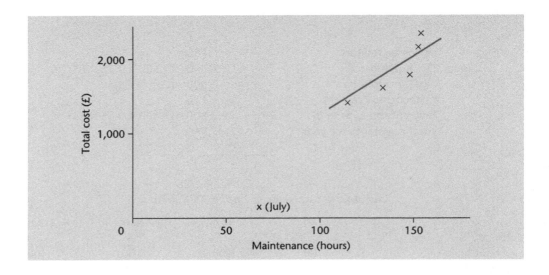

Calculate by using the highest month (June):

		£
Total cost	=	2,073
Total variable cost = 157 h × £10/h	=	1,570
Total fixed cost	=	503

Check by using the lowest month (September):

$$\text{Total cost} = \text{total fixed cost} + \text{total variable cost}$$
$$= 503 + (122 \times 10)$$
$$= £1,723$$

So, the best estimate for maintenance expenditure in November is

$$\text{Total cost} = \text{total fixed cost} + \text{total variable cost}$$
$$= 503 + (180 \times 10)$$
$$= £2,303$$

CASE STUDY	The Omega Document Case Company

Omega is a long-established firm which used to make many different kinds of leather goods. However, in 2012 it made a loss for the first time in over 20 years. This was due to fierce competition, mainly from the Far East. In response to this, it has slashed its product range to its best-selling and most profitable items. It is hoping to benefit from economies of scale and now plans to make only two types of document case: the Delta and the Alpha.

Task:

From the following information, using the pro formas provided, you are required to create a budget for the year ending 31 December 2013.

Sales forecast

	Delta	Alpha
Number of cases sold	4,000	2,500
Selling price per case	£60	£55

Standard production data

Omega has only two production departments: Cutting and Stitching.
   Unit costs:

Direct labour rates		Raw materials	
Cutting	**Stitching**	**Leather**	**Zip fasteners**
£6.00/h	£7.00/h	£3.00/unit	£1.00/unit

Product content

	Delta	Alpha
Leather	2 units	4 units
Zips	1 unit	2 units
Cutting dept labour	2 hours	1.5 hours
Stitching dept labour	1 hour	0.5 hour

Production overheads

	Cutting Department		Stitching Department	
	Fixed	**Variable**	**Fixed**	**Variable**
	£	£	£	£
Indirect labour	7,000	–	3,000	–
Indirect materials	–	3,000	–	9,000
Maintenance	2,000	1,000	500	500
Business rates	6,000	–	1,000	–
Depreciation	8,000	–	2,000	–
Electricity	1,000	2,000	500	1,000
	24,000	6,000	7,000	10,500

Marketing overheads

	£
Salaries	28,000
Advertising	24,000
Other	2,000
	54,000

Administration overheads

	£
Salaries	32,000
Telephone	5,000
Other	4,150
	41,150

Stocks forecast

	Raw materials		Completed cases	
	Leather	**Zips**	**Delta**	**Alpha**
	(units)	**(units)**	**(units)**	**(units)**
Opening stock	6,000	1,000	100	1,000
Closing stock	8,000	2,000	1,100	500

Debtors and creditors

Raw materials, labour, all overheads and debenture interest will be paid in full through the bank and cash accounts. Debtors and creditors at 31 December 2012 will pay and be paid during 2013. Debtors and creditors at 31 December 2013 are expected to be £25,000 and £10,000 respectively. One year's interest on the debenture is paid during the year.

Fixed assets

There are no disposals expected during 2013 but some new equipment will be acquired, on cash terms, for £20,000 just before the end of 2013.

Expected balance sheet as at 31 December 2012

	Cost	Depreciation provision	NBV
Fixed assets	£	£	£
Buildings	40,000	40,000	–
Machinery	200,000	50,000	150,000
	240,000	90,000	150,000
Current assets			
Raw material stock	19,000		
Finished goods stock	40,000		
Total stock		59,000	
Debtors		15,000	
Bank and cash		10,000	
		84,000	
Less: Current liabilities			
Creditors		8,000	
Net current assets			76,000
			226,000
Less: Long-term liabilities			
10% debenture 2021/22			120,000
			106,000
Financed by:			
Shareholders' capital			£
Ordinary shares			82,000
Retained profit			24,000
			106,000

Pro formas

1 Sales budget y/e 31 December 2013

	Units	Selling price	Revenue
		£	£
Delta	....	....	....
Alpha	....	....	....
		Budget revenue	

2 Production budget y/e 31 December 2013

	Delta (units)	Alpha (units)
Planned sales	....	....
Desired closing stock finished goods	....	....
Total required	....	....
Less opening stock finished goods	....	....
Budgeted production	....	....

3 Direct materials usage budget y/e 31 December 2013

	Delta Material content (units/case)	Delta Production (cases)	Delta Usage (units)	Alpha Material content (units/case)	Alpha Production (cases)	Alpha Usage (units)
Leather	....	....	....	....	....	....
Zips	....	....	....	....	....	....

	Cost/unit £	Total usage	Cost of materials used £
Leather	....	....	....
Zips	....	....	....
Budgeted material cost			_____

4 Direct materials purchases budget y/e 31 December 2013

	Leather	Zips
Desired closing stock	.... units	.... units
Units needed for production	.... units	.... units
Total required	.... units	.... units
Less opening stock	.... units	.... units
Purchases needed	.... units	.... units
Cost per unit	£.........	£.........
Budgeted purchases cost	£.........	£.........

5 Direct labour budget y/e 31 December 2013

	Labour content in product (hours)	Cases produced	Total labour hours	Rate per hour £	Total labour cost £
Cutting Dept	....	....	....	....	....
Delta	....	....	....	....	....
Alpha	....	....	....	....	....
Stitching Dept	....	....	....	....	....
Delta	....	....	....	....	....
Alpha	....	....	....	....	....
Budgeted labour hours and cost			_____		_____

6 Production overheads budget y/e 31 December 2013

	Cutting Dept (expected 13,000 direct labour hours)		Stitching Dept (expected 6,000 direct labour hours)	
	Fixed costs £	Variable costs £	Fixed costs £	Variable costs £
Indirect labour	....	....	....	....
Indirect materials	....	....	....	....
Maintenance	....	....	....	....
Business rates	....	....	....	....
Depreciation	....	....	....	....
Electricity	....	....	....	....
Budgeted overhead costs	_____	_____	_____	_____
Overhead absorption rate per direct labour hour	_____	_____	_____	_____

7 Standard budgeted unit cost of manufacturing y/e 31 December 2013

		Delta		Alpha	
	Unit cost	Units in product	Cost	Units in product	Cost
	£		£		£
Leather	....	....	....	....	....
Zips	....	....	....	....	....
Direct labour:					
Cutting	....	....	....	....	....
Stitching	....	....	....	....	....

		Delta		Alpha	
	Unit cost	Units in product	Cost	Units in product	Cost
	£		£		£
Production overheads:	....	....	....	....	....
Cutting – Fixed	....	....	....	....	....
– Variable	....	....	....	....	....
Stitching – Fixed	....	....	....	....	....
– Variable	....	....	....	....	....
Standard cost of product			_____		_____

8   Closing stock budget at 31 December 2013

	Units	Unit cost £	Total cost £	£
Direct materials:				
Leather	....	....	....	....
Zips	....	....	....	....
Finished products				
Delta	....	....	....	....
Alpha	....	....	....	....
Budgeted closing stock				_____

9   Cost of sales budget y/e 31 December 2013

	£	£
Direct materials usage (3)	....	
Direct labour (5)	....	
Production overheads (6)	....	....
Add: Opening stock finished products		....
Less: Closing stock finished products		....
Budgeted cost of sales		....

10   Marketing and administration expenses budget y/e 31 December 2013

	£	£
Marketing expenses:		
Salaries	....	
Advertising	....	
Other	....	....
Administrative expenses:		
Salaries	....	
Telephone	....	
Other	....	....
Budgeted selling and administrative expenses		....

11   Budgeted profit statement y/e 31 December 2013

	£
Sales (1)	....
Less: Cost of sales (9)	....
Gross profit	....
Less: Marketing and admin expenses (10)	....
Budgeted net profit	....
Less: Interest on debenture	....
Profit after interest	....

12 Cash budget y/e 31 December 2013 (summary form)

	£	£
Opening cash balance		....
Add receipts		....
Total cash available		....
Less payments:		
Purchases	....	
Direct labour (5)	....	
Factory overheads less depreciation (6)	....	
Marketing and admin expenses (10)	....	
Debenture interest	....	
Fixed asset purchases	....	....
Budgeted closing cash balance		....

13 Budgeted balance sheet of Omega Manufacturing as at 31 December 2013

	£ Cost	£ Depn provn	£ NBV
Fixed assets			
Buildings	....	....	....
Machinery	....	....	....
	....	....	....
Current assets			
Stocks:			
Finished goods	....		
Raw materials	....	....	
Debtors		....	
Bank and cash		....	
Less current liabilities			
Creditors		....	....
Net current assets			....
Less long-term liabilities			
10% Debenture 2021/22			....
			£_____
Financed by:			
Shareholders' capital			
Ordinary shares			....
Retained profits			....
			£_____

Questions

An asterisk * on a question number indicates that the answer is given at the end of the book. Answers to the other questions are given in the Lecturer's Guide.

Q14.1* Kellaway Ltd

Kellaway Ltd makes aluminium junction boxes for the electrical industry. It makes the boxes in three different sizes: small, medium and large. The following details are taken from next quarter's budget:

	Large	Medium	Small
Sales volume (units)	4,000	5,000	3,500
Direct labour:			
Fitters and turners (hours/unit)	1.25	0.90	0.80
Assemblers and packers (hours/unit)	0.40	0.25	0.20
Direct materials:			
Aluminium strips per unit	2.5	1.0	0.5
Packaging materials (metres)	1.25	0.75	0.5
Stocks:			
Finished goods opening stock (units)	300	400	200
Finished goods closing stock (units)	400	300	150

Rates of pay for fitters/turners and assemblers/packers are £10.00/hour and £6.00/hour respectively. Aluminium strips cost £3 each and packaging is £1/metre. Kellaway plans to have opening material stocks of 220 aluminium strips and 80 metres of packaging. The closing material stocks are 150 aluminium strips and 50 metres of packaging. The quarter's fixed production overheads of £31,700 are attached to product lines on a direct labour hour basis.

Tasks:

1 Create the production budget for the quarter.
2 Calculate the unit production cost of each type of junction box.
3 Create the materials usage budget in quantities and value.
4 Create the materials purchases budget in quantities and value.
5 Create the direct labour budget in hours and value.

Q14.2* Pierce Pommery

Pierce Pommery specializes in the manufacture of dry cider. The 1-litre bottles sell for £3.00 each, with 25% of sales on cash terms and 75% on one month's credit. The budget shows the following sales volumes:

Month	Litres
August	400,000
September	340,000
October	300,000
November	260,000
December	320,000
January	250,000

The company's policy is for opening stock of cider to equal one-fifth of each month's sales, but the stock of cider on 1 September was actually 80,000 litres. For stocks of apples, the policy is for opening stock to equal 50% of each month's usage. On 1 September, the stock of apples was actually 2,200 tonnes.

On average, 15 kilograms of apples are needed to produce 1 litre of cider (1 tonne = 1,000 kg). The cost price of apples is £50/tonne in September and October but £150/tonne in November and December as they have to be imported. Direct labour is paid in the month it is incurred and costs £0.20 a litre. Fixed overheads are £30,000 a month (including £5,000 for depreciation). Payment for apples is made two months after purchase but all other expenses are paid for one month after being incurred.

Tasks:

1 For the months of September, October, November and for the quarter as a whole, prepare the production budget (in litres) and the purchases budget (in tonnes and £).
2 For November only, prepare the cash budget. (Assume the bank balance on 1 November is £495,900 overdrawn.)

Q14.3* Norman Ropes

The sales budget for next year for a particular type of rope manufactured by Norman Ropes is as follows:

Period	Metres	Period	Metres
1	3,000	7	8,000
2	4,000	8	7,000
3	5,000	9	6,000
4	4,000	10	5,000
5	6,000	11	4,000
6	6,000	12	3,000

The stock of finished rope at the start of each period is to be equal to 25% of the sales estimate for the period. (Norman Rope's policy concerning finished product stock levels is to have a quantity of rope in stock approximately equal to one week's sales.) Exceptionally, at the beginning of period 1 there will be 1,500 metres of rope in stock. There is no work-in-progress at the end of any period.

This type of rope uses only one material, a nylon cord known as ARN. Many lengths of this cord are twisted together to form the rope. The budget assumes that each metre of rope uses 100 metres of ARN and that each metre of ARN will cost £0.04.

Materials equal to 25% of each period's usage are to be on hand at the start of the period. Exceptionally, the stock at the start of period 1 will be 125,000 metres of ARN. (Norman Rope's policy concerning raw material stock levels is to have a quantity of material in stock approximately equal to one week's usage.)

Tasks:

For the first six periods, prepare:

a) the production budget (in metres of rope);
b) the materials usage cost budget;
c) the materials purchases cost budget.

Q14.4 Bishop & Co.

Bishop & Co. manufactures vinyl pond lining for the water-garden industry. The company buys vinyl beads by the tonne and heats and rolls them into large sheets which are then cut to the required sizes. One tonne of beads produces 10,000 square metres of liner. Bishop & Co. is uncertain of demand for next year and decides to produce a flexible budget covering five activity levels from 400,000 square metres to 600,000 square metres in steps of 50,000 square metres.

The vinyl beads cost £800/tonne for purchases of up to and including 50 tonnes per year. Bishop & Co.'s supplier offers it the following bulk-purchase incentive. For annual purchases exceeding 50 tonnes, the cost of every tonne in addition to the first 50 is £750.

The direct labour cost is made up of an annual lump sum of basic pay plus a volume-related bonus operative on all production output.

The present annual capacity of the manufacturing plant is 450,000 square metres. For production above this, a new machine will have to be purchased at a cost of £500,000. (No additional labour will be necessary to operate this highly automated machinery.) Bishop & Co.'s policy on depreciation is to write off machinery in equal instalments over 10 years, assuming a zero residual value.

The cost of insurance cover is a fixed amount up to a production level of 500,000 square metres. Beyond that, there is an additional cost per unit.

Bishop & Co. is currently one of the market leaders (in terms of sales volume) in the vinyl pond liner market although it is very competitive. Bishop & Co. sets its selling price per square metre on a cost-plus basis by adding a 300% mark-up to the total production cost. This covers marketing and administration expenses and leaves a little left over for profit.

Tasks:

1 Complete the following production department budget for next year:

000 sq. m	400	450	500	550	600
	£	£	£	£	£
Vinyl beads	32,000				47,500
Direct labour	80,000				90,000
Electricity	8,000				10,000
Depreciation	22,000				34,000
Insurance	11,000				11,250
Other production costs	139,000				139,000
Total	**292,000**				**331,750**

2 If demand were to exceed 500,000 square metres and the new machinery was purchased, what effect might this have on Bishop's overall performance? What advice would you give regarding the purchase of the new machinery?

Q14.5 Chinkin Corporation

The Chinkin Corporation produces surfboards. Its sales have been 300 a month for the last few months but it is about to launch an expansion strategy aimed at increasing sales by 50% over the next four months, April to July. Sales in April are expected to be 300 boards but to increase by 50 units a month until 450 units are sold in July and each subsequent month.

The selling price of the boards is £50 and half the customers pay in the month following purchase. One-quarter take two months to pay and the other quarter pay cash on delivery, taking advantage of a 5% cash discount.

Chinkin has planned an advertising campaign for the months of April, May and June, costing a total of £40,000. Half this amount is payable in April and the remainder in two equal instalments in May and June.

To facilitate the increase in production, new plant and equipment costing £18,000 have been ordered for delivery in April, with payment in three equal monthly instalments, commencing in May. The cost of commissioning this machinery is estimated at £2,000 and will be paid to the outside contractors in April.

To lessen the impact of acquiring these fixed assets, Chinkin plans to arrange a three-month loan of £20,000 from its bank and expects to pay interest at the rate of 10% per annum. The interest will be paid in one amount on the same day as the capital sum is repaid. The money is to be transferred into its account on 3 April.

Raw materials cost £20 a unit and are paid for one month after purchase. Chinkin plans to have a monthly opening stock of raw materials equal to each month's production requirements. Similarly, its policy regarding stocks of finished boards is to have a monthly opening stock equal to each month's total sales.

Monthly fixed costs, including depreciation of £600, total £6,200 and are paid for in the month incurred.

The opening bank balance for April is expected to be £11,400 positive. Chinkin's current overdraft limit is £25,000.

Task:

Create Chinkin's monthly cash budget for the four-month period April to July and for the four-month period as a whole (work to the nearest £). Advise the corporation accordingly.

Q14.6 T Ltd

T Ltd is a newly formed company that designs customized computer programs for its clients. The capital needed to fund the company will be provided by a venture capitalist who will invest £150,000 on 1 January 2002 in exchange for shares in T Ltd.

The directors are currently gathering the information needed to help in the preparation of the cash budget for the first three months of 2002. The information that they have is given below.

Budget details

The budgeted sales (that is, the value of the contracts signed) for the first quarter of 2002 are expected to be £200,000. However, as the company will only just have commenced trading, it is thought that sales will need time to grow. It is therefore expected that 15% of the first quarter's sales will be achieved in January, 30% in February and the remainder in March. It is expected that sales for the year ending 31 December 2002 will reach £1,000,000.

Clients must pay a deposit of 5% of the value of the computer program when they sign the contract for the program to be designed. Payments of 45% and 50% of the value are then paid one and two months later respectively. No bad debts are anticipated in the first quarter.

There are six people employed by the company, each earning an annual gross salary of £45,000, payable in arrears on the last day of each month.

Computer hardware and software will be purchased for £100,000 in January. A deposit of 25% is payable on placing the order for the computer hardware and software, with the remaining balance being paid in equal amounts in February and March. The capital outlay will be depreciated on a straight-line basis over three years, assuming no residual value.

The company has decided to rent offices that will require an initial deposit of £13,000 and an ongoing cost of £6,500 per month payable in advance. These offices are fully serviced and the rent is inclusive of all fixed overhead costs.

Variable production costs are paid in the month in which they are incurred and are budgeted as follows:

January   £1,200   February   £4,200   March   £8,000

A marketing and advertising campaign will be launched in January at a cost of £10,000 with a further campaign in March for £5,000, both amounts being payable as they are incurred.

Administration overhead is budgeted to be £500 each month: 60% to be paid in the month of usage and the balance one month later.

Tax and interest charges can be ignored.

Required:

(a) Prepare the cash budget by month and in total for the first quarter of 2002.

(15 marks)

(b) Identify and comment on those areas of the cash budget that you wish to draw to the attention of the Directors of T Ltd, and recommend action to improve cash flow.

(7 marks)

(c) Briefly explain three advantages for T Ltd of using a spreadsheet when preparing a cash budget.

(3 marks)
(Total = 25 marks)

CIMA Foundation: Management Accounting Fundamentals, November 2001

Q14.7 ST plc

ST plc produces three types of processed foods for a leading food retailer. The company has three processing departments (Preparation, Cooking and Packaging). After recognizing that the overheads incurred in these departments varied in relation to the activities performed, the company switched from a traditional absorption costing system to a budgetary control system that is based on activity based costing.

The *foods* are processed in batches. The budgeted output for April was as follows:

	Output
Food A	100 batches
Food B	30 batches
Food C	200 batches

The number of activities and processing hours budgeted to process a batch of foods in each of the departments are as follows:

	Food A Activities per batch	Food B Activities per batch	Food C Activities per batch
Preparation	5	9	12
Cooking	2	1	4
Packaging	15	2	6
Processing time	10 hours	375 hours	80 hours

The budgeted departmental overhead costs for April were:

	Overheads $
Preparation	100,000
Cooking	350,000
Packaging	50,000

Required:

(a) For food A ONLY, calculate the budgeted overhead cost per batch:
   (i) using traditional absorption costing, based on a factory-wide absorption rate per processing hour; and
   (ii) using activity based costing.

(6 marks)

(b) Comment briefly on the advantages of using an activity based costing approach to determining the cost of each type of processed food compared with traditional absorption costing approaches. You should make reference to your answers to requirement (a) where appropriate.

(4 marks)

(c) The actual output for April was:

	Output
Food A	120 batches
Food B	45 batches
Food C	167 batches

Required:

Prepare a flexed budget for April using an activity based costing approach. Your statement must show the total budgeted overhead for each department and the total budgeted overhead absorbed by each food.

(10 marks)

(d) Discuss the advantages that ST plc should see from the activity based control system compared with the traditional absorption costing that it used previously.

(5 marks)

(Total 25 marks)

CIMA Intermediate: Management Accounting – Performance Management, May 2004

Review questions

1 Explain what a budget is.
2 Explain how budgets fit into the corporate planning context.
3 List the positive attributes of budgetary control systems.
4 Differentiate between fixed and flexible budgets.
5 Differentiate between incremental and zero-based budgeting.
6 Define standard cost.
7 Discuss the issues about the setting of standards.
8 Discuss the limitations of budgets.

The answers to all these questions can be found in the text of this chapter.

chapter 15

Using budgets to control operations

Introduction

Having learned how to create a budget, you will have some idea of the complexity of this task. The budget in the case study at the end of the previous chapter comprised 13 schedules; a real organization will probably have many more. Creating a budget uses a great deal of time, effort and money. So it is understandable for the people involved to heave a sigh of relief when the completed budget is accepted by top management. It must be tempting to file it away and get on with some other work. But if the budget is now forgotten about, all the resources that went into it will have been completely wasted!

The creation of the budget means that the plan is now ready to be put into action. This chapter is all about how budgets are **used** to control the activities of organizations, to take them towards their chosen destination.

<table>
<tr><td>

**Learning
objectives**

</td><td>

Having worked through this chapter you should be able to:
- explain the basic theory of budgetary control systems;
- state the common formulae for cost variances and sub-variances;
- flex the budget to the actual level of production;
- calculate cost variances and their sub-variances;
- produce a profit reconciliation statement;
- illustrate the relationships between variances;
- discuss the additional benefits of budgetary control systems;
- manage the operating cost of budgetary control systems;
- comment on the problems of 'responsibility accounting';
- discuss the limitations of budgetary control systems;
- list 10 points for good budgetary control.

</td></tr>
</table>

The budgetary control system

The basic principle of budgetary control systems is very simple and is best thought of as a cyclical four-step process (see Figure 15.1).

Although the budget is an annual statement, it is usually divided into 12 monthly periods. This is because, if something starts to go wrong, an attempt to put it right needs to be made as soon as possible to minimize the negative effect. For example, if an underground water pipe cracked in month 2, causing the cost of the metered water supply

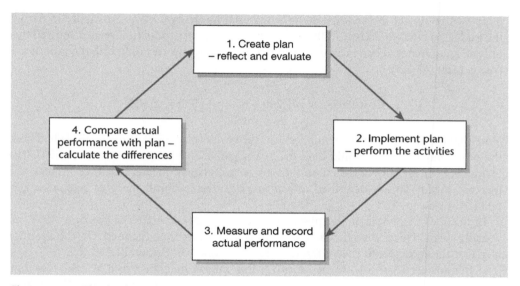

Figure 15.1 **The budgetary control loop**

unexpectedly to treble, a comparison of the actual and planned cost at the end of that month would reveal this and corrective action could be taken quickly. If the comparison was not made until the end of the year, the unnecessary extra cost would be much greater. The comparisons need to be made frequently if effective control is to be exercised.

Variances

Variances are the increases or decreases in profit which occur when things do not go according to plan. Variances are the differences referred to in step 4 of the budgetary control process (see Figure 15.1).

Profit = sales revenue − total costs

If sales revenue changes, then the profit will change. If total costs change, then profit will change.

A *variance* is a change in *profit* caused by changes in either sales revenue or costs from their budgeted levels.

Variance formulae and raw material variances

For every item of cost, e.g. raw material, the cost variance is calculated by the following formula:

Cost variance = budgeted cost − actual cost

Suppose the budget showed that 80 kg of material was to be used at a price of £15 per kg: the budgeted cost would be £1,200 (80 × 15). If the actual production record showed that only 65 kg of material had been used and that each kilogram cost only £10, then the actual cost is £650 (65 × 10).

$$\text{Cost variance} = 1,200 - 650 = +£550 = £550 \text{ F}$$

Note that the answer to this calculation is positive; it is **plus** £550. If the formula had been the other way round, it would have given a negative answer (650 − 1,200 = −550). The formulae are carefully designed so that a positive answer means that the variance will increase profit. This is described as a *favourable* variance and the plus sign is usually replaced by a capital 'F'.

In the above example, it was planned to spend £1,200 on material but only £650 was actually spent. This means that actual profit is £550 more than planned. On the assumption that the more profit the better, this result is 'good' or 'favourable'.

If the answer turns out to be negative, this means that the profit will be less than expected. This type of variance is 'bad' or '*adverse*' and the minus sign is usually replaced by a capital 'A'. (Sometimes 'U' for 'unfavourable' is used.)

Sub-variances

It is worth saying at this point that the words 'cost' and 'price' are often used to mean the same thing in colloquial English. However, in variance analysis these words are used in a precise sense to mean two different things. To avoid confusion in the calculation of variances it is a good idea to understand this clearly from the start.

'Price' refers to one item only. 'Cost' refers to the total expenditure for several items. For example, if 10 kilos of flour are bought at a *price* of £2 a kilo, the *cost* of the purchase is £20.

$$\text{Cost} = \text{price} \times \text{quantity}$$

Having got this distinction clear, the cost variance can now be analysed into its two component variances:

$$\text{Cost variance} = \text{price variance} + \text{quantity variance}$$

This enables us to find out how much of the profit change is due to a change in purchase **price** and how much is due to a change in the **quantity** used. This information may enable us to take corrective action to improve the profit or it may identify areas for further investigation.

Price variance

$$\text{Price variance} = (\text{budgeted price} - \text{actual price}) \times \text{actual quantity}$$
$$= (\text{BP} - \text{AP}) \times \text{AQ}$$

In the above example,

$$\text{Price variance} = (15 - 0) \times 65 = +325 = 325 \text{ F}$$

It is conventional always to calculate price variances at actual quantities used. This gives the difference in cost **due to price changes only**. (It is not distorted by any change in quantities used.)

Quantity variance

$$\text{Quantity variance} = (\text{budgeted quantity} - \text{actual quantity}) \times \text{budgeted price}$$
$$= (\text{BQ} - \text{AQ}) \times \text{BP}$$

In the above example,

$$\text{Quantity variance} = (80 - 65) \times 15 = +225 = 225 \text{ F}$$

It is conventional always to calculate quantity variances at budgeted prices. This gives the difference in cost **due to changes in quantity only**. (It is not distorted by any change in price.)

Reconciliation of variances

	Price variance	325 F
Add:	Quantity variance	225 F
	Cost variance	550 F

These relationships are illustrated by Figure 15.2.

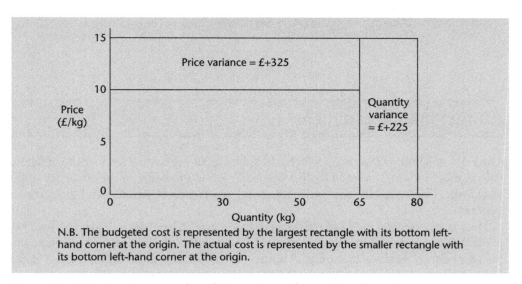

N.B. The budgeted cost is represented by the largest rectangle with its bottom left-hand corner at the origin. The actual cost is represented by the smaller rectangle with its bottom left-hand corner at the origin.

Figure 15.2 Cost variance analysed into price and quantity elements

Terminology

There are two other types of variable cost: direct labour and variable overheads. They can also be analysed into their constituent price and quantity variances. However, these sub-variances are known by different names, as follows:

	Price variance (BP – AP)AQ	Quantity variance (BQ – AQ)BP
Raw materials	Price variance	Usage variance
Direct labour	Rate variance	Efficiency variance
Variable overheads	Expenditure variance	Efficiency variance

Observe that the same basic formulae are used for each of these cost types. It is possible to calculate all six variances named above if you can remember the two formulae shown at the top of the columns.

Note that, in this context, the word 'standard' can be used instead of 'budget'.
So,

$$\text{Standard price} = \text{budgeted price}$$

and

$$\text{Standard quantity} = \text{budgeted quantity}$$

Self-assessment question S15.1

Try the following question for yourself (answer at the end of the chapter).

Roach Ltd planned to use 100 kg of material at £5 per kg for last week's output. Although its production output was exactly as planned, it used 110 kg of material and paid only £4 per kg for it. Calculate the material cost, price and usage variances.

Direct labour variances

The price of labour is the rate at which it is paid, e.g. £9 per hour. The quantity of labour (the number of hours) needed to do a particular job is a measure of the efficiency of the workforce. This is why the sub-variances are known as the *rate variance* and the *efficiency variance*.

Here is an example. SUB Ltd estimates that one particular order will need 30 hours of grade A labour, which is paid at the rate of £10 per hour. After the order has been completed, the records show that only 28 hours were taken, but these were paid at £11 per hour due to a new incentive bonus. What are the direct labour rate, efficiency and cost variances?

Rate variance $= (BP - AP) \times AQ$
$= (\text{budgeted} - \text{actual rate}) \times \text{actual hours}$
$= (10 - 11) \times 28$
$= -28$
$= 28\ A$

Efficiency variance $= (BQ - AQ) \times BP$
$= (\text{budgeted hours} - \text{actual hours}) \times \text{budgeted rate}$
$= (30 - 28) \times 10$
$= +20$
$= 20\ F$

Cost variance $= \text{budgeted cost} - \text{actual cost}$
$= (30 \times 10) - (28 \times 11)$
$= 300 - 308$
$= -8$
$= 8\ A$

Try the following question for yourself (answer at the end of the chapter).

Roach Ltd has a small finishing department employing two people. The budget showed they were expected to work for a total of 4,000 hours during the year just ended. The standard rate of pay used was £6.50 per hour. The payroll shows they actually worked a total of 4,100 hours and were paid a total of £26,650 to produce the budgeted output. Calculate the direct labour cost, rate and efficiency variances.

Idle time variance

Consider the following situation:

Budget = 100 direct labour hours @ £5/h = £500 cost
Actual = 108 direct labour hours @ £4/h = £432 cost

Variance calculations:

Labour rate $= 108(5 - 4) = 108\ F$
Labour efficiency $= 5(100 - 108) = (40)\ A$
Labour cost variance $= 500 - 432 = \underline{68}\ F$

Note that the £40 labour efficiency variance is shown in brackets as well as being followed by the capital 'A'. These brackets signify that this is a negative number.

The analysis shows that the workforce were paid less than planned for each hour worked but that the number of hours needed to complete the work was eight more than planned. It indicates that the operatives were inefficient.

But what if the 108 hours included 10 hours that were paid normally but during which no work could be done? Suppose there had been a power cut, preventing operators from using their machines? This 10 hours of idle time means that only 98 hours were actually worked although 108 hours were paid. To get a better analysis of the situation, the variance caused by the idle time needs to be isolated and shown separately.

Amended variance calculations:

$$
\begin{aligned}
\text{Labour rate} &= 108(5-4) = 108\ \text{F} \\
\text{Labour efficiency} &= 5(100-98) = 10\ \text{F} \\
\text{Idle time} &= 5(98-108) = \underline{(50)}\ \text{A} \\
\text{Total labour variance} &= \underline{\underline{68}}\ \text{F}
\end{aligned}
$$

This more detailed analysis shows that, far from being inefficient, the workforce were efficient. They took only 98 hours to complete work estimated to need 100 hours.

Idle time occurs only occasionally, but when it does it is important for its effects to be separated from the other variances. Otherwise the operatives may be unnecessarily demotivated by being identified as inefficient when they are actually efficient. When idle time occurs, the variance formulae are modified as follows:

Labour efficiency variance = (budgeted hours – actual hours worked) × budgeted rate
Idle time variance = idle hours × budgeted rate

Note that the idle time variance is always adverse and that the labour rate variance does not change.

Self-assessment question S15.3

Try the following question for yourself (answer at the end of the chapter).

Roach Ltd has a direct labour budget for June's planned output of 2,000 hours at £10 per hour. Early in July it is found that the planned output for June was achieved but 2,100 hours were paid for at £11 per hour. However, no work could be done for 300 of the hours paid due to a failure in the just-in-time stock control system. Calculate the appropriate variances.

Variable overhead variances

Variable overheads are expenses indirectly associated with production activity. Two examples are lubricants for, and maintenance of, the production machinery. The more the machinery is used, the more these items cost. They increase or decrease as activity increases or decreases.

In Chapter 9, we saw that some mechanism is needed to include a 'fair' proportion of these indirect expenses in the product cost. One method often used is to spread these expenses out among products in the same proportion as they use direct labour hours.

So, if each product A takes 8 dlh and each product B takes 4 dlh to complete, this means that not only will A have twice the labour cost of B, it will also have twice the variable overhead cost.

Using the example given above of SUB Limited, its variable overhead absorption rate is £3.00 per direct labour hour (dlh). This means that, for the particular order involved, it planned to spend £90 (30 dlh × £3.00/dlh) on variable overheads. The order was actually completed in 28 dlh and the actual cost of the variable overheads was £79.80. Calculate the variable overhead cost, expenditure and efficiency variances.

$$
\begin{aligned}
\text{Cost variance} &= \text{budgeted cost} - \text{actual cost} \\
&= 90.00 - 79.80 \\
&= +10.20 \\
&= 10.20 \text{ F}
\end{aligned}
$$

$$
\begin{aligned}
\text{Expenditure variance} &= (\text{budgeted absorption rate} - \text{actual absorption rate}) \times \text{actual dlh} \\
&= (\text{budgeted abs. rate} \times \text{actual dlh}) - (\text{actual abs. rate} \times \text{actual dlh}) \\
&= (\pounds 3.00 \times 28) - (\pounds 79.80) \\
&= 84.00 - 79.80 \\
&= +4.20 \\
&= 4.20 \text{ F}
\end{aligned}
$$

$$
\begin{aligned}
\text{Efficiency variance} &= (\text{BQ} - \text{AQ}) \times \text{BP} \\
&= (\text{budgeted dlh} - \text{actual dlh}) \times \text{budgeted absorption rate} \\
&= (30 - 28) \times 3.00 \\
&= +6.00 \\
&= 6.00 \text{ F}
\end{aligned}
$$

Note that the combination of the expenditure and efficiency variances should give the cost variance.

Try the following question for yourself (answer at the end of the chapter).

Self-assessment question S15.4

Building on the example of Roach Ltd in S15.1–3 above, it was planned to spend £4,400 on variable overheads, giving a budgeted absorption rate of £1.10/dlh. At the end of the year it was found that the actual amount spent on variable overheads was £4,592. Calculate the variable overhead cost, expenditure and efficiency variances.

Fixed overhead variances

Fixed overheads are those indirect expenses which do **not** vary with output.
This section on fixed overhead variances is covered in two parts:

(i) in a variable costing system; and
(ii) in an absorption costing system.

Variable costing treats fixed costs as period costs but absorption costing treats them as product costs. The earlier chapter of this book entitled 'Comparison of profits under absorption and variable costing' discusses the differences between the two systems in detail.

Variable costing systems

As fixed production overheads are **not** included in the product cost, the volume of goods produced has no effect. The only variable to measure is the amount of money actually spent on the fixed overheads. Therefore, a single cost variance (called 'expenditure') is calculated as follows:

$$\text{Fixed overhead expenditure variance} = \text{budgeted fixed overhead} - \text{actual fixed overhead}$$

For example,	Budgeted fixed overhead	= £300,000
Less:	Actual fixed overhead	= £321,000
	Fixed overhead expenditure variance	= £(21,000) A

Self-assessment question S15.5

Try the following question for yourself (answer at the end of the chapter).

Roach Ltd expects its total annual expenditure on fixed overheads to be £180,000 and decides to spread this evenly over its 12 accounting periods. If the amount actually spent on fixed overheads in month 8 is £16,100, what is the fixed overhead expenditure variance for that month?

Absorption costing systems

For the 'production' activity, all absorption costing systems use predetermined fixed overhead absorption rates (FOARs). For example, the budget for next year may show total fixed production overheads to be £5,500,000 and the total of direct labour hours to be 11,000. This gives a predicted FOAR of £500 per direct labour hour. This is the rate at which fixed production overheads will be attached to next year's actual activity.

These FOARs depend on two factors:

1 The total amount of expenditure on fixed overheads.
2 The total quantity of the chosen activity base (e.g. direct labour hours).

It is extremely unlikely that the predetermined rate will equal the actual rate. For that to happen, both of the factors shown above would have to be predicted with 100% accuracy. The difference between actual and budgeted expenditure causes the **fixed overhead expenditure variance**. The difference between actual and budgeted volume of activity (e.g. direct labour hours) causes the **fixed overhead volume variance**. *For the period, the total variance of fixed production overhead cost equals the total of fixed production overhead under- or over absorbed.*

Because the FOAR is based on the original budget, the fixed overhead variance formulae use some figures from the original budget as well as the flexed budget. However, the total fixed overhead cost variance follows the same pattern as the material, labour and variable overhead cost variances:

Fixed overhead (FO) total cost variance = flexed budget (FB) cost − actual cost

This can be analysed as follows:

$$\text{FB cost − act. cost} = \text{(FB cost − OB cost)} + \text{(OB cost − act. cost)}$$
$$\text{TOTAL} = \text{VOLUME} + \text{EXPENDITURE}$$

Also, the volume variance can be further analysed as follows:

$$\text{(FB cost − OB cost)} = \text{(FB hrs − OB hrs)FOAR}$$
$$= \text{(FB hrs − act. hrs)FOAR} + \text{(act. hrs − OB hrs)FOAR}$$
$$\text{VOLUME} = \text{EFFICIENCY} + \text{CAPACITY}$$

The efficiency variance is concerned with 'output per hour' or the *rate* of producing. The capacity variance is concerned with 'total hours used'. (Note that the idea of 'capacity', in the sense of the **total volume** that the production facilities are capable of producing, is inappropriate and misleading.)

For example, if the operatives are working below the planned rate (i.e. the efficiency variance is adverse), the actual number of hours worked would have to be greater than planned *in order to achieve the planned total output*. In this case the efficiency variance would be *adverse* but the capacity variance would be *favourable*. In other situations the efficiency variance could be favourable and the capacity variance could be adverse or they could both be favourable or both adverse.

Figure 15.3 illustrates the relationships between the fine variances discussed immediately above.

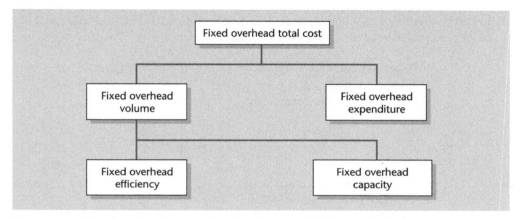

Figure 15.3 **Fixed production overhead variance relationships under absorption costing**

Comparison of systems

Note that the volume variance only occurs where a standard absorption costing system is used. Where a business adopts a standard variable costing system, no volume variance arises because fixed production overheads are treated as period costs and are debited directly to the profit and loss account. So, for variable costing systems, the 'fixed overhead total cost variance' will always equal the 'fixed overhead expenditure variance'.

Under standard absorption costing systems, fixed overheads are treated as a product cost and are attached to products. For unsold products, they are included in the *inventory valuation* on the balance sheet; for products sold in the period, they are included in *cost of sales* on the profit and loss account.

To summarise:

	FO expenditure variance	FO volume variance
Variable costing system	Yes	No
Absorption costing system	Yes	Yes

Example 15.1

FO variance calculations in standard absorption costing

Scaatefour Plc makes only one product, the Skylon, and never has any work-in-progress at the end of a production period. It operates a standard absorption costing system which uses direct labour hours as a base for its fixed overhead absorption rate (FOAR). The management accountant had calculated all the other variances before she was unexpectedly admitted to hospital as an emergency case. In order that the monthly variance analysis report can be completed, you are required to use the following data for month 11 to calculate the five fixed overhead variances.

The budgeted output for this month was 12,000 Skylons, each one budgeted to use 10 direct labour hours in production. The predetermined FOAR was calculated at £6.70 per direct labour hour. The actual production data are

Units produced	11,200
Number of direct labour hours worked	110,000
Expenditure on fixed overheads	£824,000

Solution

i) FO total cost variance

$$= \text{flexed budget cost} - \text{actual cost}$$
$$= (11{,}200 \times 10 \times 6.70) - 824{,}000$$
$$= 750{,}400 - 824{,}000$$
$$= \text{£73,600 A}$$

Sub-analysis of FO total cost variance using labour hours

ii) FO expenditure variance

> = OB cost − act. cost
> = (12,000 units × £67 per unit) − 824,000
> = 804,000 − 824,000
> = **£20,000 A**

iii) FO volume variance

> = FB cost − OB cost
> = (11,200 units × £67 per unit) − (12,000 units × £67 per unit)
> = (11,200 − 12,000)67
> = (−800)67
> = **£53,600 A**

Sub-analysis of FO volume variance using labour hours

iv) FO capacity variance

> = (act. hrs − OB hrs)FOAR
> = (110,000 − 120,000)6.70
> = (−10,000)6.70
> = **£67,000 A**

v) FO efficiency variance

> = (FB hrs − act. hrs)FOAR
> = (112,000 − 110,000)6.70
> = (2,000)6.70
> = **£13,400 F**

Try the following question for yourself (answer at the end of the chapter).

Self-assessment question S15.6

Blackpack Limited makes only one product, the darkbox, and never has any work-in-progress at the end of a production period. It operates a standard absorption costing system which uses direct labour hours as a base for its fixed overhead absorption rate. Use the following data for month 5 to calculate the five fixed overhead variances.

The budgeted output for this month was 24,000 darkboxes, each one budgeted to use 5 direct labour hours in production. The predetermined fixed overhead absorption rate was calculated at £15 per direct labour hour. The actual production data is as follows:

Units produced	20,000
Number of direct labour hours worked	132,000
Expenditure on fixed overheads	£765,000

Appendix: the algebraic basis for the FO variances in standard absorption costing

There is no need or requirement for students to know or understand the algebra presented below but many students of accountancy have good mathematical skills and will not find it difficult to grasp. However, an understanding of the underlying algebra may help students to derive the correct formulae when needed, during an examination for example.

Let

$$
\begin{aligned}
S &= \text{flexed budget cost} \\
T &= \text{actual cost} \\
N &= \text{original budget cost} \\
P &= \text{predetermined FOAR} \\
J &= \text{flexed budget hours} \\
R &= \text{actual hours} \\
K &= \text{original budget hours}
\end{aligned}
$$

Then the following formulae can be derived:

FO total cost variance

$$
\begin{aligned}
S - T &= S - N + N - T \\
&= (S - N) + (N - T)
\end{aligned}
$$

FO volume variance
  If $S = JP$ and $N = KP$, then

$$
\begin{aligned}
S - N &= JP - KP \\
&= JP - RP + RP - KP \\
&= (J - R)P + (R - K)P
\end{aligned}
$$

FO expenditure variance

$$
= N - T
$$

FO efficiency variance

$$
= (J - R)P
$$

FO capacity variance

$$
= (R - K)P
$$

The importance of the flexed budget

Suppose you were the manager responsible for a large production facility. For the year just ended, your budget for raw material costs was £9 million but your actual expenditure was only £8 million. Do you deserve a bonus?

It appears you have made a saving of £1 million, but this may not be so. There is not enough information to provide a clear answer. The £9 million budget was to achieve a certain level of production. If that level was achieved, then a bonus is probably deserved. But what if the production output was only half of what was planned? This means that only £4.5 million **should** have been spent on materials, not the £8 million actually spent! In this case, a bonus seems rather inappropriate.

To get meaningful answers when calculating the variances for the variable costs (materials, labour and variable overheads) the actual amounts must be compared with a budget which has been revised to the actual level of output. This revised budget is called the *flexed budget*; it is created **after** the actual figures are known. The effect of using the flexed budget instead of the original budget is that the variances will now show the differences between the actual costs and what those costs **should have been** for the output actually achieved. This is useful information. Variable cost variances based on the original budget will almost certainly be misleading.

<table><tr><td>

Illustration with raw materials (manufacturing wheels from raw plastic)

Original budget:	10,000 wheels using 5 kg of plastic each @ £2.00/kg
	Cost = 10,000 × 5 × 2 = £100,000
Actual expenditure:	Total cost of plastic used in period was £74,880.
	Thus, saving on budget £25,120

Is the production manager to be congratulated on this favourable variance?

Yes, congratulations are in order if 10,000 wheels were actually produced.

But what if only 6,000 wheels were actually produced (each using 5.2 kg @ £2.40/kg = £74,880 cost)?

Flex the budget to the actual level of activity:

Flexed budget: 6,000 wheels using 5 kg plastic @ £2.00 = £60,000 cost
Material price variance = $(2.0 - 2.4) \times 31,200 = (12,480)$ A
Material usage variance = $(30,000 - 31,200) \times 2 = \underline{(2,400)}$ A
Actual cost of materials = $\underline{£74,880}$

Congratulations are not appropriate in this case.

As you can see from this example, flexed budgets use the same standard amounts as the original budget (1 wheel uses 5 kg of plastic costing £2/kg). The only thing that changes is the level of output or production volume. More often than not, the actual output differs from that planned. **When calculating variances, the first step is to create the flexed budget.**

This does not mean to say that the difference between the original and flexed budget is ignored. This difference is accounted for elsewhere by the sales volume variance (see below).

</td><td>Example 15.2</td></tr></table>

Try the following question for yourself (answer at the end of the chapter).

During week 32, Maykit Ltd planned to produce 50 plastic boxes using two hours
of direct labour for each box, paid at the standard rate of £10 per hour, giving a
budgeted cost of £1,000. At the end of that week, it was found that 55 boxes had
been produced, using 105 hours of labour paid at £10 per hour and costing £1,050.
As there is no labour rate variance and the labour cost for the week was £50 greater
than planned, is it accurate to say that the labour force must be working inefficiently?

Sales variances

As sales are concerned with income rather than cost, the sales price variance will differ
from cost variances in the following way. If the actual sales price achieved is greater than
the budgeted price then the profit will increase, giving a **favourable** variance. So the
prices inside the brackets will be the opposite way round (**actual – budget**).

Sales price variance

Sales price variance = (actual price – budget price) × actual quantity
For example, Sales budget = 20,000 items @ £10; actual = 20,000 items @ £11
Sales price variance = (11 – 10) × 20,000 = 20,000 F

Sales volume variance

Sales volume variance = flexed budget profit – original budget profit

This is consistent, with the only difference between the original and flexed budgets being
the level of activity. The number of items produced is assumed to be the same as the
number of items sold and the situation one of making to order and not for stock.

Try the following question for yourself (answer at the end of the chapter).

The following data refers to Pike Ltd for the month of May. The original budget showed
400 items sold at £25 each, resulting in a profit of £2,000. The actual performance
was 300 items sold at £26 each, resulting in a profit of £1,663. When the budget was
flexed, it gave a revised profit of £1,650. Calculate the sales price variance and the sales
volume variance.

The profit reconciliation statement

When the variance analysis exercise is complete, the original budget should be reconciled to the actual results to summarize the findings of the investigation. As the flexed budget is an important part of the analysis, it should be included in the reconciliation. An example of a profit reconciliation statement is shown below.

Pike Ltd: profit reconciliation statement

		£	£
Original budget profit			2,000
Sales volume variance			(350) A
Flexed budget profit			1,650
Sales price variance			300 F
Material variances:	Usage	(140) A	
	Price	20 F	
	Cost		(120) A
Labour variances:	Efficiency	75 F	
	Rate	(25) A	
	Cost		50 F
Variable overhead variance:	Efficiency	56 F	
	Expenditure	(24) A	
	Cost		32 F
Fixed overhead expenditure variance			(249) A
Actual profit			**1,663**

Note that the adverse variances are shown in brackets. This is not compulsory but it may help students to arrive at the correct answers, especially during exams. The capital 'A' or 'F' is compulsory.

Try the following question for yourself (answer at the end of the chapter).

Self-assessment question S15.9

From the following information (all figures in £000) produce a profit reconciliation statement. Fixed overheads cost 24 less than expected; variable overhead expenditure variance = 5 F and variable overhead efficiency variance = 1 A; labour variances are rate = 14 F and efficiency = 2 A; sales price variance = 18 A; material variances are usage = 39 F and price = 27 A; original budget profit = 400 and flexed budget profit = 431; there is also an idle time variance of 12.

Variance relationships

Figures 15.4 and 15.5 illustrate the interrelationships of variances.

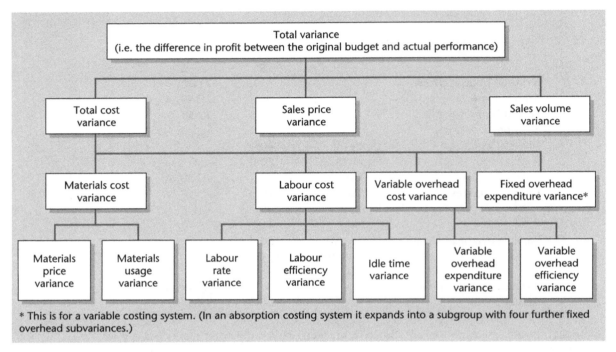

Figure 15.4 **Variance family tree**

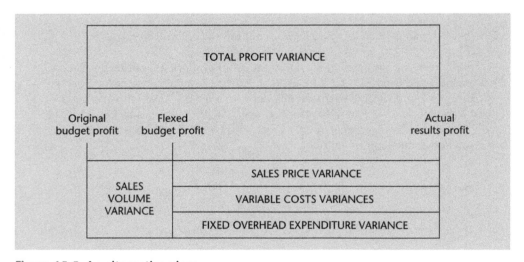

Figure 15.5 **An alternative view**

Additional benefits of the budgetary control system

As well as appropriately recording and evaluating performance, budgetary control systems have the following positive effects:

1 They communicate organizational aspirations. The annual organizational plan is distributed to budget holders who are then aware of what is expected of them.
2 They co-ordinate complex activities. For example, if there is no opening stock of finished goods and the company plans to sell 200,000 items next year, it must budget to produce at least 200,000 items.
3 They authorize budget holders. For example, if the purchasing budget shows that £1 million of materials are to be bought every month, the purchasing manager does not have to seek permission to spend this amount. The purchasing budget itself authorizes this spending.
4 They motivate budget holders. Budgets can also be used as targets. The performance levels (known as *standards*) in a budget are often set high but attainable in order to encourage improvement.

Managing the cost of the system

The process of variance investigation is time consuming and has a cost of its own. Organizations need to control this activity. The usual approach is that of 'management by exception'. If operations are going more or less as planned and the variances are small, no follow-up activity takes place. However, where the variances are significant, they are investigated. But how do you know if a variance is significant or not?

This decision is inherently subjective and may vary from business to business. Someone has to decide **in advance** what the significance levels of their organization are going to be. A percentage difference between budget and actual is determined in advance, subject to a minimum amount. For example, a given company may investigate all variances that are at least 5% different from budget provided they are at least £250 in amount. This approach is both relative and absolute. But another company may have a policy of 10% difference with a threshold of £10,000.

Responsibility accounting

Budgetary control works through people. Functional budgets are delegated to the lowest practical level, where an appropriate person is made the 'budget responsible manager'. For this to work effectively, the lines of authority must be clearly defined. This can be a problem, especially in those organizations operating a matrix approach to their management structure. Where two people are responsible for an item of income or cost, there is always room for dispute as to who should take the credit or accept the blame.

Responsibility accounting usually supports the payment of rewards, such as cash bonuses, to budget-responsible officers for meeting their targets. The theory is that the company will benefit from their increased motivation and a 'win–win' situation will occur. For this to happen, the accounting mechanisms must be structured in the same way as the responsibilities. For example, if the regional sales managers are responsible for the value of sales in their areas, the budgets and reporting mechanisms must be analysed over these areas. A single set of aggregated figures for the whole country would not allow the individual responsibilities to be defined or monitored.

This allows companies to achieve their goals through 'management by objective' (MBO) as well as 'management by exception' (MBE). A good example of the latter is the investigation of variances only when they are significant. If actual performance is not very different from budget, things are considered to be going to plan, i.e. no exceptions have occurred.

Another aspect of responsibility accounting is that of **uncontrollable** costs. Not all costs are completely within the control of management. For example, the business rates for the factory may be one item on the production manager's budget. If the cost of these rates is completely outside that person's control, he or she is likely to be demotivated when held responsible for an adverse variance. To avoid this, either the situation should be made very clear in the variance analysis reports or the uncontrollable items should be extracted and isolated in a budget of their own. Unfortunately, problems still arise from some costs that are **partially** controllable. For instance, the cost of running the computerized management information system may be partly based on the manager's ability to retain experienced staff (temporary IT staff are expensive). But it is also based on the rates of pay in the marketplace. The manager may be responsible for the first but not for the second. In this case, it would be up to that manager to justify any adverse variances arising, if he or she can.

Limitations of the budgetary control process

For many, many years, most organizations have operated a budgetary control system. This management accounting technique has been enormously successful. Yet, during the last few years there have been signs of firms moving away from traditional budgeting. IKEA (furniture), Asea Brown Boveri (engineering), Svenska Handelbanken (banking) and Borealis (petrochemicals), all huge multinational organizations based in Europe, are examples of this trend. They believe that there is more to measuring and controlling business performance than can be expressed by a traditional budget. The main influence on their thinking is the accelerating rate of change in the business environment. Many organizations are finding that their environment is not only constantly changing but changing faster and faster as time moves on.

Budgets tend to reinforce the 'old' way of doing things. Budget managers have many other responsibilities pressing on them when the budget creation deadline is imminent. To reflect changing circumstances, changes may need to be made concerning which data is shown. Consequently, the layout of the form would need to be changed, but this would have to be approved at a high level, which would take considerable time and effort. The normal 'efficient' approach to this situation is to use the same form as last year, meet the deadline and get on with the next task. Over the years, the budget format becomes more and more divorced from reality and less effective in improving performance.

Having said this, budgets are still very effective and necessary instruments of control for the vast majority of organizations. If budgets were removed without something better being put in their place, the organization would almost certainly start to deteriorate.

The manager's point of view (written by Nigel Burton)

As discussed in the previous chapter, the first major objective of budgeting is to complete a detailed review of the business, and set up a budget framework which ensures that the company is progressing down its designated strategic path. The second objective is to monitor performance against that budget, but with the minimum amount of time and effort.

The main advantage of a detailed budget is that it provides a sound basis for management by exception. Once the budget is agreed, all departmental managers know exactly what is expected of them, in terms of the level of sales to be achieved, or the amount of cost they can incur. Subject to the normal safeguards, they are authorized to spend the amount budgeted in furtherance of their departmental objectives. Moreover, the managing director knows that he or she has nothing to worry about, providing managers are performing within the budgeted parameters. The MD simply reviews the numbers for any significant variances, and then gets on with the job of running the business.

The key to effective management by exception is the IT system. Information must be presented in such a way as to minimize any further analysis work. My company, for instance, used a simple but effective system for monitoring sales. This showed orders due out this month, by volume, sales value and marginal income (contribution), set against the budget for the month. Initially, it summarized these items for the whole company, but there was a feature which allowed the user to 'drill down' through the layers of product group and product line, to individual customer/product level. It took a matter of moments, therefore, on arriving at the office each morning, for me to update myself in detail on the progress of this month's sales. I knew exactly which customers and which products had so far failed to meet expectations. I was so familiar with our performance at all times that the monthly management accounts served merely to confirm what I already knew. Not only did this allow me to spend my time more productively, but also it gave me a detailed knowledge of our current situation from which to answer the regular stream of questions from our head office in the USA.

We had a similar 'drill down' system with which to interrogate previous months' results. By the simple expedient of ranking sales on the basis of variance from budget, an analysis of the causes of shortfalls and overachievements was the work of a few minutes. By presenting the information in the right format, all the traditional, painstaking sales analysis work was completely eliminated. It should be borne in mind that users at different levels in the company, e.g. managing director, sales manager or sales executive, may need the information in a different format, so a cleverly designed system should address the needs of all.

Analysis of manufacturing variances is another case in point. As we have seen above, each production batch will generate at least six variances. In any given month, the factory will produce hundreds of batches, so an enormous amount of variance information is produced. Each batch's variances will tell a slightly different story. In chemicals manufacturing, no two batches are ever the same. The raw materials may have slight differences in specification, the chemical reactions might not work in precisely the same way, and even atmospheric temperatures and humidity might play their part. As a result, processes may need a further input of materials, or perhaps more reaction time or a longer cooling period. Each divergence from the standard generates manufacturing variances. How much time should be spent analysing it all? While a manufacturing process is at the development stage, the production staff will clearly wish to examine all the information in detail, looking for clues which will help them to improve the efficiency of the processing. Once the process has stabilized, however, the production staff will, for the most part, ignore small variations on batches, and look for regular trends which indicate that a process change is required. They will only look at individual batches where there is either a significant variance or a complete batch failure.

Standards may sometimes be set as targets, in order to encourage greater efficiency in the factory. This can be a two-edged sword. The standards are incorporated in the product costs, so, if they are drawn too tightly (showing low costs), there is a risk that the salespeople might be misled into thinking that they can reduce their selling prices. Production's failure to achieve the standards will emerge as adverse manufacturing variances on the profit and loss account, but will be seen as a local production problem, rather than an issue for the whole of the company. Conversely, if the standards are drawn too slackly (showing high costs), production will have a nice, comfortable time. However, the resultant higher costs might discourage salespeople from quoting more competitive prices and generating more business. In my view, standards should always be set at expected performance and not at 'target' levels. However, if there is still a requirement for a target, production can always be asked to produce at a specified level which will result in favourable variances. If they achieve this consistently, it can then be transferred into the product costs, and everyone is happy.

As in many areas of management accounting, the secret of success is to keep it simple but effective. When setting up new systems, there is a natural tendency to over-elaborate. One wants to feel that a thorough and professional job has been done, and perhaps too little thought is directed at the practical aspects of managing the system when it is up and running. I have already described some of the benefits and pitfalls of the activity-based costing system, which my US head office decided to install throughout the organization (see Chapter 10, on activity-based costing). One of the more complex aspects of this system was variance reporting. Normal standard costing principles were used, so the normal manufacturing variances described earlier in this chapter were generated. However, to make the product costs more accurate, and therefore of greater value to the salesforce, the standards were changed every three months. Actual performance was then monitored against the new standards, but, as the original standards were still the basis of the budget, we had another set of variances capturing the difference between the original and revised standards. Somehow, for every batch produced, the number of variances had grown to 16! The monthly variance printout was three-quarters of an inch thick. We were swamped with information and, as a result, gave less attention to this area than we might otherwise have done.

A similar example of overkill occurred with our performance-monitoring reporting. We had developed a simple graphical representation of eight key measurements which we felt reflected our overall performance as a company on a monthly basis. These included the percentage of batches achieving specification without rework, the percentage of orders dispatched on time, and the number of customer complaints received. By combining these eight measurements, we arrived at a single company performance indicator. It was crude, perhaps, but effective, as it helped to focus the minds of employees throughout the company on the need for high-quality performance. Our head office was quite taken with this concept, and decided to adopt it throughout the organization. However, head office increased the number of measurements to 30, some of which were rather dubious as performance monitors. Purchase price variance was one example. Does a favourable PPV reflect a good performance by the purchasing department? Not necessarily. If the market price was coming down, perhaps the variance should have been twice the size. Conversely, a 10% adverse variance could be a fine performance if the market price had actually gone up by 20%. So the selection of performance monitors should be done with a great deal of care. Nevertheless, we duly submitted our data (a time-consuming exercise in itself), and the worldwide results were published in a vast monthly tome. This contained so much information, much of it flawed or inconsistent, that no one ever bothered to look at it, and the motivational impact was completely lost.

A really good information system, whether it is performance monitoring or budgetary control, will tell the users exactly what they need to know, nothing more, nothing less. And it will do so with the minimal amount of input from the users. Experience will help in deciding the right level, although even experienced managers can fall into the trap of immersing themselves in excessive amounts of data. It is one of the features of this technological age that there is more information available than the human mind can reasonably assimilate, and one of the most important business skills is the ability to specify exactly the information you want and the format in which you want it. Another significant business skill is obtaining the necessary programming time in the IT department, but that is another story!

Summary

- The budgetary control process is a continuous closed-loop system.
- It consists of planning, recording, comparing, evaluating and acting.
- The differences between budget and actual are known as variances.
- Cost variances can be analysed into their constituent price and quantity variances.
- The budget should be flexed before the cost variances are calculated.
- Fixed overhead variances are different in absorption and variable costing systems.
- Sales volume variance is the difference in the original and flexed budget profits.
- Profit reconciliation statements give a complete summary of the variance analysis.
- Spin-offs include communication, co-ordination, authorization and motivation.
- System operating costs are controlled by a 'management by exception' approach.
- Budget holders can be demotivated if held responsible for non-controllable costs.
- Budgetary control systems do not measure the effect of missed opportunities.
- A few large successful organizations claim to have recently abandoned budgeting.
- The vast majority of organizations still operate budgetary control systems.

Ten points for good budgetary control

1 Areas of responsibility are clearly defined.
2 Budgets are held at the lowest practical management level.
3 Non-controllable items are clearly identified.
4 Reporting system is routine/automatic.
5 Reporting periods are short.
6 Reports are produced soon after the period end.
7 Variance significance levels are pre-established.
8 Significant variances are always investigated.
9 Corrective action is taken where possible.
10 Senior management exemplify the importance of the budgetary control system.

Further reading

Atkinson, A., Banker, R., Kaplan, R. and Young, S. (2001) *Management Accounting*, 3rd edition, Prentice Hall, Harlow. See Chapter 11, 'Using budgets to achieve organisational objectives'.

Budding, G. T. (2004) 'Accountability, environmental uncertainty and government performance: evidence from Dutch municipalities', *Management Accounting Research*, Vol. 15, Issue 3, September.

'FA kicks off new budget control system' (2004) *Computer Weekly*, 30 November.

Horngren, C., Bhimani, A., Datar, S. and Foster, G. (2002) *Management and Cost Accounting*, 2nd edition, Prentice Hall Europe, Harlow. See chapters on 'Flexible budgets, variances and management control 1 & 2'.

Merchant, K. A. (1998) *Modern Management Control Systems: Text and Cases*, Prentice Hall, Englewood Cliffs, NJ.

Otley, D. (1987) *Accounting Control and Organisational Behaviour*, Heinemann Professional Publishing, Oxford. See Chapters 5 and 9, 'Performance appraisal' and 'Accounting for effective control'. (Other chapters concentrate on the 'human' aspects of budgetary control.)

Player, S. (2003) 'Beyond the budget games', *Intelligent Enterprise*, Vol. 6, Issue 16, 10 October Supplement.

Shim, J. and Siegel, J. (2005) *Budgeting Basics and Beyond*, 2nd edition, Wiley, Hoboken, NJ.

Upchurch, A. (2003) *Management Accounting, Principles and Practice*, 2nd edition, Financial Times/Prentice Hall, Harlow. See chapters 'Budgetary control' and 'Analysis of variances'.

Weetman, P. (2002) *Management Accounting, an Introduction*, 3rd edition, Financial Times/ Prentice Hall, Harlow. See chapters 'Standard costs' and 'Performance evaluation and feedback reporting'.

Answers to self-assessment questions

S15.1

Budget: 100 kg @ £5/kg = £500 cost
Actual: 110 kg @ £4/kg = £440 cost

Price variance $= (BP - AP) \times AQ$
$= (5 - 4) \times 110 = 110$ F

Usage variance $= (BQ - AQ) \times BP$
$= (100 - 110) \times 5 = (50)$ A

Cost variance $=$ budget cost $-$ actual cost
$= 500 - 440 = 60$ F

Note: The combined price and usage variances should equal the cost variance.

S15.2

$$\text{Rate variance} = (\text{budgeted rate} - \text{actual rate}) \times \text{actual hours}$$
$$= (\text{BR} \times \text{AH}) - (\text{AR} \times \text{AH})$$
$$= (6.50 \times 4{,}100) - 26{,}650$$
$$= 26{,}650 - 26{,}650$$
$$= \text{zero (The actual rate paid must also} = £6.50/\text{hour.})$$

$$\text{Efficiency variance} = (\text{budgeted hours} - \text{actual hours}) \times \text{budgeted rate}$$
$$= (4{,}000 - 4{,}100) \times 6.50$$
$$= (-100) \times 6.50$$
$$= -650$$
$$= 650 \text{ A}$$

$$\text{Cost variance} = \text{budgeted cost} - \text{actual cost}$$
$$= (4{,}000 \times 6.50) - 6{,}650$$
$$= 26{,}000 - 26{,}650$$
$$= -650$$
$$= 650 \text{ A}$$

Note: As the rate does not vary, the efficiency variance should equal the cost variance.

S15.3

$$\text{Rate variance} = (\text{budgeted rate} - \text{actual rate}) \times \text{actual hours paid}$$
$$= (10 - 11) \times 2{,}100$$
$$= -2{,}100$$
$$= 2{,}100 \text{ A}$$

$$\text{Efficiency variance} = (\text{budgeted hours} - \text{actual hours worked}) \times \text{budgeted rate}$$
$$= (2{,}000 - 1{,}800) \times 10$$
$$= +2{,}000$$
$$= 2{,}000 \text{ F}$$

$$\text{Idle time variance} = \text{idle hours} \times \text{budgeted rate}$$
$$= 300 \times 10$$
$$= -3{,}000$$
$$= 3{,}000 \text{ A}$$

$$\text{Labour cost variance} = \text{budgeted cost} - \text{actual cost}$$
$$= (2{,}000 \times 10) - (2{,}100 \times 11)$$
$$= 20{,}000 - 23{,}100$$
$$= -3{,}100$$
$$= 3{,}100 \text{ A}$$

S15.4

$$\text{Cost variance} = \text{budgeted cost} - \text{actual cost}$$
$$= 4{,}400 - 4{,}592$$
$$= -192$$
$$= 192 \text{ A}$$

$$\text{Expenditure variance} = (\text{budgeted absorption rate} - \text{actual absorption rate}) \times \text{actual dlh}$$
$$= (\text{budgeted abs. rate} \times \text{actual dlh}) - (\text{actual abs. rate} \times \text{actual dlh})$$
$$= (1.10 \times 4{,}100) - (4{,}592)$$
$$= 4{,}510 - 4{,}592$$
$$= -82$$
$$= 82 \text{ A}$$

$$\text{Efficiency variance} = (\text{BQ} - \text{AQ}) \times \text{BP}$$
$$= (\text{budgeted dlh} - \text{actual dlh}) \times \text{budgeted absorption rate}$$
$$= (4{,}000 - 4{,}100) \times 1.10$$
$$= -110$$
$$= 110 \text{ A}$$

Note: The combination of the expenditure and efficiency variances should give the cost variance.

S15.5

Fixed overhead monthly budget = 180,000/12 =	15,000
Less: Actual expenditure in month 8	= <u>16,100</u>
Fixed overhead expenditure variance	= −1,100
	= 1,100 A

S15.6

Solution to Blackpack Limited

i) FO total cost variance

$$= \text{flexed budget cost} - \text{actual cost}$$
$$= (20{,}000 \times 5 \times 15) - 1{,}465{,}000$$
$$= 1{,}500{,}000 - 1{,}465{,}000$$
$$= £35{,}000 \text{ F}$$

Sub-analysis of FO total cost variance using labour hours

ii) FO expenditure variance

$$= \text{OB cost} - \text{act. cost}$$
$$= (24{,}000 \times 5 \times 15) - 1{,}465{,}000$$
$$= 1{,}800{,}000 - 1{,}465{,}000$$
$$= £335{,}000 \text{ F}$$

iii) FO volume variance

$$= \text{FB cost} - \text{OB cost}$$
$$= (20{,}000 \times 5 \times 15) - (24{,}000 \times 5 \times 15)$$
$$= (1{,}500{,}000) - (1{,}800{,}000)$$
$$= \pounds 300{,}000 \text{ A}$$

Sub-analysis of FO volume variance using labour hours

iv) FO capacity variance

$$= (\text{act. hrs} - \text{OB hrs})\text{FOAR}$$
$$= (132{,}000 - 120{,}000)15$$
$$= (12{,}000)15$$
$$= \pounds 180{,}000 \text{ F}$$

v) FO efficiency variance

$$= (\text{FB hrs} - \text{act. hrs})\text{FOAR}$$
$$= (100{,}000 - 132{,}000)15$$
$$= (-32{,}000)15$$
$$= \pounds 480{,}000 \text{ A}$$

S15.7

As the actual output is different from that planned in the original budget, the first step is to **flex the budget** to the activity level of 110 items.

Flexed budget (activity level = 55 items):

$$\text{Cost} = 55 \text{ units} \times 2 \text{ hours/unit} \times \pounds 10/\text{hour} = \pounds 1{,}100$$

$$\begin{aligned}
\text{Labour cost variance} &= \text{budgeted cost} - \text{actual cost} \\
&= 1{,}100 - 1{,}050 \\
&= +50 \\
&= 50 \text{ F}
\end{aligned}$$

$$\begin{aligned}
\text{Labour efficiency variance} &= (\text{budgeted hours} - \text{actual hours}) \times \text{budgeted rate} \\
&= (110 - 105) \times 10 \\
&= +50 \\
&= 50 \text{ F}
\end{aligned}$$

$$\begin{aligned}
\text{Labour rate variance} &= (\text{budgeted rate} - \text{actual rate}) \times \text{actual hours} \\
&= (10 - 10) \times 105 \\
&= 0
\end{aligned}$$

These results show that the workforce are working **efficiently**; the statement made in the question is not accurate.

S15.8

$$\text{Sales price variance} = (\text{actual price} - \text{budgeted price}) \times \text{actual quantity sold}$$
$$= (26 - 25) \times 300$$
$$= +300$$
$$= 300 \text{ F}$$

$$\text{Sales volume variance} = \text{flexed budget profit} - \text{original budget profit}$$
$$= 1,650 - 2,000$$
$$= -350$$
$$= 350 \text{ A}$$

S15.9

Profit reconciliation statement

		£000	£000
Original budget profit			400
Sales volume variance			31 F
Flexed budget profit			431
Sales price variance			(18) A
Material variances:	Usage	39 F	
	Price	(27) A	
	Cost		12 F
Labour variances:	Efficiency	(2) A	
	Idle time	(12) A	
	Rate	14 F	
	Cost		0
Variable overhead variance:	Efficiency	(1) A	
	Expenditure	5 F	
	Cost		4 F
Fixed overhead expenditure variance			24 F
Actual profit			**453**

CASE STUDY 1 | Anomira Ltd

Anomira Ltd is a wholly owned subsidiary of an industrial conglomerate. It produces one standard size of sealing compound used in the motor vehicle industry. As the new management accountant of this company, you have been asked to explain why the actual results differed from the budget for the year just ended. You ascertain the following information.

The budget was for a volume of 100,000 units produced and sold, each using 2 kg of material at £3.00 per kg. The total of variable overheads was expected to be £100,000 and the fixed overheads £250,000. Total sales revenue was planned to be £1,500,000 and the 50,000 direct labour hours planned were expected to cost £250,000. The variable overhead absorption rate is £2.00 per direct labour hour.

The actual performance for last year showed production of 90,000 units and no change in stock levels over the year. Sales revenue was £1,440,000 and 196,000 kg of material were used, costing £529,200. Variable overheads were £94,500 and fixed overheads £255,000. The total cost of direct labour was £232,750 for 49,000 hours. However, 1,000 of these hours were completely non-productive due to a breakdown of the heating system during exceptionally bad winter weather causing the factory to be temporarily closed.

Tasks:

1 Perform a variance analysis (in as much detail as the information will allow) reconciling the actual profit to the budgeted profit.

(40 marks)

2 Suggest possible explanations for any significant variances you have found.

(20 marks)

3 Discuss budgetary control and responsibility accounting in organizations. Include comments on any dangers/limitations inherent in this technique.

(40 marks)
(Total 100 marks)

CASE STUDY 2	Windsurfers of Perth Limited

Windsurfers of Perth Limited makes and sells windsurfing boards in the UK. It buys the board already made (complete with all fittings) but it manufactures the sails and assembles the finished product. It operates a **standard variable costing system** and performs variance analysis on a monthly basis.

	Standard variable cost for one windsurfer
Sailcloth	60 square metres at £7.00 per square metre
Labour	20 hours at £8 per hour
Board	£400
Variable overheads	£50

Windsurfers Limited budgeted to sell 90 units in May at a price of £1,500 each. It estimates that its fixed overheads are £240,000 a year (incurred evenly throughout the year). Variable overheads are absorbed per windsurfer (not per direct labour hour). Opening and closing stocks were zero for May.

The actual performance for May was as follows:

Item	Detail
Sales	81 windsurfers
Revenue	£109,350 total
Sailcloth	4,800 square metres, costing £38,400
Labour	1,540 hours, costing £13,860
Board	£420 per windsurfer
Variable overheads	£3,240 total
Fixed overheads	£21,000 total

Tasks:

a) Perform a variance analysis for May in as much detail as the information will allow. Produce a profit reconciliation statement and comment on your findings.

(70 marks)

b) Windsurfers of Perth Limited holds the purchasing department responsible for the price at which materials are purchased and the manufacturing department responsible for the quantities of materials used. Comment on this policy.

(15 marks)

c) Sometimes, managers blame adverse variances on poor standard setting. Explain how accurate standards can be set and describe the dangers of setting inaccurate standards.

(15 marks)
(Total 100 marks)

Questions

An asterisk * on a question number indicates that the answer is given at the end of the book. Answers to the other questions are given in the Lecturer's Guide.

Q15.1* Welco Ltd

Welco Ltd manufactures one type of hydraulic jack. The labour force, who are all paid at the same rate, assemble and finish two bought-in components. Each jack uses two metal castings and one rubber seal. The jacks are very popular and Welco sells all it can make. It budgets to make a profit of £4,400 each month.

The budget is as follows:

	Standard (1 item)		Budget (1,100 items)
		£	£
Rubber seals	(1 @ £2)	2	2,200
Metal castings	(2 @ £3)	6	6,600
Direct labour	(10 minutes)	1	1,100
Fixed overhead		7	7,700
		16	17,600
Sales revenue		20	22,000
Profit		4	4,400

The £7 fixed overhead consists of production, marketing and administration overheads. It is based on production and sales of 1,100 jacks (the budgeted activity level for each month).

Last month, the actual results were as follows:

Number of jacks made and sold	1,050
	£
Rubber seals (1,060 @ £1.95)	2,067
Metal castings (2,108 @ £3.25)	6,851
Direct labour (190 hours @ £5.90)	1,121
Fixed overhead incurred	7,600
	17,639
Sales revenue (1,050 @ £19)	19,950
Actual profit	2,311

Tasks:

1 Flex the budget to the actual level of activity.
2 Analyse the variances in as much detail as the figures will allow.
3 Create a profit reconciliation statement.

Q15.2* Stanley & Co.

Stanley & Co. manufactures door frames from a bought-in wooden moulding. The budget for one door frame has costs of £20 for materials and £6 for labour. Each frame has a standard usage of 5 metres of wooden moulding at a standard price of £4.00 per metre. Each frame has a standard time of 0.50 hours and the standard rate of pay is £12.00 per hour.

The budget for April was for 2,200 frames with a material cost of £44,000 and a labour cost of £13,200.

However, 2,100 frames were actually produced in April, taking 1,000 hours to make at a total labour cost of £13,000. Also, 11,550 metres of wooden moulding were used at a total cost of £43,890.

Tasks:

1 Calculate the cost, quantity and price variances for materials and labour in April.
2 Suggest possible reasons for these variances.
3 If 50 of the 1,000 hours paid were during a power cut which prevented work continuing, what changes would you make to your answers to tasks 1 and 2?

Q15.3* Ivanblast computer game

Bigcheque Ltd has created a new computer game called Ivanblast. It knows it will only have a five-week period from launch in order to market this successfully before pirating will reduce its sales to virtually zero. The budget for this period is

			£
Sales:	25,000 games	@ £50	= 1,250,000
Production materials:	25,000 blank CDs	@ £1.10	= 27,500
Variable overheads:	25,000 games	@ £0.50	= 12,500
Fixed overheads:		=	800,000
Net profit		=	410,000

(Note that, like many firms with highly automated production facilities, Bigcheque Ltd considers its production labour to be all fixed in nature. So, **all** labour costs are included in the fixed overheads.)

The actual results for the five-week period are shown below (no stocks of raw materials or finished computer games were left over at the end of the period).

			£
Sales:	30,000 games	@ £45	= 1,350,000
Production materials:	30,250 blank CDs	@ £1.00	= 30,250
Variable overheads:		=	15,000
Fixed overheads:		=	850,000
Net profit		=	454,750

Tasks:

1 Prepare a variance analysis for the period in as much detail as the figures allow.
2 Produce a statement reconciling the budgeted profit with the actual profit.
3 Comment on your findings.

Q15.4* Flipside Limited

Flipside Ltd manufactures a single-size lubrication unit for use in wind turbines etc. It operates a standard absorption costing system and uses variance analysis to control its operations. The figures below refer to the year just ended.

Production costs:	Standard costs (1 item)	Original budget (10,000 items) £	Actual results (11,000 items)
Material A	5 kg @ £2.00/kg	100,000	66,000 kg @ £1.50/kg
Material B	10 kg @ £4.00/kg	400,000	99,000 kg @ £5.00/kg
Direct labour	2 hrs @ £15.00/dlh	300,000	20,900 dlh @ £16.00/dlh
Variable overhead	2 hrs @ £3.00/dlh	60,000	20,900 dlh @ £3.00/dlh
Fixed overhead	2 dlh @ £7.00/dlh	140,000	20,900 dlh @ £7.50/dlh

The standard selling price used in the original budget is £150. However, due to increased competition, this was reduced to £139 with effect from the first day of the year. (This revised price remained in operation throughout the year.)

Tasks:

1 Calculate all possible variances from the above information in as much detail as possible.
2 Create a statement reconciling the original budget profit (before all other overheads, e.g. marketing, administration) to the actual profit.
3 Comment on your findings.

Q15.5 Elbo Ltd

Elbo Ltd makes roof tiles. It has two production departments: moulding and packing. It makes two different sizes of tile, the Handi and the Jiant. The following table shows the standard costs of labour per pallet of tiles (one pallet contains 144 tiles):

Department	Labour type	Standard hourly rate £	Standard production hours per pallet Handi	Jiant
Moulding	A	5.00	4	6
Moulding	C	4.00	5	8
Packing	A	5.00	1	2
Packing	B	4.50	2	3

During October, 400 pallets of Handis, and 150 pallets of Jiants were actually produced and the following labour hours and costs were incurred:

Labour type	Moulding department Actual hours worked	Actual pay (£)	Packing department Actual hours worked	Actual pay (£)
A	2,600	12,480	695	3,336
B	–	–	1,250	5,875
C	3,180	12,720	–	–
Totals	5,780	25,200	1,945	9,211

Tasks:

For the month of October:

1 Create the labour budget (hours and £) for (a) Handis, and (b) Jiants.
2 Calculate the budgeted direct labour cost of one pallet of Handis and one pallet of Jiants.
3 Calculate the budgeted total labour cost of each department and of the whole factory.
4 Calculate the direct labour cost variance for each department and for the factory.
5 For each department and labour type, analyse the cost variances into their rate and efficiency variances.
6 Comment on your findings.

Q15.6 Fablus Limited

Fablus Limited makes a single product, the NL. It operates a standard absorption costing system. The budget for 2012 shows sales of 500,000 NLs at £0.25 giving a profit of £12,500.

Standard absorption cost for one unit of NL:

		£
Materials	1 kg plastic @ £0.05/kg	0.050
Direct Labour	15 minutes @ £0.50/h	0.125
Variable Overheads	15 minutes @ £0.10/h	0.025
Fixed Overheads	15 minutes @ £0.10/h	0.025
Standard cost of production		**0.225**

Actual results for 2012:

Number of NLs actually made = 452,000 which were sold at £0.30 each.

Item	Details	Cost £
Materials	480,000 kg	18,000
Direct labour	100,000* hours @ £0.55/h	55,000
Variable overheads		12,000
Fixed overheads		12,000

* Due to a power cut, only 95,000 hours were actually worked.

Required:

Assuming there were no opening or closing stocks, calculate as many variances as the information will allow and present them in the form of an operating statement reconciling the actual and budget profits.

Q15.7* Triform Limited

Triform Limited operates a standard absorption costing system. During last month, it made only one product, the TR2. Using the following information, you are required to calculate as many variances as possible, discuss their causes and reconcile the budgeted profit with the actual profit.

Standard cost card (for one unit of TR2)

		£
Direct materials	4 kg @ £5/kg	20
Direct labour	3 hours @ £7/hour	21
Variable overhead	3 hours @ £3/hour	9
Fixed overhead	3 hours @ £4/hour	12
Standard cost		62
Standard profit margin		14
Standard selling price		76

Budgeted output and sales for last month = 800 units of TR2

Actual results for last month (700 units of TR2 produced and sold)

		£
Sales revenue	700 @ £79	55,300
Direct materials used	3,100 kg @ £4.25/kg	13,175
Direct labour hours worked	2,350 hours @ £6.40/hour	15,040
Variable overhead incurred		6,700
Fixed overhead incurred		9,200

Q15.8 JK plc

JK plc operates a chain of fast-food restaurants. The company uses a standard marginal costing system to monitor the costs incurred in its outlets. The standard cost of one of its most popular meals is as follows:

		£ per meal
Ingredients	(1.08 units)	1.18
Labour	(1.5 minutes)	0.15
Variable conversion costs	(1.5 minutes)	0.06
The standard price of this meal is		1.99

In one of its outlets, which has budgeted sales and production activity level of 50,000 such meals, the number of such meals that were produced and sold during April 2003 was 49,700. The actual cost data was as follows:

		£
Ingredients	(55,000 units)	58,450
Labour	(1,200 hours)	6,800
Variable conversion costs	(1,200 hours)	3,250
The actual revenue from the sale of the meals was		96,480

Required:

(a) Calculate
   (i) the total budgeted contribution for April 2003;
   (ii) the total actual contribution for April 2003.

(3 marks)

(b) Present a statement that reconciles the budgeted and actual contribution for April 2003. Show all variances to the nearest £1 and in as much detail as possible.

(17 marks)

(c) Explain why a marginal costing approach to variance analysis is more appropriate in environments such as that of JK plc, where there are a number of different items being produced and sold.

(5 marks)
(Total = 25 marks)

CIMA Intermediate: Management Accounting – Performance Management, May 2003

Q15.9 TBS

TBS produces two products in a single factory. The following details have been extracted from the standard marginal cost cards of the two products:

Product	S3	S5
	£/unit	£/unit
Selling price	100	135
Variable costs:		
Material X (£3 per kg)	30	39
Liquid Z (£4.50 per litre)	27	45
Direct labour (£6 per hour)	18	24
Overheads	12	16

TBS uses a standard marginal costing system linked with budgets.

Budgeted data for the month of October included:

	S3	S5
Sales (units)	10,000	10,000
Production (units)	12,000	13,500
Fixed costs:		
Production		£51,000
Administration		£34,000

Actual data for the month of October was as follows:

	S3	S5
Sales (units)	12,200	8,350
Production (units)	13,000	9,400
Selling prices per unit	£96	£145
Variable costs:		
Material X	270,000 kg costing	£786,400
Liquid Z	150,000 litres costing	£763,200
Direct labour	73,200 hours costing	£508,350
Overheads		£347,000
Fixed costs:		
Production		£47,550
Administration		£36,870

Required:

a) Calculate the budgeted profit/loss for October.

(2 marks)

b) Calculate the actual profit/loss for October.

(3 marks)

c) As a management accountant in TBS you will be attending the monthly management team meeting. In preparation for that meeting you are required to:

   (i) Prepare a statement that reconciles the budgeted and actual profit/loss for October, showing the variances in as much detail as is possible from the data provided.

(15 marks)

   (ii) State, and then briefly explain, the main issues in your profit reconciliation statement.

(5 marks)

(Total = 25 marks)

CIMA Intermediate: Management Accounting – Performance Management, November 2004

Review questions

1 Explain the basic theory and cyclical nature of budgetary control systems.
2 State the common formulae for cost variances and sub-variances.
3 Discuss the importance of flexing the budget to the actual level of production.
4 Describe the purpose of a profit reconciliation statement.
5 Give examples of the possible relationships between variances.
6 Discuss the additional benefits of budgetary control systems.
7 Explain how the operating costs of budgetary control systems can be managed.
8 Comment on the problems of 'responsibility accounting'.
9 Discuss the limitations of budgetary control systems.
10 List 10 points for good budgetary control.

The answers to all these questions can be found in the text of this chapter.

Answers to end-of-chapter questions

Q5.1 Bodgit Ltd – Solution

	£	Workings	£
1 a) Materials	15	Sales price	50
Direct labour	8	Less: Variable cost	30
Variable overheads	7	Unit contribution	20
Variable cost	**30**		

b) BEP = fixed costs/unit contribution = 3,000/20 = 150 chairs

c) Total contribution = fixed costs + profit
   $200 \times 20 = 3,000 + \text{profit}$
   Profit = £1,000

d) Total contribution = fixed costs + profit
   $N \times 20 = 3,000 + 4,000$
   $N = 7,000/20$
   = 350 chairs

2 a) BEP = fixed costs/unit contribution

Workings	£
Materials	18 (15 × 1.20)
Direct labour	8
Variable overheads	7
Variable cost	33
Sales price	48
Unit contribution	15

   = (3,000 + 1,000)/15
   = 267 chairs

b) Total contribution = fixed costs + profit
   $350 \times 15 = 4,000 + \text{profit}$
   Profit = 5,250 − 4,000
   Profit = £1,250

c) Margin of safety = (actual − BEP)/actual
   = (350 − 267)/350
   = 83/350
   = **24% of sales**

d) Total contribution = fixed costs + profit
   $N \times 15 = 4,000 + 4,000$
   $N = 8,000/15$
   $N = $ **533 chairs**

3 The answers to these questions should be viewed as estimates because the variable costing financial model is based on several assumptions and approximations. For example, total revenue and total cost are shown as straight lines on the breakeven chart. In reality, they are curved as the selling price and total cost *per unit* tend to decrease as the volume of activity increases.

Also, breakeven charts are applicable only to single products (or constant sales mixes of several products). In reality, almost all manufacturers make more than one product. For breakeven purposes this necessitates a theoretical apportionment of the firm's fixed assets between different products. Some degree of approximation and subjectivity is unavoidable in this process.

Q5.2 Concord Toy Company – Solution

Operating Unit 1

Workings

Unit contribution = sales price – variable cost = 2.00 – 1.50 = £0.50
Sales forecast = £800,000/£2 = 400,000 pens

1 $\text{BEP} = \dfrac{\text{fixed costs}}{\text{contribution/Unit}} = \dfrac{£150,000}{£0.5} = 300,000 \text{ units}$

Breakeven point in £ sales = 300,000 × £2/pen = **£600,000**

2 $\text{Margin of safety} = \dfrac{\text{planned sales} - \text{breakeven sales}}{\text{planned sales}} = \dfrac{£800,000 - £600,000}{£800,000}$

$= 25\%$

3 ROCE at 400,000 pens: Profit = total contribution – total fixed cost
$= (400,000 \times £0.50) - 150,000$
$= 50,000$

$\text{ROCE} = \dfrac{50,000}{300,000} = 16.7\%$

4 For 450,000 pens: Total contribution = 450,000 × £0.50 = £225,000
Less total fixed cost   = £150,000
Equals net profit   = **£75,000**

When a firm operates at maximum capacity, problems usually occur due to the lack of 'leeway' or safety margin if anything goes wrong. These problems affect throughput and profitability adversely.

5 Total contribution   = total fixed cost + profit
$N \times$ unit contribution = total fixed cost + profit

$N = \dfrac{\text{total fixed cost} + \text{profit}}{\text{unit contribution}}$

$N = \dfrac{150,000 + 60,000}{£0.50}$

$N = 420,000 \text{ pens}$

6 Possible actions to increase profitability:
   ● Review selling prices in the light of the effects on sales volume of the price elasticity of demand. Price reductions can lead to increased profitability if elasticity is relatively high and price increases can have the opposite effect.
   ● Review the potential for cost reduction in fixed overheads.
   ● Review the potential for cost reduction in variable costs.

Operating Unit 2

1 $\text{ROCE} = \dfrac{700,000}{3,600,000} \times 100 = 19.4\%$

2

	Buggy	**Scooter**	**MP3 player**
Selling price	20	10	10
Variable cost	6	2	4
Unit contribution	14	8	6

Working in 'bundles' of 1 buggy + 1 scooter + 1 MP3 player, the contribution of one 'bundle' = 14 + 6 + 8 = 28

$$\text{BEP} = \frac{\text{total fixed cost}}{\text{unit contribution}} = \frac{2,100,000}{28} = 75,000 \text{ bundles}$$

			£000
BEP occurs at:	75,000 buggies	@ £20 =	1,500
	75,000 scooters	@ £10 =	750
	75,000 MP3 player	@ £10 =	750
	225,000 products		**= 3,000 sales**

3

	Forecast	**−10%**	**−20%**	**Breakeven**
	£000	**£000**	**£000**	**£000**
Sales	4,000	3,600	3,200	3,000
Variable costs	1,200	1,080	960	900
Contribution	2,800	2,520	2,240	2,100
Fixed costs	2,100	2,100	2,100	2,100
Profit	700	420	140	Nil

4 Unit 2 should not drop the MP3 player immediately as it has a positive contribution. If the company does drop the MP3 player, does not use the spare capacity released and fixed costs remain unchanged, its profit will be:

	£
Sales	3,000
Variable costs	800
Contribution	2,200
Fixed costs	2,100
Profit	100

i.e. it will be worse off than it is at present. The MP3 player should not be discontinued unless it can be replaced by a product or products that provide at least £600,000 contribution or unless, by dropping the product, fixed costs can be reduced by at least £600,000. For example, if the MP3 player was dropped 75,000 more scooters would have to be produced and sold to maintain profits at £700,000.

5 The danger is that this 20% price increase will cause a fall in sales volume.
New unit contribution = 12 − 4 = 8
Current total contribution = £600,000
No. of units needed = 600,000/8 = 75,000 units
If the price of the MP3 player was raised to £12, it must sell at least 75,000 units (current volume = 100,000 units) to prevent the company's profit falling below £700,000.

6 Additional information required on the new product would be:
- the selling price per unit;
- the variable cost per unit;
- the contribution per unit;
- the expected unit sales per year;
- the length of the contract;
- the cost of the new plant;
- the residual value of the new plant;
- the life of the new plant;
- the annual depreciation charge of the new plant;
- the rate of interest on the bank loan.

Q5.3 Rover's 'last chance saloon' – Solution

1 Retail price = 22,000
Trade price = 16,500 (22,000 × 75%)
Rover's total cost price = 13,200 (16,500 × 80%)
At BEP, total contribution = total fixed costs
(Unit contribution × 140,000) = total fixed costs

a) Variable cost = 6,600 (13,200 × 50%)
Selling price = 16,500
Unit contribution = 9,900
Total fixed costs = **£1,386,000,000** (140,000 × 9,900)
= **£3,800,000/day**

b) Variable cost = 8,580 (13,200 × 65%)
Selling price = 16,500
Unit contribution = 7,920
Total fixed costs = **£1,109,000,000** (140,000 × 7,920)
= **£3,000,000/day**

c) Variable cost = 10,560 (13,200 × 80%)
Selling price = 16,500
Unit contribution = 5,940
Total fixed costs = **£832,000,000** (140,000 × 5,940)
= **£2,300,000/day**

2 Total contribution = total fixed cost + profit
$N \times 7,920 = 1,109,000,000 + 100,000,000$
$N = 1,209,000,000/7,920$
$N = 152,652$ cars

3   £

Total contribution = 200,000 × £7,920 = 1,584,000,000
Less: Total fixed cost   = 1,109,000,000
Profit   = £475,000,000

4 Profit = £10,000,000,000 × 20% = £2,000,000,000
Total contribution = total fixed cost + profit
$$N \times 7,920 = 1,109,000,000 + 2,000,000,000$$
$$N = 3,109,000,000/7,920$$
$$N = 392,551 \text{ cars}$$

Q6.1 Burgabar Corporation – Solution

£000	West Ham	Hackney	Forest Gate	Mile End	Total
Sales	100	120	120	140	480
Variable costs	20	24	24	28	96
Contribution	80	96	96	112	384
Salaries & wages	32	32	34	34	132
Fixed costs	30	30	32	34	126
Head office	20	24	24	28	96
Total fixed costs	82	86	90	96	354
Profit	(2)	10	6	16	30

If West Ham is closed and fixed costs remain unchanged (except as stated in question):

For Burgabar Group:	£000	£000
Total contribution (96 + 96 + 112)		304
Total fixed costs	354	
Less West Ham's salaries & wages	(32)	
Less reduction in head office costs	(10)	
Add redundancy pay	8	
Revised total fixed cost		320
Revised group loss for next year		(16)

Advice: The immediate closure of the West Ham branch would lose the group £46,000 in the next year. It would turn a group profit of £30,000 into a loss of £16,000.

If head office costs could be reduced by £10,000 without closing West Ham, all the branches would show a profit if sales remained the basis of apportionment for head office charges.

A positive strategy would be to aim to increase West Ham's annual sales from £100,000 to £105,000. This 5% increase would increase West Ham's contribution to £84,000 and turn its £2,000 loss into a £2,000 profit. Also, group profit would increase from £30,000 to £34,000.

The best option is to pursue a sales drive at West Ham (and possibly at the other branches at the same time) aimed at a minimum 5% improvement. The worst thing Burgabar could do is to close the West Ham branch immediately.

Q6.2 Profoot Ltd – Solution

1 Current year

	P1	P2	
Variable costs per pair:	£	£	
Materials	15.00	15.00	
Labour – Machining (£8/hour)	2.00	2.00	
– Assembly (£7/hour)	3.50	3.50	
– Packing (£6/hour)	0.50	0.50	
Total unit variable cost	21.00	21.00	
Selling price	40.00	40.00	
Unit contribution	19.00	19.00	
Annual sales demand (pairs)	14,000	10,000	
Total contribution	£266,000	£190,000	£456,000
Less: Total fixed costs			£300,000
Net profit			**£156,000**

2 Next year – full demand met

	P1	P2	PDL
Variable costs per pair:	£	£	£
Materials	15.00	20.00	32.50
Labour – Machining (£8/hour)	2.00	4.00	4.00
– Assembly (£7/hour)	3.50	3.50	7.00
– Packing (£6/hour)	0.50	0.50	0.50
Total unit variable cost	21.00	28.00	44.00
Selling price	40.00	50.00	65.00
Unit contribution	19.00	22.00	21.00
Order of preference	3	1	2
Annual sales demand (pairs)	14,000	7,000	5,000
Total contribution – per type	£266,000	£154,000	£105,000
– per total			£525,000
Less: Total fixed costs (£300,000 × 1.02)			£306,000
Net profit			**£219,000**

3 Next year – maximum of 8,500 machine hours

	P1	P2	PDL
Unit contribution	19.00	22.00	21.00
Machine hours/pair	0.25	0.50	0.50
Unit contribution/machine hour	76.00	44.00	42.00
Order of preference	1	2	3
Production*	**14,000**	**7,000**	**3,000**
Total contribution – per type	£266,000	£154,000	£63,000
– total			£483,000
Less: Total fixed costs (£300,000 × 1.02)			£306,000
Net profit			**£177,000**

* Production workings:

Preference	Model	Demand	Mh/pair	Total mh	Cum. mh
1	P1	14,000	0.25	3,500	3,500
2	P2	7,000	0.50	3,500	7,000
3	PDL	3,000	0.50	1,500	8,500

4 Additional machine

Shortfall in production of PDLs = 5,000 − 3,000 = 2,000 pairs
Shortfall in machine hours   = 2,000 × 0.50 = 1,000 mh

This is within the capacity of the new machine. So purchasing the machine will allow the shortfall to be eliminated.

Total extra contribution from machine = 2,000 pairs × £21 = £42,000
But, additional fixed cost depreciation = 420,000/10 = £42,000
Thus, net effect on profit   = nil

Q6.3 King & Co. – Solution

Budget

	Total cost £000	Fixed cost £000	Variable cost £000
Manufacturing	3,000	2,000	1,000
Sales & admin	1,500	1,000	500
Total	4,500	3,000	1,500

	Total £000	Unit £
Sales commission (@ 5%)	250	0.25
Other variable costs	1,250	1.25
All variable costs	1,500	1.50
Sales revenue	5,000	5.00
Contribution	3,500	3.50

Contract

	Unit £	Total £000
Other variable cost	1.25	62.5
Badge	0.50	25.0
All variable costs	1.75	87.5
Sales revenue	4.00	200.0
Contribution	2.25	112.5

Comment: As all fixed overheads will be recovered by the budgeted sales, the contribution from this one-off contract will translate directly into profit. The managing director's rejection of this contract will lose the company £112,500.

The breakeven price would be the variable cost of £87,500 (£1.75 a cap). So King & Co. would make a healthy profit even at a price of half the amount offered. The managing director should think again.

Q7.1 Burton Brothers – Solution

Assuming the machine is sold to Bridge & Co.

Item	Cash	Avoidable	Future	Note	Amount	Relevant in/(out)
Owing by Wey	Y	Y	N	1	(590 – 180 – 150) = 260	–
Costs to date	Y	N	N	2	£273,480	–
Completion: direct labour	Y	Y	Y	3	2,000 × (10 – 4)	(12,000)
Completion: contracted materials	Y	Y	Y	4	24,000 – 6,000	(18,000)
Completion: regularly used materials	Y	Y	Y	5	204,000/4	(51,000)
Completion: materials not regularly used	Y	Y	Y	3	204 – 24 – 51	(129,000)
Completion: production overheads	N	N	Y	6	2,000 × £88	–
Additions: materials	Y	Y	Y	5	45,000 – 13,500	(31,500)
Additions: substitute materials	Y	Y	Y	7		(12,000)
Additions: direct labour	Y	Y	Y	3	400 × (10 – 4)	(2,400)
Additions: production overheads	N	N	Y	6	400 × £88	–
Scrap value of machine as it stands	Y	Y	Y	7		(6,000)
Selling price to Bridge & Co.	Y	Y	Y	3		400,000
Net relevant cash flow in/(out)						**£138,100**

Notes:
1 This income will not now happen; it is not a future item.
2 Sunk cost.
3 Avoidable.
4 Committed cost, effectively of £6,000; other £18,000 is avoidable.
5 Replacement cost.
6 Non-cash item.
7 Opportunity cost.

Advice: Although Bridge & Co.'s offer of £400,000 is much less than the £590,000 agreed by Wey Ltd, despite the extra modifications Burton Brothers will be £138,100 better off in cash terms if it accepts it.

Q7.2 Eezikum – Solution

Item	Cash	Avoidable	Future	Note	Amount	Relevant in/(out)
UK cancellation fees	Y	Y	Y	1	11 × £10,000	(110,000)
UK lost fees	Y	Y	Y	1	11 × £15,000	(165,000)
UK out-of-pocket expenses	Y	Y	Y	2	11 × £2,500	27,500
New equipment	Y	Y	Y	1	100,000 – 40,000	(60,000)
Lost interest on deposit a/c	Y	Y	Y	3	100,000 × 9/12 × 12%	(9,000)
US fees	Y	Y	Y	2	125 × £10,000	1,250,000
US out-of-pocket expenses	Y	Y	Y	1	125 × 2,000	(250,000)
Airfares	Y	Y	Y	1	2 × £14,500	(29,000)
Health insurance	Y	Y	Y	1		(6,000)
Travel insurance	Y	N	Y	4		–
Net cash flow in/(out)						**£648,500**

Notes:
1 Avoidable cost.
2 Avoidable income.
3 Opportunity cost.
4 Sunk cost.

The net benefit of accepting the US tour is £648,500.

Q7.3 Carbotest Corporation – Solution

Item	Cash	Avoidable	Future	Note	Amount	Relevant in/(out)
Contract price		Y	Y	Y		152,000
Components – 35,000	Y	Y	Y	1	$35,000 \times £3$	(105,000)
– 5,000	Y	Y	Y	2	$5,000 \times £1$	(5,000)
– scrap value	Y	Y	Y	3		(1,000)
Harness	Y	Y	Y	4	$1,000 \times £9$	(9,000)
Skilled labour – pay	Y	N	Y	5		–
– abandoned work	Y	Y	Y	6	60,000 – 48,000	(12,000)
Supervision	Y	N	Y	7		–
Machines – depreciation	N	N	Y	8		–
– resale value	Y	Y	Y	9		(5,000)
– lease costs	Y	Y	Y	10	$6 \times £500$	(3,000)
Accommodation	Y	N	N	11		–
– planning permission						
Temporary building	Y	Y	Y	12	£8,000 + £2,000	(10,000)
Car park – construction cost	Y	N	Y	13		–
Fixed overheads	N	N	Y	14		–
Net cash flow						**£2,000**

Notes:
1 Replacement cost.
2 Modification cost.
3 Opportunity cost.
4 All at replacement cost as harness is already in regular use.
5 Unavoidable cost, will be paid irrespective of decision.
6 Lost cash contribution = opportunity cost.
7 Unavoidable, permanent employee.
8 Non-cash expense.
9 Opportunity cost.
10 Replacement cost.
11 Committed cost.
12 Construction and demolition costs.
13 Postponed, not avoided.
14 Non-cash, unavoidable.

Note that net cash inflow of £2,000 is very close to breakeven. Are the effort and risk involved worth it? Suppose unforeseen difficulties appear. To what extent will the postponement of the car park demotivate employees? On balance, I would **not** recommend acceptance of the contract.

Q9.1 Lewington Ltd – Solution

Workings

	Cutting	Assembly	Finishing
OAR/mh	$\dfrac{1,600,000}{40,000}$	$\dfrac{2,000,000}{25,000}$	$\dfrac{1,400,000}{14,000}$
	= £40/mh	= £80/mh	= £100/mh
OAR/dlh	$\dfrac{1,600,000}{10,000}$	$\dfrac{2,000,000}{40,000}$	$\dfrac{1,400,000}{20,000}$
	= £160/dlh	= £50/dlh	= £70/dlh

1 **Machine hour rates**   £

Direct materials   3,300
Direct labour   4,500
Prime cost   7,800
Production overheads:
    Cutting   50 mh × £40/mh   = 2,000
    Assembly 25 mh × £80/mh   = 2,000
    Finishing 10 mh × £100/mh = 1,000
                                                                       5,000
Production cost   **12,800**   Cost/unit = **£42.67**

2 **Direct labour hour rates**   £

Direct materials   3,300
Direct labour   4,500
Prime cost   7,800
Production overheads:
    Cutting   20 dlh × £160/dlh = 3,200
    Assembly 45 dlh × £50/dlh   = 2,250
    Finishing 20 dlh × £70/dlh   = 1,400
                                                                       6,850
Production cost   **14,650**   Cost/unit = **£48.83**

3 **Mixed rates**   £

Direct materials   3,300
Direct labour   4,500
Prime cost   7,800
Production overheads:
    Cutting   50 mh × £40/mh = 2,000
    Assembly 45 dlh × £50/dlh = 2,250
    Finishing 20 dlh × £70/dlh = 1,400
                                                                       5,650
Production cost   **13,450**   Cost/unit = **£44.83**

4 *Comment*: The choice of OAR makes a significant difference to the production cost (over 10% in this case). This illustrates the approximate nature of absorption costing.

Q9.2 Graham and Sara – Solution

1 a) Direct material cost

	Men's £000	Women's £000	Total £000
Materials	78	26	104
Direct labour	18	30	48
Variable overheads	4	4	8
Variable production cost	100	60	160
Fixed production overheads	12	4	16
Total production cost	112	64	176
Increase in stock	2	1	3
Cost of sales	110	63	173
Marketing overheads	8	4	12
Administration overheads	4	4	8
Total cost	122	71	193
Sales revenue	118	78	196
Profit/(loss)	(4)	7	3

b) Direct labour cost

	Men's £000	Women's £000	Total £000
Materials	78	26	104
Direct labour	18	30	48
Variable overheads	4	4	8
Variable production cost	100	60	160
Fixed production overheads	6	10	16
Total production cost	106	70	176
Increase in stock	2	1	3
Cost of sales	104	69	173
Marketing overheads	8	4	12
Administration overheads	4	4	8
Total cost	116	77	193
Sales revenue	118	78	196
Profit/(loss)	2	1	3

c) Variable overhead cost

	Men's £000	Women's £000	Total £000
Materials	78	26	104
Direct labour	18	30	48
Variable overheads	4	4	8
Variable production cost	100	60	160
Fixed production overheads	8	8	16
Total production cost	108	68	176
Increase in stock	2	1	3
Cost of sales	106	67	173
Marketing overheads	8	4	12
Administration overheads	4	4	8
Total cost	118	75	193
Sales revenue	118	78	196
Profit/(loss)	–	3	3

2 Summary of alternative profit/(loss) (£000)

	Men's	Women's	Total
Variable production cost	(2)	5	3
Direct material cost	(4)	7	3
Direct labour cost	2	1	3
Variable overhead cost	–	3	3

These results show the arbitrary nature of the absorption costing system regarding the internal distribution of overheads between departments/products. Note that the overall total figure is not affected.

The objective of the absorption costing system is to ensure all the production overheads are absorbed. It is **not** primarily concerned with '**accurate**' (in the sense of 'caused by') product or departmental costs.

Q9.3 Stellar Showers – Solution

Table showing apportionments and allocations

	Moulding	Assembly	Packaging	Q. control	Stores	Total
M/c electr.	30,000	8,000	2,000	–	–	40,000
Stores	–	–	–	–	80,000	80,000
Heating	2,400	4,200	4,000	200	2,200	13,000
Lighting	600	1,600	1,000	100	700	4,000
Superv'n*	20,000	25,000	20,000	–	–	65,000
Prod. mgr	4,000	28,500	2,500	–	–	35,000
Bus. rates	2,400	6,400	4,000	400	2,800	16,000
Fire ins.	4,400	3,600	1,800	–	200	10,000
QC pay	–	–	–	30,000	–	30,000
Depr'n	7,500	6,000	3,000	–	1,500	18,000
Total	71,300	83,300	38,300	30,700	87,400	311,000
Qual. con.	5,117	15,350	5,117	(30,700)	5,116	–
Total	76,417	98,650	43,417	–	92,516	311,000
Stores	9,252	67,074	16,190	–	(92,516)	–
Total	85,669	165,724	59,607	–	–	311,000

* Allocated.

1

	Moulding	Assembly	Packaging
Overhead absorption rate	$\frac{85,669}{34,967}$	$\frac{165,724}{63,986}$	$\frac{59,607}{10,998}$
	£2.45/mh	£2.59/dlh	£5.42/dlh

2 Batch of 800 SS40Ts:

Moulding	$1,500 \times 2.45 =$	3,675
Assembly	$3,500 \times 2.59 =$	9,065
Packaging	$1,000 \times 5.42 =$	5,420
Direct materials	$=$	16,000
Direct labour	$=$	8,800
		42,960

Unit production cost $= £42,960/800 = $ **£53.70**

Workings

Apportionment of machine electricity (total cost £40,000):
Most **rational** basis of apportionment is 'wattage'. Total wattage $= 6,000$

	Moulding	Assembly	Packaging	Q. con.	Stores	Total
Proportion	$\dfrac{4,500}{6,000}$	$\dfrac{1,200}{6,000}$	$\dfrac{300}{6,000}$	–	–	$\dfrac{6,000}{6,000}$
	15/20	4/20	1/20	–	–	20/20
Overhead cost	£40,000	£40,000	£40,000	–	–	£40,000
Apportionment	**£30,000**	**£8,000**	**£2,000**	–	–	**£40,000**

Apportionment of production manager's pay (total cost £35,000):
Most **rational** basis of apportionment is 'added value'. Total added value $= £7.0$ million

	Moulding	Assembly	Packaging	Q. con.	Stores	Total
Proportion	$\dfrac{0.8}{7.0}$	$\dfrac{5.7}{7.0}$	$\dfrac{0.5}{7.0}$	–	–	$\dfrac{7.0}{7.0}$
	8/70	57/70	5/70	–	–	70/70
Overhead cost	£35,000	£35,000	£35,000	–	–	£35,000
Apportionment	**£4,000**	**£28,500**	**£2,500**	–	–	**£35,000**

Apportionment of business rates (total cost £16,000):
Most **rational** basis of apportionment is 'area'. Total area $= 2,000$ sq. m

	Moulding	Assembly	Packaging	Q. con.	Stores	Total
Proportion	$\dfrac{300}{2,000}$	$\dfrac{800}{2,000}$	$\dfrac{500}{2,000}$	$\dfrac{50}{2,000}$	$\dfrac{350}{2,000}$	$\dfrac{2,000}{2,000}$
	6/40	16/40	10/40	1/40	7/40	40/40
Overhead cost	£16,000	£16,000	£16,000	£16,000	£16,000	£16,000
Apportionment	**£2,400**	**£6,400**	**£4,000**	**£400**	**£2,800**	**£16,000**

Apportionment of lighting (total cost £4,000):
Most **rational** basis of apportionment is 'area'. Total area $= 2,000$ sq. m

	Moulding	Assembly	Packaging	Q. con.	Stores	Total
Proportion	$\dfrac{300}{2,000}$	$\dfrac{800}{2,000}$	$\dfrac{500}{2,000}$	$\dfrac{50}{2,000}$	$\dfrac{350}{2,000}$	$\dfrac{2,000}{2,000}$
	6/40	16/40	10/40	1/40	7/40	40/40
Overhead cost	£4,000	£4,000	£4,000	£4,000	£4,000	£4,000
Apportionment	**£600**	**£1,600**	**£1,000**	**£100**	**£700**	**£4,000**

Apportionment of heating oil (total cost £13,000):
Most **rational** basis of apportionment is 'volume'. Total volume = 6,500 cu. m

	Moulding	Assembly	Packaging	Q. con.	Stores	Total
Proportion	$\dfrac{1,200}{6,500}$	$\dfrac{2,100}{6,500}$	$\dfrac{2,000}{6,500}$	$\dfrac{100}{6,500}$	$\dfrac{1,100}{6,500}$	$\dfrac{6,500}{6,500}$
	12/65	21/65	20/65	1/65	11/65	65/65
Overhead cost	£13,000	£13,000	£13,000	£13,000	£13,000	£13,000
Apportionment	**£2,400**	**£4,200**	**£4,000**	**£200**	**£2,200**	**£13,000**

Apportionment of fire insurance (total cost £10,000):
Most **rational** basis of apportionment is 'WDV'. Total WDV = £50,000

	Moulding	Assembly	Packaging	Q. con.	Stores	Total
Proportion	$\dfrac{22,000}{50,000}$	$\dfrac{18,000}{50,000}$	$\dfrac{9,000}{50,000}$	–	$\dfrac{1,000}{50,000}$	$\dfrac{50,000}{50,000}$
	22/50	18/50	9/50	–	1/50	50/50
Overhead cost	£10,000	£10,000	£10,000	–	£10,000	£10,000
Apportionment	**£4,400**	**£3,600**	**£1,800**	**–**	**£200**	**£10,000**

Apportionment of depreciation (total cost £18,000):
Most **rational** basis of apportionment is 'fixed asset cost'. Total FA cost = £120,000

	Moulding	Assembly	Packaging	Q. con.	Stores	Total
Proportion	$\dfrac{50}{120}$	$\dfrac{40}{120}$	$\dfrac{20}{120}$	–	$\dfrac{10}{120}$	$\dfrac{120}{120}$
	5/12	4/12	2/12	–	1/12	12/12
Overhead cost	£18,000	£18,000	£18,000	–	£18,000	£18,000
Apportionment	**£7,500**	**£6,000**	**£3,000**	**–**	**£1,500**	**£18,000**

Apportionment of quality control (total cost £30,700):
Most **rational** basis of apportionment is 'QC work hours'. Total hours = (40 − 4) = 36

	Moulding	Assembly	Packaging	Q. con.	Stores	Total
Proportion	$\dfrac{6}{36}$	$\dfrac{18}{36}$	$\dfrac{6}{36}$	–	$\dfrac{6}{36}$	$\dfrac{36}{36}$
	1/6	3/6	1/6	–	1/6	6/6
Overhead cost	£30,700	£30,700	£30,700	–	£30,700	£30,700
Apportionment	**£5,117**	**£15,350**	**£5,117**	**–**	**£5,116**	**£30,700**

Apportionment of stores costs (total cost £92,516):
Most **rational** basis of apportionment is 'issues'. Total issues = 20,000

	Moulding	Assembly	Packaging	Q. con.	Stores	Total
Proportion	$\dfrac{2,000}{20,000}$	$\dfrac{14,500}{20,000}$	$\dfrac{3,500}{20,000}$	–	–	$\dfrac{20,000}{20,000}$
	4/40	29/40	7/40	–	–	40/40
Overhead cost	£92,516	£92,516	£92,516	–	–	£92,516
Apportionment	**£9,252**	**£67,074**	**£16,190**	**–**	**–**	**£92,516**

Q11.1 Clamco – Solution

Workings

January	
Direct labour	120,000
Direct materials	90,000
Variable production overhead	18,000
Variable cost	228,000
Fixed production overhead	72,000
Absorption cost	300,000

Variable cost/unit = £228,000/6,000 units = £38/unit
Absorption cost/unit = £300,000/6,000 units = £50/unit
Fixed production overhead/unit = £72,000/6,000 units = £12/unit

Physical stock changes (number of units)

	Jan	Feb	Mar	Qtr
Opening stock	0	2,000	1,000	0
Actual production	6,000	5,000	7,000	18,000
Actual sales	4,000	6,000	7,000	17,000
Closing stock	2,000	1,000	1,000	1,000

1 a) Absorption costing (£000) (abs. prod. cost = £50/unit)

	Jan	Feb	Mar	Qtr
Opening stock	0	100	50	0
Add: Production cost	300	250	350	900
Less: Closing stock	100	50	50	50
Under/(over)absorption	0	12	(12)	0
Cost of sales	200	312	338	850
Sales revenue	256	384	448	1,088
Gross profit	56	72	110	238
Non-production overhead	25	25	25	75
Net profit	**31**	**47**	**85**	**163**

b) Variable costing (£000) (var. prod. cost = £38/unit)

	Jan	Feb	Mar	Qtr
Opening stock	0	76	38	0
Add: Production cost	228	190	266	684
Less: Closing stock	76	38	38	38
Cost of sales	152	228	266	646
Sales revenue	256	384	448	1,088
Gross profit	104	156	182	442
Production overheads	72	72	72	216
Non-production overhead	25	25	25	75
Total fixed overheads	97	97	97	291
Net profit	**7**	**59**	**85**	**151**

2 Reconciliation of profits (£000)

	Jan	Feb	Mar	Qtr
Absorption net profit	31	47	85	163
Variable net profit	7	59	85	151
Difference	**24**	**(12)**	**–**	**12**
Increase in stock (units)	2,000	(1,000)	–	1,000
Production overheads in stock				
increase (@ £12 a unit)	24	(12)	–	12

Q11.2 Rivilin plc – Solution

Workings

	£/unit
Variable production cost	20 – variable costing production and stock value
Fixed production cost	12 – £9,600/800 units – planned absorption rate
Absorption production cost	32 – absorption costing production and stock value

Stock movements (units)

	April	May	June
Opening stock	–	–	50
Production	800	750	820
Sales	(800)	(700)	(850)
Closing stock	–	50	20
Change in level	–	+50	–30

1 Variable costing profit statement (£)

	April	May	June
Opening stock	–	–	1,000
Production (@ £20)	16,000	15,000	16,400
Less: Closing stock	–	1,000	400
Cost of sales	16,000	14,000	17,000
Sales (@ £60)	48,000	42,000	51,000
Gross profit	32,000	28,000	34,000
Less: Production overheads	9,600	9,600	9,600
Less: Non-production overheads	10,000	10,000	10,000
Net profit	12,400	8,400	14,400

2 Absorption costing profit statement (£)

	April	May	June
Opening stock	–	–	1,600
Production (@ £32)	25,600	24,000	26,240
Less: Closing stock	–	1,600	640
Cost of sales	25,600	22,400	27,200
Under/(over)recovery of fixed production overheads	–	(50 × £12) 600	(20 × £12) (240)

Adjusted cost of sales	25,600	23,000	26,960
Sales (@ £60)	48,000	42,000	51,000
Gross profit	22,400	19,000	24,040
Less: Non-production overheads	10,000	10,000	10,000
Net profit	12,400	9,000	14,040

3 Explanation of profit differences

April – no stock movement – identical profits
May – stock increase – absorption profits higher by £600 (50 × £12)
June – stock decrease – absorption profits lower by £360 (30 × £12)

Q11.3 The Valley Fireworks Corporation – Solution

Workings

Direct labour	180
Direct materials	60
Variable production overhead	10
Variable cost	250
Fixed production overhead	80
Absorption cost	330

Fixed production overhead/unit = £96,000/1,200 units = £80/unit
Underabsorption = (1,200 – 1,100) units × £80/unit fixed overhead = £8,000

Physical stock changes (number of units)

	Q1	Q2	Q3	Q4	Year
Opening stock	10	290	550	690	10
Actual production	300	300	200	300	1,100
Actual sales	20	40	60	980	1,100
Closing stock	290	550	690	10	10

1 a) Absorption costing (£000) (abs. prod. cost = £330/unit)

	Q1	Q2	Q3	Q4	Year
Opening stock	3,300	95,700	181,500	227,700	3,300
Add: Production cost	99,000	99,000	66,000	99,000	363,000
Less: Closing stock	95,700	181,500	227,700	3,300	3,300
Under/(over)absorption	–	–	8,000	–	8,000
Cost of sales	6,600	13,200	27,800	323,400	371,000
Sales revenue	10,000	20,000	30,000	490,000	550,000
Gross profit	3,400	6,800	2,200	166,600	179,000
Non-production overhead – fixed	36,000	36,000	36,000	36,000	144,000
– variable @ £20	400	800	1,200	19,600	22,000
Net profit	(33,000)	(30,000)	(35,000)	111,000	13,000

b) Variable costing (£000) (var. prod. cost = £250/unit)

	Q1	Q2	Q3	Q4	Year
Opening stock	2,500	72,500	137,500	172,500	2,500
Add: Production cost	75,000	75,000	50,000	75,000	275,000
Less: Closing stock	72,500	137,500	172,500	2,500	2,500
Cost of sales	5,000	10,000	15,000	245,000	275,000
Sales revenue	10,000	20,000	30,000	490,000	550,000
Gross profit	5,000	10,000	15,000	245,000	275,000
Production overheads – fixed	24,000	24,000	24,000	24,000	96,000
Variable non-production overhead	400	800	1,200	19,600	22,000
Fixed non-production overhead	36,000	36,000	36,000	36,000	144,000
Net profit	(55,400)	(50,800)	(46,200)	165,400	13,000

2 Reconciliation of profits (£000)

	Q1	Q2	Q3	Q4	Year
Absorption net profit	(33,000)	(30,000)	(35,000)	111,000	13,000
Variable net profit	(55,400)	(50,800)	(46,200)	165,400	13,000
Difference	**22,400**	**20,800**	**11,200**	**(54,400)**	–
Increase in stock (units)	280	260	140	(680)	–
Production overhead in stock increase (@ £80/unit)	**22,400**	**20,800**	**11,200**	**(54,400)**	–
Net profit using variable costing	(55,400)	(50,800)	(46,200)	165,400	13,000
Adjustment for fixed production overheads in stock change	22,400	20,800	11,200	(54,400)	–
Net profit using absorption costing	(33,000)	(30,000)	(35,000)	111,000	13,000

3 The profit figures derived from variable costing give a realistic view of performance for each period as they do not carry forward any fixed production overheads incurred in one period to the next. This enables managers to monitor performance and to create useful internal reports.

The profit figures derived from absorption costing are created using the basic rule for the treatment of fixed production overheads which has to be followed for external reporting purposes. It enables managers to monitor the cumulative profits which will ultimately be used by the owners of the business to judge the performance of its managers.

Q14.1 Kellaway Ltd – Solution

1 Production budget

Production = sales + closing stock – opening stock

	Large	Medium	Small
Sales	4,000	5,000	3,500
+ Closing stock	400	300	150
– Opening stock	(300)	(400)	(200)
= Production	**4,100**	**4,900**	**3,450**

2 Unit production costs

	Large	Medium	Small
Direct labour:			
Fitters/turners	$1.25 \times 10 = 12.50$	$0.90 \times 10 = 9.00$	$0.80 \times 10 = 8.00$
Assemblers/packers	$0.40 \times 6 = 2.40$	$0.25 \times 6 = 1.50$	$0.20 \times 6 = 1.20$
Direct materials:			
Aluminium	$2.5 \times 3 = 7.50$	$1.0 \times 3 = 3.00$	$0.5 \times 3 = 1.50$
Packaging	$1.25 \times 1 = 1.25$	$0.75 \times 1 = 0.75$	$0.5 \times 1 = 0.50$
Production overhead*	$1.65 \times 2.00 = 3.30$	$1.15 \times 2.00 = 2.30$	$1.00 \times 2.00 = 2.00$
Unit production cost	**£26.95**	**£16.55**	**£13.20**

Total dlh = 4,100(1.25 + 0.40) + 4,900(0.90 + 0.25) + 3,450(0.80 + 0.20)
= 6,765 + 5,635 + 3,450 = 15,850
* Overhead absorption rate = £31,700/15,850 = £2.00/dlh.

3 Materials usage quantity budget

	Large	Medium	Small	Total
Aluminium	$2.5 \times 4,100 = 10,250$	$1.0 \times 4,900 = 4,900$	$0.5 \times 3,450 = 1,725$	**16,875 strips**
Packaging	$1.25 \times 4,100 = 5,125$	$0.75 \times 4,900 = 3,675$	$0.50 \times 3,450 = 1,725$	**10,525 metres**

Materials usage cost budget
Aluminium = 16,875 strips @ £3 = £50,625
Packaging = 10,525 metres @ £1 = £10,525

4 Materials purchases budget

	Aluminium (strips)	Packaging (metres)
Usage	16,875	10,525
+ Closing stock	150	50
– Opening stock	(220)	(80)
= Purchases	**16,805**	**10,495**
	@ £3	@ £1
Purchases	**£50,415**	**£10,495**

5 Direct labour budget

F/T = Fitters/Turners
A/P = Assemblers/Packers

	Large	Medium	Small	Total
F/T	$4,100 \times 1.25 = 5,125$	$4,900 \times 0.9 = 4,410$	$3,450 \times 0.8 = 2,760$	12,295 dlh
A/P	$4,100 \times 0.4 = 1,640$	$4,900 \times 0.25 = 1,225$	$3,450 \times 0.2 = 690$	3,555 dlh

F/T 12,295 @ £10.00 = £122,950
A/P 3,555 @ £6.00 = £21,330

Q14.2 Pierce Pommery – Solution

1 Production budget

Production = sales + closing stock − opening stock

000 litres	Sept	Oct	Nov	Qtr	Dec
Sales	340	300	260	900	320
Closing stock	60	52	64	64	50
Opening stock	80	60	52	80	64
Production	**320**	**292**	**272**	**884**	**306**

Purchases budget

Production = sales + closing stock − opening stock

Tonnes	Sept	Oct	Nov	Qtr	Dec
Usage	4,800	4,380	4,080	13,260	4,590
Closing stock	2,190	2,040	2,295	2,295	
Opening stock	2,200	2,190	2,040	2,200	
Purchases	**4,790**	**4,230**	**4,335**	**13,355**	
Cost/tonne	£50	£50	£150	£150	
Purchases (£)	**239,500**	**211,500**	**650,250**	**1,101,250**	

2 Cash budget

	Workings	November
Cash sales	Nov 260,000 × £3 × 25%	195,000
Credit sales	Oct 300,000 × £3 × 75%	675,000
Total in		870,000
Apple purchases	from September	239,500
Direct labour	272,000 × £0.20	54,400
Overheads (excl. depreciation)	from October	25,000
Total out		318,900
Cash in/(out)		551,100
Opening balance		(495,900)
Closing balance		**55,200**

Q14.3 Norman Ropes – Solution

Period	Norman Ropes – Model answer						
	1	2	3	4	5	6	7
a) Production budget (metres of rope)							
Add: Sales	3,000	4,000	5,000	4,000	6,000	6,000	8,000
Less: Opening stock	1,500	1,000	1,250	1,000	1,500	1,500	2,000
Add: Closing stock	1,000	1,250	1,000	1,500	1,500	2,000	1,750
Production (metres)	**2,500**	**4,250**	**4,750**	**4,500**	**6,000**	**6,500**	**7,750**
b) Materials usage cost budget							
Usage (metres of ARN)	250,000	425,000	475,000	450,000	600,000	650,000	775,000
Cost (£)	**10,000**	**17,000**	**19,000**	**18,000**	**24,000**	**26,000**	**31,000**
c) Materials purchases cost budget							
Add: Cost of materials used	10,000	17,000	19,000	18,000	24,000	26,000	31,000
Less: Opening stock	5,000	4,250	4,750	4,500	6,000	6,500	7,750
Add: Closing stock	4,250	4,750	4,500	6,000	6,500	7,750	
Purchases (£)	**9,250**	**17,500**	**18,750**	**19,500**	**24,500**	**27,250**	

Q15.1 Welco Ltd – Solution

1 Flexed budget (1,050 units)

	£
Seals (1,050 @ £2)	2,100
Castings (2,100 @ £3)	6,300
Labour ((1,050/6) h @ £6)	1,050
Fixed overheads	7,700
Total costs	17,150
Revenue (1,050 @ £20)	21,000
Profit	3,850

2 Materials variances

	Seals		**Castings**	
Usage:				
	(BQ – AQ)BP		(BQ – AQ)BP	
	(1,050 – 1,060)2		(2,100 – 2,108)3	
	–20	= 20 A	–24	= 24 A
Price:				
	(BP – AP)AQ		(BP – AP)AQ	
	(2.00 – 1.95)1,060		(3.00 – 3.25)2,108	
	+53	= 53 F	–527	= 527 A
Cost:				
	Budget cost – actual cost		Budget cost – actual cost	
	2,100 – 2,067		6,300 – 6,851	
	+33	= 33 F	–551	= 551 A

Direct labour variances

Efficiency: (BQ − AQ)BP = (175 − 190)6 = −90 = **90 A**
Rate: (BP − AP)AQ = (6.00 − 5.90)190 = +19 = **19 F**
Cost: Budget cost − actual cost = 1,050 − 1,121 = −71 = **71 A**

Fixed overhead variance

Cost: Budget FO − actual FO = 7,700 − 7,600 = +100 = **100 F**

Sales variances

Price: (AP − BP)AQ = (19 − 20)1,050 = −1,050 = **1,050 A**
Volume: Flexed budget profit − original budget profit
3,850 − 4,400 = −550 = **550 A**

3 Profit reconciliation statement

Original budget profit				**4,400**
Sales volume variance				550 A
Flexed budget profit				**3,850**
Sales price variance				1,050 A
Materials:	Seals:	Usage	20 A	
		Price	53 F	
		Cost		33 F
	Castings:	Usage	24 A	
		Price	527 A	
		Cost		551 A
Direct labour:		Efficiency	90 A	
		Rate	19 F	
		Cost		71 A
Fixed overhead expenditure				100 F
Actual profit				**2,311**

Q15.2 Stanley & Co. – Solution

Workings

Flexed budget (for 2,100 frames)

£
Materials: 2,100 × 5.0 m × £4.00/m = 10,500 m × £4.00/m = 42,000
Labour: 2,100 × 0.50 h × £12.00/h = 1,050 h × £12.00/h = 12,600
Total = 54,600

Actual performance (for 2,100 frames)

Materials:	11,550 m × £3.80/m	= 43,890
Labour:	1,000 h × £13.00/h	= 13,000
		Total = 56,890

1 Variance calculations

Materials usage:	(BQ – AQ)BP	
	(10,500 – 11,550)4.00	= **(4,200) A**
Materials price:	(BP – AP)AQ	
	(4.00 – 3.80)11,550	= **2,310 F**
Materials cost:	Budgeted cost – actual cost	
	42,000 – 43,890	= **(1,890) A**
Labour efficiency:	(BQ – AQ)BP	
	(1,050 – 1,000)12.00	= **600 F**
Labour rate:	(BP – AP)AQ	
	(12.00 – 13.00)1,000	= **(1,000) A**
Labour cost:	Budgeted cost – actual cost	
	12,600 – 13,000	= **(400) A**

2 Possible explanations for variances

Materials usage = (4,200) A	– wastage from poorer-quality materials
	– wastage due to demotivated workforce
	– out-of-date standards
Materials price = 2,310 F	– lower-priced substitute material used
	– unexpected discounts achieved
	– lower prices from new supplier
	– out-of-date standards
Labour efficiency = 600 F	– motivated workforce due to pay rise
	– more highly skilled type of labour used
	– out-of-date standards
Labour rate = (1,000) A	– recent pay rise
	– some overtime at premium rates may have occurred
	– out-of-date standards

3 Amendments

The payment of 'idle time' during the power cut affects the labour efficiency variance only.

Labour efficiency:	(BQ – AQ *worked*)BP	
	(1,050 – 950)12.00	= 1,200 F
Idle time:	Idle hours × budgeted rate	
	–50 × 12.00	= (600) A
Combined (as previous)		= 600 F

It was originally thought that the operatives had worked efficiently by saving 50 hours at £12 = £600 (50/1,050 = 4.8% improvement on standard). It is now clear that they were twice as efficient as originally thought as they saved 100 hours at £12 = £1,200 (100/1,050 = 9.5% improvement on standard).

Q15.3 Ivanblast – Solution

Flexed budget:			**£**
Sales:	30,000 games	@ £50 =	1,500,000
Production materials:	30,000 blank CDs	@ £1.10 =	33,000
Variable overheads:	30,000 games	@ £0.50 =	15,000
Fixed overheads:		=	800,000
Net profit		=	652,000

1 Variance analysis

Sales volume Variance	= flexed budget profit – original budget profit = 652,000 – 410,000 = +242,000 = **242,000 F**
Sales price variance	= (AP – BP)AQ = (45 – 50)30,000 = –150,000 = **150,000 A**
Material quantity variance	= (BQ – AQ)BP = (30,000 – 30,250)1.10 = –275 = **275 A**
Material price variance	= (BP – AP)AQ = (1.10 – 1.00)30,250 = +3,025 = **3,025 F**
Material cost variance	= budgeted cost – actual cost = 33,000 – 30,250 = +2,750 = **2,750 F**
Variable overhead cost variance	= budgeted variable overhead – actual variable overhead = 15,000 – 15,000 = **0**
Fixed overhead expenditure variance	= budgeted fixed overhead – actual fixed overhead = 800,000 – 850,000 = –50,000 = **50,000 A**

2 Budget reconciliation statement

	£	£
Original budget profit		**410,000**
Sales volume variance		<u>242,000</u> F
Flexed budget profit		**652,000**
Sales price variance		150,000 A
Material quantity variance	275 A	
Material price variance	<u>3,025</u> F	
Material cost variance		2,750 F
Var. ohd cost variance		–
Fix. ohd expenditure variance		50,000 A
Actual profit		**<u>454,750</u>**

3 The 10% reduction in sales price seems to have paid off as the number of games sold increased by 20%. The net effect of the sales volume and sales price variances is £92,000 favourable.

A total of 275 CDs were wasted. This could have been caused by deciding to purchase slightly inferior CDs than originally planned at the slightly cheaper price of £1.00 as opposed to £1.10. However, the favourable material price variance of £3,025 shows this was a good idea. On the other hand, the material quantity variance may be the result of simply not building normal production wastage into the budget, If so, this planning error has now been revealed and should not be repeated in future.

The adverse fixed overhead expenditure variance of £50,000 should not have occurred and should be investigated.

The net result of the period's activities is that the actual profit is £44,750 (11%) greater than originally planned.

Q15.4 Flipside Limited – Solution

Workings

Standard:	Quantity	Price	Cost (£)
Material A	5 kg	2.00 £/kg	10.00
Material B	10 kg	4.00 £/kg	40.00
Direct labour	2 dlh	15.00 £/dlh	30.00
Variable overhead	2 dlh	3.00 £/dlh	6.00
Fixed overhead	2 dlh	7.00 £/dlh	<u>14.00</u>
Production cost			100.00
Selling price			150.00
Standard profit			**50.00**

Original budget output = 10,000 units
Actual budget output = 11,000 units

Original budget:	Quantity	Price	Cost (£)
Material A	50,000 kg	2.00 £/kg	100,000
Material B	100,000 kg	4.00 £/kg	400,000
Direct labour	20,000 dlh	15.00 £/dlh	300,000
Variable overhead	20,000 dlh	3.00 £/dlh	60,000
Fixed overhead	20,000 dlh	7.00 £/dlh	140,000
Production cost			1,000,000
Sales revenue	10,000 units	150.00 £/unit	1,500,000
Profit			**500,000**

Flexed budget:	Quantity	Price	Cost(£)
Material A	55,000 kgs	2.00 £/kg	110,000
Material B	110,000 kgs	4.00 £/kg	440,000
Direct labour	22,000 dlh	15.00 £/dlh	330,000
Variable overhead	22,000 dlh	3.00 £/dlh	66,000
Fixed overhead	22,000 dlh	7.00 £/dlh	154,000
Production cost			1,100,000
Sales revenue	11,000 units	150.00 £/unit	1,650,000
Profit			**550,000**

Actual performance:	Quantity	Price	Cost (£)
Material A	66,000 kg	1.50 £/kg	99,000
Material B	99,000 kg	5.00 £/kg	495,000
Direct labour	20,900 dlh	16.00 £/dlh	334,400
Variable overhead	20,900 dlh	3.00 £/dlh	62,700
Fixed overhead	20,900 dlh	7.50 £/dlh	156,750
Production cost			1,147,850
Sales revenue	11,000 units	139.00 £/unit	1,529,000
Profit			**381,150**

1 Variance analysis

Material A

Cost var.	110,000	less	99,000	=		**11,000 F**
Price var.	2.00	less	1.50	×	66,000	**33,000 F**
Usage var.	55,000	less	66,000	×	2.00	**−22,000 A**

Material B

Cost var.	440,000	less	495,000	=		**−55,000 A**
Price var.	4.00	less	5.00	×	99,000	**−99,000 A**
Usage var.	110,000	less	99,000	×	4.00	**44,000 F**

Direct labour

Cost var.	330,000	less	334,400	=		**−4,400 A**
Rate var.	15.00	less	16.00	×	20,900	**−20,900 A**
Efficiency var.	22,000	less	20,900	×	15.00	**16,500 F**

Variable overheads

Cost var.	66,000	less	62,700	=		**3,300 F**
Expenditure var.	3.00	less	3.00	×	20,900	**0**
Efficiency var.	22,000	less	20,900	×	3.00	**3,300 F**

Fixed overheads

Cost var.	154,000	less	156,750	=		**−2,750 A**
Expenditure var.	140,000	less	156,750	=		**−16,750 A**
Volume var.	154,000	less	140,000	=		**14,000 F**
Efficiency var.	22,000	less	20,900	×	7.00	**7,700 F**
Capacity var.	20,900	less	20,000	×	7.00	**6,300 F**

Sales price variance

139.00	less	150.00	×	11,000	**−121,000 A**

Sales volume variance

550,000	less	500,000	=	**50,000 F**

2 Profit reconciliation statement (before admin & marketing overheads)

		£	£
Original budget profit			**500,000**
Sales volume variance			50,000 F
Flexed budget profit			**550,000**
Sales price variance			−121,000 A
Material A:	Price variance	33,000 F	
	Usage variance	−22,000 A	
	Cost variance		11,000 F
Material B:	Price variance	−99,000 A	
	Usage variance	44,000 F	
	Cost variance		−55,000 A
Direct labour:	Rate variance	−20,900 A	
	Efficiency variance	16,500 F	
	Cost variance		−4,400 A
Variable overheads:	Expenditure variance	0	
	Efficiency variance	3,300 F	
	Cost variance		3,300 F
Fixed overheads:	Efficiency variance	7,700 F	
	Capacity variance	6,300 F	
	Volume variance	14,000 F	
	Expenditure variance	−16,750 A	
	Cost variance		−2,750 A
Actual profit			**381,150**

3 Comments

Sales

The sales price decreased from the budgeted £150 to the actual £139. The price elasticity of demand was positive and the net effect was adverse as follows:

Sales price variance	=	121,000 A
Sales volume variance	=	50,000 F
		71,000 A

Variable costs

Material A had a favourable price variance and an adverse usage variance. This could be caused by sourcing lower-priced materials which were also lower quality causing higher wastage to occur.

Material B had an adverse price variance and a favourable usage variance. This could be caused by sourcing higher-quality materials at more expensive prices. The better-quality materials may have caused lower wastage to occur.

The adverse effect was a cost variance of £11,000 favourable for material A and £55,000 for material B.

The favourable labour efficiency variance of £16,500 may have been caused by the increase in pay from £15/hour to £16/hour. Pay rises tend to motivate operatives. However, the resulting adverse labour rate variance of £20,900 results in an adverse labour cost variance of £4,400.

Variable overheads are absorbed on a labour hour basis so their efficiency variance would follow the labour efficiency. The variable overhead expenditure variance shows a zero variance and could be caused by excellent budgeting and control. The cost variance was £3,300 favourable.

Fixed overheads

The adverse cost variance of £2,750 shows that more was spent on fixed overheads than planned. This was due to the adverse expenditure variance of £16,750. The fixed overhead absorption rate is based on direct labour hours. The favourable volume variance of £14,000 was made up of £6,300 F (capacity) due to working less hours than planned and £7,700 A (efficiency) from working at a faster rate per hour than planned.

In summary

Original budget profit	500,000
Sales variances	71,000 A
Variable cost variances	45,100 A
Fixed overhead variances	2,750 A
Actual profit	381,150

The management performance appears to have been poor. After eliminating the effect of the change in sales volume, the actual profit was £158,850 below the flexed budget profit. The increase in the sales price accounts for most of the bad performance but the adverse variance for material B is also very significant and needs to be investigated urgently. (Standards should also be checked to make sure they are up to date so as to avoid significant planning variances.)

Q15.7 Triform Limited – Solution

Standard cost card (for one unit of TR2)

		£
Direct materials	4 kg @ £5/kg	20
Direct labour	3 hours @ £7/hour	21
Variable overhead	3 hours @ £3/hour	9
Fixed overhead	3 hours @ £4/hour	12
Standard cost		62
Standard profit margin		14
Standard selling price		76

Budget for last month (800 units of TR2)

	Quantity	Price	Cost (£)
Direct materials	800 × 4 = 3,200	£5/kg	16,000
Direct labour	800 × 3 = 2,400	£7/hour	16,800
Variable overhead	800 × 3 = 2,400	£3/hour	7,200
Fixed overhead	800 × 3 = 2,400	£4/hour	9,600
Total cost			49,600
Total sales revenue	800	£76	60,800
Total profit margin	800	£14	11,200

Flexed budget for last month (700 units of TR2)

	Quantity	Price	Cost (£)
Direct materials	700 × 4 = 2,800	£5/kg	14,000
Direct labour	700 × 3 = 2,100	£7/hour	14,700
Variable overhead	700 × 3 = 2,100	£3/hour	6,300
Fixed overhead	700 × 3 = 2,100	£4/hour	8,400
Total cost			43,400
Total sales revenue	700	£76	53,200
Total profit margin	700	£14	9,800

Actual results for last month (700 units of TR2 produced and sold)

	Quantity	Price	Cost (£)
Direct materials	3,100	£4.25	13,175
Direct labour	2,350	£6.40	15,040
Variable overhead	2,350	£2.8510638	6,700
Fixed overhead	2,350	£3.9148936	9,200
Total cost			44,115
Total sales revenue	700	£79	55,300
Total profit margin			11,185

Standard hours of production (SHP) – *a measure of output*

SHP = actual number of units produced × standard labour time/unit = $700 \times 3 = 2,100$

Formulae (for a standard absorption costing system)

(FAOR = Fixed Overhead Absorption Rate = £4/hour)

Fixed overhead total cost variance

= flexed budget total cost – actual total cost

= $8,400 - 9,200 = 800$ A

Fixed overhead expenditure variance

= original budget total cost – actual total cost

= $9,600 - 9,200 = 400$ F

Fixed overhead volume variance

= flexed budget cost – original budget cost

= $8,400 - 9,600$

= $1,200$ A

Fixed overhead efficiency variance

= (flexed budget hours – actual hours worked) × standard FOAR

= $(2,100 - 2,350) \times 4 = 1,000$ A

Fixed overhead capacity variance

= (actual hours worked – original budget hours) × standard FOAR

= $(2,350 - 2,400) \times 4 = 200$ A

Sales

Sales volume variance = flexed budget profit – original budget profit

= $9,800 - 11,200$

= $1,400$ A

Sales price variance = (actual selling price – standard selling price)

× actual sales volume

= $(79 - 76) \times 700$

= $2,100$ F

Variable overheads

(VAOR = Variable Overhead Absorption Rate = £3/hour)

Total variable overhead variance

= flexed budget VO cost – actual VO cost

= $6,300 - 6,700 = 400$ A

Variable overhead expenditure variance

= (flexed budget VOAR − actual VOAR) × actual hours

= (flexed budget VOAR × actual hours) − (actual VOAR × actual hours)

= (flexed budget VOAR × actual hours) − actual VO incurred

= $(3 \times 2{,}350) - 6{,}700$

= $7{,}050 - 6{,}700$

= **350 F**

Variable overhead efficiency variance

= (flexed budget hours − actual hours worked) × flexed budget VOAR

= $(2{,}100 - 2{,}350) \times 3$

= $(-250) \times 3$

= **750 A**

Materials

Material price variance

= (flexed budget price − actual price) × actual quantity of materials

= $(5.00 - 4.25) \times 3{,}100$

= **2,325 F**

Material usage variance

= (flexed budget quantity − actual quantity used) × flexed budget price

= $(2{,}800 - 3{,}100) \times 5$

= $(-300) \times 5$

= **1,500 A**

Total material cost variance

= flexed budget cost − actual cost incurred

= $14{,}000 - 13{,}175$

= **825 F**

Direct labour

Labour rate variance

= (standard rate − actual rate) × actual labour hours worked

= $(7.00 - 6.40) \times 2{,}350$

= **1,410 F**

Labour efficiency variance

= (flexed budget hours − actual labour hours worked) × standard rate

= $(2{,}100 - 2{,}350) \times 7$

= $(-250) \times 7$

= **1,750 A**

Total labour cost variance

= flexed budget labour cost − actual labour cost incurred

= 14,700 − 15,040

= **340 A**

Profit reconciliation statement

	£	£	£
Original budget profit			11,200
Sales volume variance			1,400 A
Flexed budget profit			9,800
Sales price variance			2,100 F
	Favourable	**Adverse**	
Materials price	2,325		
Materials usage		1,500	
Materials cost			825 F
Labour rate	1,410		
Labour efficiency		1,750	
Labour cost			340 A
Variable overhead expenditure	350		
Variable overhead efficiency		750	
Variable overhead total cost			400 A
Fixed overhead expenditure	400		
Fixed overhead volume efficiency		1,000	
Fixed overhead volume capacity		200	
Fixed overhead total cost			800 A
Actual profit			**11,185**